THE STORY OF CANADA

THE STORY OF
CANADA

by

Donald grant Creighton

HOUGHTON MIFFLIN COMPANY BOSTON

The Riverside Press Cambridge

1960

CONTENTS

ILLUSTRATIONS

9

Illustrations

MAPS

1

FURS AND THE FLEUR-DE-LIS

I

The ships were ready. Charles de Mouy, Seigneur de la Meilleraye and Vice-Admiral of France, had solemnly required the commander, the captains, and the sailors to swear that they would conduct themselves truly and loyally in the service of His Most Christian Majesty, Francis I. The last farewells had been said. The two vessels, each about sixty tons in burden, with their small company of sixty-one souls in all, moved slowly out of the harbour and beyond the jutting promontory on which stood the little town. The narrow, twisting streets, the substantial merchant houses, the walls and great defensive towers of St. Malo receded slowly into the distance. The wind freshened. They were out in the Channel now, heading west. And Jacques Cartier, the Breton master-pilot, who bore the King's commission, stood on deck, shading his eyes against the sun and studying his course.

It was Monday, 20th April 1534. The typical Renaissance monarch, Francis I, had been nearly twenty years on the throne of France, and Henry VIII, his great rival in arts, sports, and conquest, had married Anne Boleyn only a little over a year before. These men and their contemporaries formed the first generation of West Europeans who had known of the existence of the vast, shadowy, half-fabulous lands beyond the western ocean. Already the knowledge was affecting their lives and prospects in subtle, indirect, but increasingly important ways: and for no group of men did the discovery of the New World have more immediate, practical consequences than for the fishermen of Brittany, Normandy, and the West Country ports of England. It was nearly forty years ago that John Cabot had first glimpsed the shores of north-eastern North America and had sailed home to astound his contemporaries with what was really the best fishing story in the history of Western Europe. He had, in fact, discovered one of the greatest fisheries in the world. Out from the long, jagged coastline which curved north-eastward from the future New England to Newfoundland, there stretched the submerged continental shelf, which had subsided into the ocean geological ages before, and now formed a series of marine uplands, covered by relatively shallow seas, which came to be called Banks. Here, where the water teemed with marine life and where the Gulf Stream met the cold Labrador Current, were the incomparable breeding places of a wide variety of fish, including the prolific cod, 'the beef of the ocean'.

On May 10th, when Cartier reached the ice-choked waters off Cape Bonavista on the east coast of Newfoundland, he was obviously following a course which fishermen had already made familiar. In a single generation, the Newfoundland fishery had become an industry of major importance for the Atlantic powers in general and for France and Portugal in particular. In France, a large continental country, there was a capacious market: fish, which were required in any case for fast days, were at all times a favourite staple article of diet. Out in the waters off Newfoundland, there were inexhaustible supplies; and the catch, preserved in salt, could be transported without deterioration in the small ships and on the long slow Atlantic voyages of the day. With its sunny, favourable climate, France could readily acquire cheap, copious supplies of the solar salt, produced by the evaporation of sea water, which was used lavishly in the cure. France, in fact, had many advantages. And her fishermen had been pressing them vigorously along the coasts of Newfoundland and Cape Breton Island and into the Strait of Belle Isle.

Other unknown adventurers had preceded Cartier thus far. But, beyond the Strait of Belle Isle, the daring originality of his first voyage began. Leaving Labrador—'the land God gave to Cain' he was inclined to call it—and the rugged, inhospitable, and stormy shores of Newfoundland behind him, Cartier plunged south and west. It was midsummer now, and the days were hot, the skies intensely blue, and the air unbelievably radiant. In a leisurely, inquiring fashion, the French ships skirted the islands and ventured up the deep bays of the Gulf of St. Lawrence. The bright, coloured landscape of northern summer was richly rewarding. Cartier looked admiringly at dense, fragrant pine forests, lush, green meadows, and fields of wild wheat, oats, and peas in flower 'as thick and fine as ever I saw in Brittany'. And when the French landed, they found strawberries, raspberries, gooseberries, and 'Provins roses'.

Cartier had found and explored the Gulf of St. Lawrence; but he had missed the great river which drained into it. The St. Lawrence—the 'River of Canada' as the French came to call it—was the great central geographical fact in the whole French enterprise in North America; and it was Cartier's happy destiny to complete the discovery which he had begun so promisingly in 1534. Yet the little flotilla of ships—the *Grande Hermine*, the *Petite Hermine*, and the *Emerillon*—which sailed from St. Malo on 19th May 1535, did not at first enjoy the good fortune which had attended the original expedition. They started a month later. They were buffeted and dispersed by violent western gales on the Atlantic; and it was not until late summer was waning into autumn that Cartier began to sail westward up the narrowing Gulf of the St. Lawrence. The information, supplied by his Indian guides, 'that one could make one's way so far up the river that they had never heard of anyone reaching the head of it' seemed to end the possibility of an easy, direct passage to the Far East; and Stadacona and Hochelaga, the two Huron-Iroquois villages which he found on the present sites of the port of Quebec and the city of Montreal, were poor, primitive communities which mocked whatever hopes he may have held of cultivated and wealthy native monarchies.

There were disappointments as the French sailed westward through the reddening autumnal forest. But there were compensations as well. Like so many of his successors, Cartier yielded inevitably to the enchantment and compulsion of the great river. The country through which he passed was richly impressive; and at Hochelaga, his journey's end, he climbed the high hill, which he called 'Mount Royal' and gazed out over the landscape for more than thirty leagues around. Up from the south-west, through level fields which were golden with ripe Indian corn and autumn foliage, the St. Lawrence, youthful, wilful, and turbulent, flowed furiously through the rapids of the future Lachine. From the north-west came another great river, which the French learnt to call the Ottawa; and beyond were the low sombre Laurentian Highlands, the beginnings of the enormous geological system of the Precambrian Shield. The St. Lawrence, the Indians assured Cartier, was navigable 'for more than three moons'; and they hinted at the precious metals which lay somewhere in the mysterious recesses of the country of the Ottawa.

Cartier could not help but be deeply moved by such a prospect. Yet it was not he, nor his later associate, the court favourite, Jean François de la Rocque, Sieur de Roberval, who was destined to found New France and to unravel the giant puzzle of the St. Lawrence—Great Lakes system. Cartier's final venture, a large-scale effort in exploration and colonization, which occupied the years 1541–3 ended ingloriously in failure; and it was left to the fishermen who had preceded him to carry on the work which he, for all his official support, had been unable to complete. In the half-century which followed Cartier's last attempt, the North Atlantic fishery expanded vigorously in an atmosphere tense with international rivalries. From Brittany, the Bay of Biscay, and the Channel ports, French fishing vessels were driven ever westward by a triple competitive compulsion. The English West Country fishermen had entered the struggle for the fishery with skill and determination. They had evolved a new and ingenious technique, the 'dry fishery', by which the fish were spread out on beaches, rocks, or stages to be dried by the sun, and only small quantities of the precious salt, in which England was so sadly deficient, were needed. They had done more than this. They had aggressively pre-empted the Avalon peninsula, in south-eastern Newfoundland, as a semi-permanent base for their new dry-curing industry.

Inevitably, the French fishery was affected by this successful challenge. In the past, the French, relying upon what was called the 'green' cure, had packed their wet, fresh-caught fish in quantities of the solar salt with which the nation was so cheaply and plentifully endowed. The heavily salted product of the 'green' fishery was well adapted for consumption in the closer domestic markets of France itself; the 'dry' fishery produced a hard lasting cure which was admirably suited to long-distance trade in southern countries. The French, as well as the English, could compete for these fine foreign markets. They could take over their rivals' new technique without ever abandoning their own original method. What they could not seem to do was to find and occupy a satisfactory permanent establishment in Newfoundland; and they were driven outwards, a dispersed rather than a concentrated band, towards the marginal areas of the fishery—to Cape Breton, Nova Scotia, Gaspé, and the Gulf of the St. Lawrence.

All the time they were drawing closer to the continent, and to the continent's native inhabitants. The dry fishery—unlike the green fishery, which could be pursued mostly at sea—required frequent and fairly prolonged occupancy of good harbours and beaches for the curing of the catch. Contact with the Indians followed naturally, and, with it, barter for the one article of value which they possessed, their furs. The fur trade, whose first casual transactions go back as far at least as the days of Cartier, prospered rapidly in the last decades of the century. And then, at length, some of the French venturers made the decision which ended this ambiguously dual commercial existence. Some of them ceased for ever to be fishermen. They became the first fur traders of North America.

II

On the 22nd June 1603 a slight, spare, dark Frenchman, rather below average height, brought his ship to anchor in a narrow stretch of the River St. Lawrence which the Indians called 'Quebec'. It was Samuel Champlain, a soldier, navigator, and cartographer of some experience, who had been born at Brouage, a small port in the Province of Saintonge, and who had already made one Atlantic voyage to the West Indies and Central America. This time he had come out to the New World as an associate of a group of fur traders; and his presence on the St. Lawrence, below the sheer heights of Quebec, was a sure indication that the new northern fur trade was entering upon the first great, expansive phase of its existence. In France, the increasingly widespread use of the felting process and the growing popularity of the broad-brimmed, high-crowned fur-felt hats had created a rising demand for beaver fur. It was a narrow, capricious market, subject to all the whims of taste and vagaries of fashion which characterize a luxury trade, but made attractive also by a luxury trade's high prices and occasional extravagant rewards.

The fur trade, in fact, was already well started upon its erratic and astonishing career. It was to make—and hideously to mar—New France. It was to bring much good—and quantities of evil. But all that was best in all that it ever gave to the French Empire in North America was personified in Samuel Champlain. He was straightforward, unassuming, sympathetic, and devout. He had all the curiosity, perseverance, quiet wisdom, and amazing fortitude of the born explorer and colonizer. He was made to find new worlds and found new nations. But, as conditions were in France and French overseas enterprise in the first half of the seventeenth century, he could make his contribution only in and through a company organization. The fishery had been a dispersed, highly individualistic industry, with hundreds of small enterprisers drawing on inexhaustible resources to serve a capacious and steady demand. The fur trade was different. In the fur trade, the market was limited and uncertain; the supply, produced by a few small bands of migratory Indians, was never copious. And the fur traders had barely begun their new business when they began to realize very clearly that the commercial company, equipped by royal charter with monopoly powers, was the only possible answer to their growing perplexities. The French state, under Henry IV and his cautious minister Sully, was prepared, on the whole, to fall in with the fur traders' wishes. France preferred to play an inactive role in the business of overseas colonization. But the privileges of the Crown were to be granted only in the hope of a real increase in the extent of the Crown's dominions. The fur traders, as a basic condition of their monopoly, were required to bring out settlers to the New World. Henry IV hoped thus to lay the modest bases of a French Empire in North America at the expense of the fur trade.

All this was already obvious when Champlain first faced the great rock of Quebec in the summer of 1603. The character of the French enterprise in north-eastern North America had been determined; but the centre from which the fur traders would organize and direct their efforts still remained uncertain. Champlain did not revisit the St. Lawrence in 1604; and for the next few years the principal fur-trading company, led by Pierre du Gua, Sieur de Monts, attempted, not very successfully, to establish itself on the Bay of Fundy, in the maritime region which the French came to call Acadia. It was not until 1608 that Monts' Company, with Champlain in control of local operations, shifted back to the St. Lawrence and to Quebec. The first great decision in the development of the French Empire in North America had been taken. The St.

Lawrence River enabled the fur-trading monopolists at once
to expand and to centralize their endeavours. It was the one
great river system in North America which led from the eastern
seaboard into the heart of the continent. It gave entrance to
an enormous dominion—cool, heavily forested, and intricately
watered—which was territory designed by nature for the
prosecution of the beaver trade.

This vast communication system might have been little used
and its resources relatively unexploited if it had not been for
the assistance and support of the native tribes. The French
were compelled to rely upon the Indians, just as the Indians
became increasingly dependent upon the iron tools, utensils,
and fire-arms of the French. Inevitably the fur traders became
involved in the politics of the interior; inevitably they were
forced to accept the friendship of the tribes dominating the
St. Lawrence. And, at the moment when Champlain was
superintending the construction of the *habitation* on the 'point
of Quebec', the political state of affairs in the great river valley
was, on the whole, distinctly favourable for the kind of enterprise which the fur traders had in mind. Stadacona and Hochelaga, the Huron-Iroquois villages of Cartier's day, with their
stockades, and lodges, and simple agriculture, had completely
vanished; and the Montagnais and Algonquins, migratory and
primitive hunting Indians from the north, had taken posssesion
of the St. Lawrence transport route. In their successful offensive, the northern hunting Indians may have been assisted by
the iron tools and weapons which, ever since Cartier's explorations, the French had been bartering along the shores of the
Gulf and the lower St. Lawrence. In any case, by the time
Champlain arrived in 1603, the Iroquois had retreated south-
west to their historic habitat in northern New York State. The
Indians who had displaced them would bring their savage
hunting skills to the aid of the fur trade. But they would demand
a price for their services; and the price could be nothing less
than the military assistance of the French in the struggle against
their ancient enemies, the Iroquois.

Furs and the Fleur-de-lis

Champlain was ready to grant what the northern Indians desired. He showed no hesitation in accepting the political necessities which the St. Lawrence River had imposed. As early as the 27th May 1603, when he first met the Montagnais at the old fur-trading rendezvous at Tadoussac, he contracted what was, in effect, the original French-Indian pact. Around him the dark natives, with their feathered scalp-locks, their breech-clouts, their rough leggings of hide, and their shapeless garments of skin and furs, sat silently in solemn conclave. The Indian interpreter, whom the French had brought with them, spoke of the grandeur of France and the might of the French Crown; and in his soft, flowing, musical Algonquin speech, the Montagnais chief replied gravely that 'he was well content that His said Majesty should people their country, and make war on their enemies, and that there was no nation in the world to which he wished more good than to the French'.

It was an alliance which Champlain felt he had to honour at the first opportunity; and in June 1609, after the de Monts' Company had occupied the new headquarters at Quebec for only a year, he was off westward with 'our allies, the Montagnais', to join other northern Indian war-parties in a planned attack on the Iroquois. On a day in late July, by the shores of a large and lovely lake which came later to be called Lake Champlain, the Father of New France first saw the soldiers of the great Indian Confederacy which was to harass French power in North America for the next century. The two native armies, in absurd, unconscious imitation of the formal order of west European battles, drew up their forces openly in fighting array. Champlain in his casque and cuirass walked forward, like some medieval champion, until he was within some thirty yards of the enemy; and then, at the first sign that the Iroquois meant to draw their bows, he levelled his arquebus, fired at the chiefs, knocked two of them down, and scattered their army in terrified confusion.

Yet all this was only a beginning. It was simply the first instalment of the heavy price which the fur-trading colony would have to pay. The costly base at Quebec, the friendship with the hunting Indians, the military domination of the lower St. Lawrence valley all formed merely the first phase in the inevitable westward expansion of the fur trade. The Montagnais and Algonquins, made more efficient by the metal tools and weapons of the French, rapidly began to exhaust the beaver in the regions most accessible to the lower St. Lawrence; and the fur trade, with its complex company organization and its high overhead costs, was drawn further into the interior in an instinctive search for the copious supplies which alone could ensure its survival. It was not until 1612, after four years of killing competition which had followed the cancellation of the de Monts' monopoly, that the fur traders were ready for the next stage of the westward advance. In that year Champlain succeeded in drawing the principal merchants engaged in the trade into a new company, often called Champlain's Company, which was fortunate enough to secure a monopoly grant from the Crown; and with this solid basis of support, the trade could afford to make the efforts which were essential for expansion. In 1615, in the last and greatest of his western explorations, Champlain journeyed up the Ottawa River to the 'sweetwater sea', Lake Huron, and wintered with the Huron Indians of Georgian Bay. The Hurons were Iroquoian in origin, with relatively stable settlements and a semi-agricultural economy; and the fur trade, pushed forward by these jealously eager middlemen, was extended throughout the whole region between the Upper and Lower Lakes.

It was an enormous commercial empire. And yet the imposing extent of this dominion was mockingly contradicted by the essential feebleness of the fur-trading state. Quebec was a commercial outpost; and the fur trade, by its very nature, was fundamentally hostile to white settlement. White settlement would mean, sooner or later, the destruction of the forests, the extinction of the animals, the departure of the Indians, and the westward flight of the fur trade. All the fur-trading companies, including Champlain's, though they were obliged by the express terms of their charters to bring out settlers from France, failed with monotonously cynical regularity to fulfil the obligations of their contracts. It was not until 1617 that Louis Hébert, the first bona-fide settler, arrived at Quebec. It was not until 1628 that they first began seriously to cultivate the fields around Champlain's fort. Clergy, of course, were not lacking. The Récollets, or Begging Friars, reformed Franciscans of the strict rule, came out with Champlain in 1615; and the Jesuits, who were to make New France the scene of one of their most arduous and tragic missionary enterprises, followed ten years later. There was a world of difference between the exalted evangelical aims of the religious orders and the mundane commercial purposes of the fur traders; and yet, in a curious but fundamental way, they shared a common interest. The main concern of both lay in the Indians, in the native population of the region. New France was a mission to the heathen and a fur-trading outpost; it was not primarily a white settlement. And in these early days only a few dozen fur traders, clerks, interpreters, missionaries, and servants made up the little population of Quebec.

At the very heart of New France, there was an essential, an irremediable weakness. Yet the fur trade was a continental undertaking whose existence depended upon its continual expansion; and the fur-trading colony, by its very nature, was driven irresistibly onward to found a vast inland commercial empire and to incur the rivalries which its ambition inevitably provoked. The quarrel, which Champlain had espoused, of the Montagnais, Algonquins, and Hurons against the Iroquois, was simply the first primitive phase of an ever deepening conflict. The Iroquois were established at the headwaters of the Hudson-Mohawk system; and the Hudson, the only other river of the Atlantic Seaboard, beside the St. Lawrence, which broke through the mountain barrier into the west, became a stream of great significance in the grand strategy of the struggle for North America. In the second and third decades of the seventeenth century, the Dutch began to found their first trading posts on the Hudson; and it was not very long before the Iroquois became the pugnaciously active middlemen of a new Dutch-English fur-trading system in much the same way as the Hurons had already become the western distributing agents of the commercial empire based on Quebec.

It was not long, either, before the Iroquois were ready aggressively to take the initiative. The whole first phase of the war, in which, in the main, the northern Indians had carried the offensive victoriously into the domain of their enemies, was now drawing to a close; and the tragic failure of the invasion of 1615, in which Champlain accompanied the Hurons in their attack upon the main stronghold of the Onondagas, was an ominous sign of the drastic approaching change of fortunes. The movable wooden tower which, in imitation of the engines of sixteenth-century French siege warfare, Champlain had persuaded his Indians to construct, was only a partial success; the Onondagas defended their palisaded fortress vigorously against the bungling attacks of their enemies; and in the end, despairing of the arrival of their expected allies, the Hurons trailed north-westward in defeat. It was the end of a long chapter of advance and victory. The little battle of October 1615, fought under the falling leaves of autumn, was full of sinister portent for the future of French Canada.

III

In 1627, Quebec and the lower St. Lawrence had been occupied by the French for nineteen years. And, as if to emphasize the fact that these first two decades had been a period of tentative and exploratory beginnings, France, in that year, took a step which seemed to mark a decisive break with all its inglorious past in the New World. A completely new and powerful company, the Company of New France, was formed to assume control of the French enterprise in the St. Lawrence valley. It was true, of course, that the Company of New France, however great its strength, was still only a commercial organization. It was also true that the history of the northern fur-trading colony had been one long, sorry tale of successive commercial organizations. But the Company of New France was surely different. It was a superlative, a transcendent company. Its patron and principal organizer was no less a person than Cardinal Richelieu. Its backers were not the humble merchants of Rouen and St. Malo, but the great financiers of Paris; and it began its career with the ample capital of three hundred thousand livres, divided among one hundred shareholders or associates. It was to do great things for New France. It had accepted heavy responsibilities in return for the grant of its monopolistic trading privileges. It had agreed—and this was the most formidable of all its undertakings—to bring the population of the colony to a total of four thousand by 1643, at the expiration of its fifteen-year monopoly of trade.

The Company of New France was an imposing organization. Its tragedy was that it was doomed to suffer calamities on the same scale as its pretensions. These were still the early days of European dominion in North America—the days of competing explorations, claims and counter claims, unsubstantial settlements, and transitory conquests. As early as 1621, in complete disregard of the prior claims of the French to Acadia, James I of Great Britain had granted the entire maritime region from Cape Gaspé to the St. Croix River to Sir William Alexander, later Earl of Stirling. Six years later, in 1627, England and France were at war; and David, Lewis, and Thomas Kirke, a buccaneering trio of sailor brothers who had decided to make a little personal gain out of this fortunate situation, obtained letters of marque from the British government and sailed westward to seize French ships and capture French posts. In 1628 they made a rich and easy prize of the first great colonizing expedition which the luckless Company of New France had dispatched. In 1629 they helped to establish Sir William Alexander the younger in his father's new province of Nova Scotia and sailed up the St. Lawrence to capture Quebec and to complete the virtual destruction of French power in North America.

The wheel spun. But Charles I, the new King of England, was never a consistently lucky monarch, and it soon spun again. In 1632, when peace was at length concluded between the two countries, France had its North American possessions returned to it; and by the summer of 1633 Champlain was back again in Quebec as Governor of New France. Outwardly, everything may have seemed the same; and so, in a dishearteningly literal sense of the phrase, it was. The ambitious hopes, the grandiose plans of the Company of New France, were laid aside, and for ever. It was, so far as French commercial enterprise went, a powerful company; but it was only a company, and the cheerfully efficient piracies of the Kirke brothers had virtually finished it. From that moment it degenerated into an inactive organization of absentee shareholders and landlords who had neither the will nor the means to give positive direction and support to the development of the colony. Their trading monopoly was disposed of to a succession of sub-companies which enjoyed far from uniform success in its exploitation. Their colonizing obligations were perfunctorily acquitted by means of grants of land, in feudal fashion, to persons of some substance on condition that these North American seigneurs would people their property with settlers. These few new landlords had as little conscience as their feudal overlord, the Company of New France; and in 1643, by which time the Company had solemnly promised to bring out at least four thousand colonists, there were probably considerably fewer than four hundred people in Quebec.

Champlain, the Father of New France, died on Christmas Day, 1635. Under his successors, the colony which he had founded preserved its original character and direction almost unaltered. It remained an outpost of militant evangelical Christianity and of aggressive commercial enterprise. The Company of New France, and its various subsidiaries, and the Society of Jesus, which had now completely replaced the original Récollet mission, dominated the life of the tiny settlements on the St. Lawrence. The Company nominated the

Governor, granted land, and provided an extremely simple, benevolently authoritarian government. The Jesuits, together with representatives of two orders of nuns, the Ursulines and the Hospitalières, supplied the colony with its schools and hospitals and supervised its religious and cultural life.

There were a handful of settlements now—at Beauport, a little below Quebec; at Three Rivers, at the junction of the St. Maurice and the St. Lawrence; and finally, in 1642, a daring, strongly palisaded outpost up the river on the island of Montreal. Beyond these patches of civilization lay the vast, treacherous world of the forests, the tumbling waterways, the ravaged, rocky uplands of the Precambrian Shield. And it was here, in the interior, that the main interest of the colony was inevitably centred. At the end of the long communication line of the St. Lawrence and Ottawa rivers, were the Hurons, the fur traders' most effective middlemen; and the Huron mission, which was to end in the ordeal of martyrdom and the glory of sainthood, was the greatest of the Jesuits' evangelical enterprises in this northern world.

The French hold on their North American possessions was feeble, spasmodic, and uncertain. In Acadia, a few picturesque adventurers quarrelled for the possession of an almost un-peopled country. In the St. Lawrence valley, where authority was at least concentrated and unquestioned, progress, though greater, was far from satisfactory. The chartered trading company and the enterprise of private individuals, upon which the French Crown had relied for the extension and maintenance of its dominions in North America, had obviously and lament-ably failed as instruments of empire; and the outposts which French fishermen and fur traders had founded in a half-century of effort, had become little more than the inviting prey of France's European rivals and native North American antagonists. In 1654, a fleet of the new Puritan Common-wealth of New England swept French power easily and swiftly from the Acadian region; and six years earlier—a vastly more terrible calamity—the long-dreaded, fearfully awaited Iroquois invasions of the French fur-trading empire had begun. In two seasons, the summer of 1648 and the early spring of 1649, the Iroquois, backed by the power of Dutch armaments, destroyed the villages of Huronia, tortured the Jesuit missionaries to death, and completed the wreck and dispersal of the Huron nation.

The outer defences were down. The heart of the fur-trading colony lay open to attack; and the Iroquois closed in upon it. They menaced its principal settlements, attacked its outposts, ambushed its stragglers, and tried to strangle its economic life by a systematic fur blockade. The colony existed precariously, dangerously, almost despairingly; and Adam Dollard, Sieur des Ormeaux, and his little band of Frenchmen and Indians, fighting and dying inside their flimsy palisaded fort near the Long Sault on the Ottawa River, in a vain attempt to stem the onslaught of hundreds of attacking Iroquois, formed a symbol both of the peril in which the colony stood and the fortitude by which alone it managed to continue its existence.

2

UP THE WATERWAYS TO THE WEST

I

Close to a newly constructed wooden fort, on a small island, at the lower end of Lake Champlain, a large and strangely contrasted company of armed men was assembling on a September day in 1666. The Indians were there, of course; the militiamen from the three districts of Montreal, Three Rivers, and Quebec, in their distinctive costumes of blue, white, and red, had gathered in large numbers. But these informal soldiers of the fur-trading colony, who had fought through the nearly twenty years of raids, surprises, and skirmishes of the Iroquois war, were a fairly familiar sight in the wooded valleys of the Richelieu and lower St. Lawrence rivers. The really startling incongruity in that still autumn scene of blue water and scarlet falling leaves was the presence of a small army of professional soldiers of what, under Louis XIV, would soon come to be known as the greatest military state in Europe. There were six hundred of them. There were soldiers from the regiments of Allier, Chambellé, Poitou, and Orléans. There were companies of the Carignan-Salières regiment in their black, wide-brimmed beaver hats, their grey tunics, and their mauve stockings. Musketeers, pikemen, grenadiers, old campaigners of the Swiss and Italian wars, veterans of the struggles against the Turks and the Hungarians—they filled the echoing lake with the stir and movement of their arrival.

It was exactly fifty-one years since Champlain and his Hurons had set out on their ill-fated invasion of the Onondaga country. It was fifty-one years since the French tactical plans had miscarried, and Champlain himself had been wounded in the knee, and the Huron army, foiled and fearful, had retreated north-westward through the snows of early winter. That defeat and retreat had been, for New France, the prelude to a half-century of slow and painful growth and gradually increasing peril. It had been a terrible half-century. But it was over now; and there could be no more reassuring proof of its termination than the presence of the regulars of some of the crack regiments of Europe in the ravaged fur-trading colony of the lower St. Lawrence.

All during the previous summer, they had kept arriving at Quebec. Twenty-four companies, twenty of whom belonged to the Carignan-Salières regiment, were now stationed in the colony under the command of the tall old soldier, Alexandre de Prouville, Marquis de Tracy; and their coming had coincided with the arrival of a new Governor, Sieur Daniel Rémy de Courcelle, of the first Intendant, Jean Talon, of whole shiploads of bachelor colonists, young girls, and settlers with their families, and ample stores of supplies, equipment and armament. Every event of that wonderful summer of 1665 proclaimed the fact that a completely new stage in the history of the fur-trading colony had begun. The bleak, niggardly, hazardous days of the chartered companies were over. New France had become a royal province, directly subject to the French Crown, a recognized part of the most imposing empire of western Europe.

And now the young Sun-King of that imposing empire was about to chastise the savage presumption of his native North American enemies. In a great flotilla of canoes and small boats Tracy's little army paddled off southward over the placid waters of the lake. It was still quiet, golden autumn weather when the troops disembarked at the upper end of Lake George. Drums beating, banners flying, they marched off, in their brilliant uniforms, through the autumn glow of the forest towards the Mohawk country. Then the weather broke. Through blinding rain and wind, Tracy drove his men forward, in forced night marches, in the vain hope of catching the elusive, retreating savages. The villages were deserted; the central Mohawk stronghold stood abandoned. All that the French could do was to wreck the Indian bastions and palisades, destroy the native villages, burn the great standing piles of corn and provisions, and then toil back, through the wild autumnal weather, to Quebec. Tracy, with his overwhelming strength, could not, of course, force the prudent Indians to a pitched encounter in the European fashion. He could not win —he and his troops had no experience—in the stealthy war of sudden attacks and swift surprises which the Indians had made their own. What he could and did do, was to convince the Iroquois that a great military power had come to the rescue of its forgotten colony and that New France no longer waited miserably upon the defensive.

New France had, in fact, for a brief but brilliant period in its existence, become a matter of interest and concern for the newly reorganized and powerful French state. The death of Mazarin in 1661 and the young Louis XIV's purposeful grasp of the control of his own government marked a significant point in the history of the centralized Bourbon monarchy. Between the wars of the two Cardinals, Richelieu and Mazarin, and the more terrible wars of the mature Louis XIV, there lay a few brief years of recovery and peaceful reorganization; and the spirit of this short, constructive period was best typified by that tirelessly efficient exemplar of the new profession of civil servant, the Controller-General of Finances, Jean Baptiste Colbert. Under Colbert's supervision, France began a systematic effort to pull its half-lost, half-forgotten colonial empire together; and the establishment of royal government in Quebec was simply one part of an ambitious programme which sought, by means of either war or diplomacy, to recover and integrate the scattered French possessions in the Western Hemisphere.

The work was undertaken at once, and with determination. Before he came on to New France, the Marquis de Tracy had spent a successful year of reconquest and reorganization in the Caribbean region. He had recaptured Guiana, and restored order in Martinique and Guadeloupe; and Acadia, the outpost of the St. Lawrence, which had been captured under Cromwell, was restored to France in 1667 by the Treaty of Breda. Once again the French Empire in the North Atlantic, the West Indies, and the continent of North America was complete. Placentia in Newfoundland, Port Royal and St. Jean in Acadia, Martinique, Guadeloupe and Guiana in the Caribbean, Quebec, Three Rivers, and Montreal in the valley of the St. Lawrence—it was a long, widely scattered, strangely varied string of all too feeble settlements. Yet what could it not become! It was an enormous and splendid empire in the making. Colbert and his band of devoted bureaucrats bent their brows over their maps and charts, their dispatches and account books. They knew exactly what they wanted to do. They were sustained by the unshakeable convictions of seventeenth-century mercantilism. They would unite the fisheries of the North Atlantic and the sugar plantations of the West Indies with the potential cereal-producing regions of the St. Lawrence, and make of the whole one richly diversified, strongly integrated empire.

In this grandiose imperialistic design, New France had a role of fundamental importance to play. It could only play it effectively, the planners reasoned, if its own character were basically altered. It had been a missionary and fur-trading outpost. It must become what its very name implied, a France overseas, with French government, institutions, social organization, and something at least of the rich variety of French economic life. In the first few years after 1663, when the colony formally became a royal province, this plan was put energetically into execution. It was easy enough for the Crown to nominate a royal Governor who would be the titular head of the colony and its commander-in-chief. It was natural enough to copy the bureaucratic organization of a province of continental France, and to appoint an intendant—one of the class of trained professional civil servants upon which the French monarchy was coming increasingly to rely—as the administrator of justice, the financial expert, the economic planner of the new New France. Under François de Laval—Montmorency, the first bishop, who had arrived in the colony a few years before the establishment of royal government, the work of organizing the community in a system of parishes served by a secular clergy was proceeding apace; and the seigniory, granted to capable enterprisers on terms borrowed from French feudal law yet sharply modified in the interests of settlement, was a device readily available for the great work of colonization and solid community building.

For a few years all was activity, achievement, and expectation. It was true that the French tended to favour the St. Lawrence valley rather than Acadia and that only a few score new colonists were added to the small settlements of Acadians already established in the Annapolis valley and around the Basin of Minas. In the long stretch of territory between Quebec and Montreal, however, the sense of growth, the belief in a prosperous future, were electrically inspiring. Most of the little army which Tracy had led into the Mohawk country in 1666 returned to France; but about four hundred officers and men took their discharge and settled in the colony, and St. Ours, Berthier, Chambly, Verchères, Contrecœur, La Valtrie, and Saurel were among the officers who accepted grants of seigniories from Talon and whose names live on yet in the place names of Quebec.

Every year a few hundred state-encouraged and state-aided immigrants—bachelor colonists, young married couples, husbands and wives with families of young children—arrived at Quebec; and every year a few score of orphan girls or daughters of poor families—marriageable young women whose colonial destiny was matrimony—were shipped out to New France at the King's charge as 'filles du Roi'. The population of the tiny colony rapidly increased. In 1672, when the period of the great migration came to an end, there were nearly five hundred Frenchmen in Acadia and nearly seven thousand in Quebec. It was only a beginning, of course. The little settlements along the St. Lawrence and the Acadian coasts were still infinitesimal, negligible, almost contemptible. Yet had they not made a solid start towards permanence? Did they not provide the satisfactory basis for the concentrated, populous, and prosperous colonies of the future?

II

It might have been. It would have been if Colbert and the mercantilist planners at Versailles had been able to effect their will. But natural tendencies, as well as official purposes, had their part to play; and natural tendencies, in their irrepressible natural fashion, opposed or limited, as often as not, the realization of the official plan. The three regions of the French western empire developed in their own distinct ways, at their own rates of speed, and in comparative isolation from one another. The French fishery in the North Atlantic was a big and prosperous affair, but its main interest was the home market, not foreign trade, and it failed to produce numerous or considerable settlements in Newfoundland or Acadia. The colony on the lower St. Lawrence was more populous and solidly established than ever; but all official attempts to diversify its economy with agriculture, lumbering and shipbuilding had to struggle against the invincible tendency towards commercial expansion into the hinterland. The trading strength which was so confidently and vigorously displayed in the continental interior was curiously contradicted by the commercial feebleness repeatedly shown on the Atlantic Ocean. The French venturers in the New World were a race of continental not maritime traders; and it was New England, not New France, which successfully carried out the commercial integration of the northern and southern Atlantic possessions of both France and England.

Up the Waterways to the West

The destiny of the Frenchmen of the St. Lawrence valley lay in the west. They turned their backs upon the Gulf and the lower reaches of the great river; they turned their backs upon the rewarding network of commercial opportunities which was opening up along the Atlantic Seaboard and among the Atlantic islands. And every vital impulse in the colony seemed to carry them westward along the St. Lawrence and the Ottawa and into the unexplored and inviting interior. The routes were open again. The Iroquois had been humbled, if not defeated; and the Hurons, who had once performed the essential functions of western middlemen for the French, no longer occupied their old strategic location—no longer even existed as a distinct nation. If the French wished to carry their trade goods to the west, and to bring its furs back with them, they would have to go themselves. And if they went, what a vast dammed-up accumulation of riches would they discover! Beyond the Lower Lakes, in the region of Lake Huron and Lake Michigan were unknown Indian tribes which had never trafficked in furs and whose only knowledge of the precious iron tools and weapons of the French was derived from the blunted knives and battered hatchets which the fleeing Hurons had carried with them in their desperate retreat. The curiosity of these Indians had been stimulated; their appetites had been whetted. They would trade, and trade as perhaps no Indians had traded since the days when the first French ships crept up the river towards Quebec.

Even this was not all. It was not simply the unexploited markets and the abundant sources of supply that lured the French into the interior; they were driven westward also by a new, more vigorous, and more efficient type of competition. It came not only from the south whence there had always been competition in the fur trade, but from the north as well. In 1664, a year before the Marquis de Tracy and the twenty companies of the Carignan-Salières regiment arrived in Quebec, England had captured New Netherland from the Dutch; and in 1668, two years after the humbling of the Iroquois, Médard

Chouart, Sieur des Groseilliers, and Pierre Esprit Radisson—two renegade French fur traders who had left Quebec in a rage at the treatment they had received—succeeded in persuading the English court and the London merchants to undertake an expedition for direct trade by sea with Hudson Bay. Competition from the Dutch, pushed north-westward via the Hudson-Mohawk system and through the distributing agencies of the Iroquois, had harassed the French for nearly half a century. Cheap English guns and tools, stout English woollen cloth, and copious supplies of West Indies rum would make that competition more keenly effective in future. But, after all, the rivalry of the Hudson River was known and expected. The rivalry of Hudson Bay—the second of the two great discoveries to which Henry Hudson had given his name—was startlingly, disconcertingly new. And on the 2nd May 1670, when Charles II granted a royal charter to the 'Governor and Company of the Adventurers of England trading into Hudson's Bay', there began a new and ultimately far more exacting phase in the struggle of the colony of the St. Lawrence for the prize of the western trade.

From the beginning of royal government, the officers of the French Crown in North America thought instinctively in the sweeping terms of continental geopolitics. Jean Talon, the first Intendant, laid down the broad lines of French grand strategy; Louis de Buade, Comte de Frontenac, the second governor, who in 1672 succeeded Rémy de Courcelle, pushed vigorously forward towards the same general objectives. The hope of making Canada a solid commercial and agricultural base for the French Empire in the west was never, of course, forgotten. The prospect of strengthening the economy of the St. Lawrence through its diversification was never abandoned. But it was odd how invariably and inevitably these prudent, prosaic plans seemed to yield to the grandiose designs of western empire. The Upper Lakes, the economic and military crossroads of the continent, the focus of the three great water transport systems of North America, must be secured and strongly held by New France. French explorers, officers, fur traders, and missionaries must press forward, north-west and south-west, in the two wide enveloping attacks which would recover lost trading territory and gain new untouched areas for exploitation. All this might be achieved by peaceful means. Commercial enterprise, judicious diplomacy, Indian alliances, and fur-trading posts might successfully do the trick. The competition of the Hudson River and Hudson Bay could be peacefully frustrated. But, if not, it could be crushed by the destruction of the sources of power from which it sprang.

On a June day in 1671, at Sault Ste. Marie, the focal point of the Upper Lakes, the French asserted their formal claims of western empire. The Sieur de St. Lusson, appointed by Talon as the Crown's representative, was the central figure in the solemn and brilliant ceremony. With him stood the French explorers and fur traders, the Jesuit missionaries, and a little company of regular soldiers; and all around a great crowd of watching, attentively listening Indians was congregated. The *Te Deum* was chanted as a huge cross was raised against the blue sky. The salvoes of musketry went echoing across the water as the royal arms of France were lifted high in the air at the top of a tall cedar post and the white and gold fleur-de-lis standard fluttered out above them. St. Lusson, clad in his gorgeous uniform, laid formal claim, not only to the whole region of the Upper Lakes, but also to 'all other countries, lakes, tributaries, contiguous and adjacent thereto, as well discovered as to be discovered, which are bounded on the one side by the North and West Seas and on the other by the South Sea, including all its length and breadth'. Three times St. Lusson shouted aloud the claims of the French King; three times he took symbolic possession of this vast western empire by raising a sod of turf with his sword.

This was only a formal—an impressively formal—beginning. At once the French set themselves to unravel and master the central geographical mysteries of the continent; and, during the next decade, by a sustained effort which for a small colony was stupendous, they mapped the natural transport system of the interior, appropriated the vital fur-trading routes, and established their key commercial and military outposts north and south of the Great Lakes. In the late summer of 1671, in what was frankly an exploratory invasion of the territory claimed by the Hudson's Bay Company, Paul Denis, Sieur de St. Simon and the Jesuit Father Albanel, led a small party on the incredible overland journey up the Saguenay River, across Lake Mistassini and down the Rupert River to James Bay. Only a year later, the Canadian-born *coureur-de-bois* Louis Jolliet and Father Jacques Marquette set out together from the Strait of Michilimackinac on the first of the long journeys down the 'great river named Messipi'. In 1678, Daniel Greysolon Du Lhut travelled westward beyond the head of Lake Superior to win the friendship of the Sioux, pacify the inter-tribal Indian warfare, and wrest new fur-trading markets for Montreal from the grasp of the Hudson's Bay Company. Finally, in 1682, little more than a decade after St. Lusson had proclaimed the western continental dominion of Louis XIV, the sombre, ambitious, and overbearing La Salle brought this long forced march of exploration to its climax by descending the Mississippi River to its mouth.

New France had made its decision. It had yielded to the compulsions of western empire; and it must now accept the burdens, distresses, and rivalries which western empire inevitably entailed. The colony had not changed—and showed no real signs of changing—in the way in which Colbert and the French mercantilists had fondly hoped it might. The enormous expansion which had followed the establishment of royal government had simply confirmed and hardened the cast of character which the first fur traders had impressed upon it. It was all too probable now that the seigniories which Talon had granted would not become the basis of a prosperous agriculture for export; there was no doubt at all that the little industries which the Great Intendant had started in Quebec were making no progress. And the type of three-cornered trade which Massachusetts had built up—with the fish of Newfoundland, the flour, provisions, and lumber of the St. Lawrence, the sugar and molasses of the West Indies, and the manufactures of the Mother Country as the main commodities of a profitable triangular commerce—seemed utterly beyond the interest or the capacity of the French.

They did not want to venture on to the ocean. They could not be persuaded to remain on the seigniories. They went west—and nothing could stop them. The costs of western enterprise—the long transport route, the upkeep of the forts and posts, the price of the fickle friendship of the Indians— were always high. The returns of the trade were inevitably subject to the whims of French fashions and the limitations of the small luxury market which it served; and during the 1670's the price of fur fell disastrously, in part as a result of the copious supplies which the exploitation of new western territory had brought down to Montreal. The colony, poised precariously upon its narrow economic base, was now in serious trouble. But how could its inherent difficulties be avoided? The authorities at Quebec imposed a system of licences which was intended to limit the number of *coureurs-de-bois* and hence to control the volume of supply. The whole colony anxiously debated the question, at once economic and moral, of selling brandy to the Indians. It was all useless. The natural forces of the fur-trading colony burst irresistibly through these paper prohibitions and swept along the waterways to the west. Only seventy-five men were permitted by the regulations to go into the interior; but in 1679 the Intendant Duchesneau admitted that he was powerless to control the numbers and gloomily estimated that there were between five hundred and six hundred *coureurs-de-bois* in the upper country.

Colbert's grand design had failed. The colony on the St. Lawrence was inevitably committed to western expansion. Henceforth it would have to make shift to live with the economic chances and reverses, the social costs of its chosen staple trade. But these were not the only burdens which those who

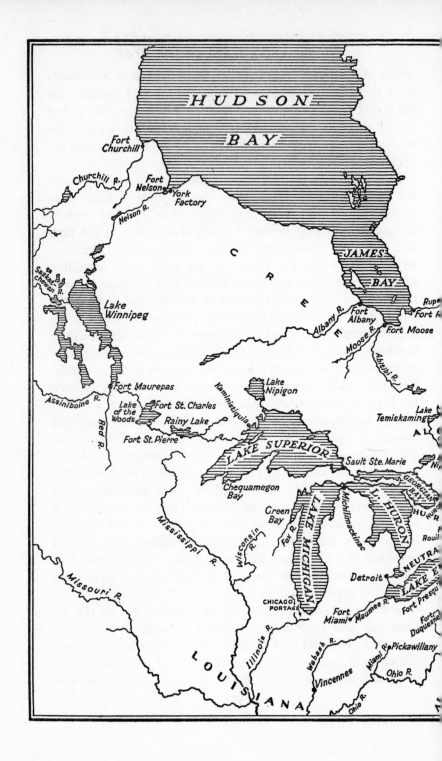

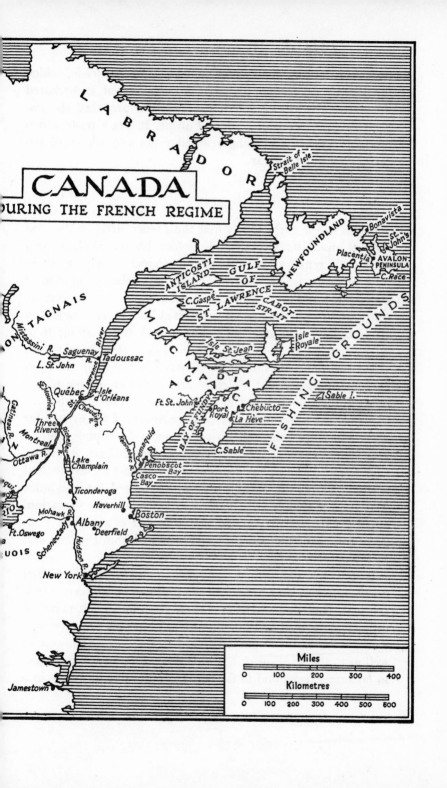

trafficked in furs would have to bear. The fur trade, which thrust swift and far into the heart of the continent, exacerbated the native rivalries of North America and provoked the imperialistic ambitions of western Europe. It was a trade which brought violence and danger at all times and which all too easily could end in war.

III

It was in the early 1680's that the French drive to the west entered upon its second and violent phase. England and France still remained in that ambiguous, increasingly uncertain state of peace which ended abruptly with the Revolution of 1688; but the official concord of western Europe imposed no restraints on the commercial rivalries of French and English on Hudson Bay; and still less could it stop the Iroquois from attempting by force to recover their lost western markets. In 1681, the Senecas, the most westerly of the Five Iroquois Nations, suddenly and violently attacked their native neighbours in the Illinois country, who by now had become the customers of the new south-western department of the French fur trade which La Salle and his agents were developing. Only a year later, in 1682, the highly versatile Pierre Esprit Radisson, who found the English service as unsatisfactory as he had formerly found the French and who changed his allegiance with greater facility as he gained experience in the operation, sailed for Hudson Bay as the representative of a French company and outwitted and captured his rivals from England and New England.

It was the old armed struggle—the struggle which had nearly wrecked New France in the first half of the seventeenth century—back once more. Yet there were important points of difference, as well as obvious similarities. This time the war would have to be fought on two fronts, to the north-west as well as to the south-west; and this time, also, New France was in far better heart and in far better condition to do battle in a far-flung conflict than it ever had been during the long bloody attrition of the first Iroquois war. New companies of regulars arrived from France to stiffen the defence; and the colony's militia was a growing force of about a thousand men to which the veterans of the Carignan-Salières regiment contributed their experience, and the new generation of young French-Canadians, born in the little settlements on the St. Lawrence, gave their instinctive knowledge of their native country and its ways. Already New France was developing its own distinctive type of forest warfare—a warfare characterized by the Indian devices of swift movement, sudden violent attack, and elusive retreat; and the expedition which the Chevalier de Troyes led on its six-hundred-mile journey across the height of land and down the Abitibi and Moose rivers to the English forts on Hudson Bay was a brilliant example of this long-range strategy and these surprise tactics.

The French could turn the native North American methods against their unsuspecting English opponents with complete and shattering effect. But they had not yet learnt completely how to cope with their inveterate enemies and unacknowledged teachers, the Iroquois. The attempt, in 1684, to overawe the Confederacy with an ostentatious show of force was a dismal failure. The full-scale invasion of the Seneca country which the new Governor, Denonville, undertook in 1687 was in effect little more than Tracy's punitive expedition of 1665 repeated over twenty years after, and with nothing of the original intimidating shock of novelty. The whole Confederacy was goaded into furious reprisals. The savage campaign of retaliation which the Iroquois now commenced bore an all too terrible resemblance to the sanguinary offensive of thirty years before. At dawn on the 5th of August 1689, under cover of a violent storm of rain and hail, some fifteen hundred of them descended upon the little village of Lachine, close to Montreal, and massacred about three score of its inhabitants. That August night of horror was the worst disaster which the fur-trading colony ever sustained at the hands of its ancient savage enemies.

Up the Waterways to the West

By this time the English Revolution had occurred and the war between England and France had formally opened. The new conflict—the War of the League of Augsburg, as it was called—altered the nature of the struggle between New France and the English colonies in North America much less than might have been expected. The French army which Louvois had created was the pride and terror of Europe; the navy which Colbert, as Minister of Marine, had carefully rebuilt, was a powerful instrument of warfare capable of doing battle with the English fleet on something like equal terms. But the War of the League of Augsburg was fought mainly in Europe and European waters; and the North American theatre was regarded as a relatively unimportant sideshow in which neither of the great antagonists was eager to mount a land or naval offensive of any real significance. In effect, the initiative was left to the colonial governments; and the plans of campaign which New France and the English colonies undertook afford a curious revelation of the character, the strength, and the weaknesses of each.

In 1690 both sides took action. Frontenac had returned as Governor to Quebec, and he and the authorities of New York and New England simultaneously planned offensives against each other's territory. Both strategic designs called for operations on a large scale; both were based upon the idea of a combined attack by a naval expedition and a land force; and both, though their sea approaches and naval objectives obviously differed, relied originally upon the Hudson River–Lake Champlain–Richelieu River route as the main pathway of their attacks by land. Fundamentally, the two strategic plans were much alike; but how differently, with what significantly contrasting touches, were they modified in detail and executed in practice!

The ships which were to undertake the French naval attack against New York failed to arrive in time; the great advance in force southward down the Richelieu and Hudson valleys was abandoned as too difficult and costly; and, in the end, Frontenac's offensive took on the increasingly characteristic French-Canadian form of three lightning and deadly frontier raids. The party that set out from Montreal followed the Lake Champlain route to Schenectady; the guerrilla company from Three Rivers hacked its way through the wilderness and fell upon Salmon Falls, a little frontier village in New Hampshire; and the Quebec expedition toiled up the Chaudière River and down the Kennebec and forced the surrender of the settlement in Casco Bay. With these raids, the French completed their apprenticeship in the toilsome and terrible art of forest warfare. The Iroquois had no more to teach them. They had appropriated the Iroquois method, developed it, exploited it with ruthless efficiency to the consternation of their English enemies and the secret admiration of the Indians themselves.

In the meantime, however, the English counter-offensive was slowly getting under way. It was just as characteristic of the spirit of the English Seaboard colonies as Frontenac's raiding parties had been of the nature of the fur-trading state. It was pugnaciously strong at sea, where the French attack had completely miscarried in weakness; and it was feeble on land, where the skill and endurance of the inland commercial empire of the French was so dramatically revealed. The colonial army which assembled under Major John Schuyler at the head of Lake Champlain failed to carry out the expected attack on Montreal; but, in the meantime, Sir William Phips had sailed out from Boston harbour in command of the greatest armament which the sea traders and sea fighters of New England had yet launched. He captured Port Royal—and with it the keys of Acadia—with ease. In the autumn he returned in triumph with a fleet of thirty ships and sailed up the St. Lawrence to Quebec. 'No,' roared old Frontenac furiously to the English envoy who had come demanding the surrender of the town, 'I will answer your general only with the mouths of my cannon and the shots of my muskets, that he may learn that a man like me is not to be summoned in this fashion.' Yet for all this defiant rejoinder, Frontenac did not exploit his opportunities very vigorously; and it was the ineptitudes of the besiegers rather than the skill of the besieged which caused the siege to fail. Within a week Phips had sailed away down the St. Lawrence in discomfiture. The direct attack on Quebec had certainly miscarried. But it had come perilously close to succeeding. The populous, prosperous colonies of the Atlantic Seaboard had given an ominous show of what they could do, even alone, when they were really roused; and the fortress of the fur-trading colony of the St. Lawrence had almost fallen nearly three-quarters of a century before its time.

After this defeat, the English were in no mood to resume large-scale operations. And after the great English naval victory at La Hogue, the French were in no position to undertake a major land-and-sea attack. The battle of La Hogue put an end to Colbert's ambitious dream of French supremacy at sea; and France turned to the guerrilla warfare of the type of naval strategy known as *guerre de course*. The organized privateering attacks on enemy commerce which were the chief features of *guerre de course* were, in effect, the naval counterpart of the swift surprises and frontier raids of *la petite guerre* of the French-Canadians. This was the kind of battle by which the War of the League of Augsburg was to be fought to a finish in the North Atlantic and in northern North America; and no other form of strategy and tactics could have better suited the strange fighting genius of the fur-trading colony.

Frontenac, who was to die in the province he had come back to defend, was the inspiration of this greatest of all French-Canadian offensives; and Pierre Le Moyne, Sieur d'Iberville, who had been born in the then outpost of Montreal and was the embodiment of all the best fighting qualities which the St. Lawrence valley had inspired, became the war's greatest paladin on both land and sea. A tall, powerful, resourceful man, with a great mop of yellow hair, he had gained his apprenticeship on the Troyes expedition to Hudson Bay and Frontenac's raid on Schenectady; and now in these last years of the War of the League of Augsburg, he moved with equal ease and consistently smashing military success, from continent to ocean and from ocean to island. He ravaged the northern coast of New England; he swept Hudson Bay clean of English shipping; he virtually destroyed English power in Newfoundland. He was perhaps the most conspicuous of that splendid company—Radisson, Groseilliers, Jolliet, Du Lhut, La Salle, and Iberville's own brothers, Maricourt and Ste. Hélène—who had made good the French claim to northern North America and who, with their own strength and in their own way, had defended it against all comers.

3

THE GRAND STRATEGY OF EMPIRE

I

In 1697, when the bewigged plenipotentiaries of Europe ended the War of the League of Augsburg by the Peace of Ryswick, New France reached and passed a point of crucial importance in its history. For over thirty years, ever since royal government had been established and Tracy had arrived at Quebec with the stout companies of the Carignan-Salières regiment, the colony had steadily increased in strength. True, it had not developed exactly as the officialdom of Versailles had desired. It was painfully obvious now that the New France which Colbert and the mercantilist bureaucrats had planned—the New France of the diversified economy, flourishing agriculture, and thriving ocean trade—showed little sign of becoming a reality. These paper doctrinaire projects had certainly been frustrated. The colony had not grown as perhaps it ought to have grown. But, at the same time, it had undeniably waxed in size and strength. It had become, in fact, an enormous oceanic and continental empire which stretched westward from Newfoundland and Acadia to beyond Lake Superior, and southward from Hudson Bay to the Gulf of Mexico.

It had reached—though nobody knew it at the time—the pinnacle of its success. It stood—though this was only realized later—at the ultimate height of its power. The settlement which followed the War of the League of Augsburg was, in effect, a recognition, on the part of all France's enemies in North America, of the extent and power of her imperialistic venture in the New World. It was an admission which had to be made, not only by the Seaboard Colonies and their Motherland, but also by the members of the Iroquois Confederacy, who were far older opponents than the English, and who had been fighting the fur-trading colony for nearly a century. The diplomacy which ended in the Peace of Ryswick was followed, three years later, by the equally elaborate and prolonged negotiations which had their happy conclusion in a general concord among the French and the Indian tribes. In the early autumn of 1700, an immense company of thirteen hundred native warriors assembled in a grand council at Montreal. The Five Iroquois Nations—Mohawks, Oneidas, Onondagas, Cayugas, and Senecas—were represented in force. There were Abenaki from Acadia, Illinois and Miami from the Mississippi regions, Ottawas and Hurons from the Lake Superior country, and Crees, Assiniboines, and Sioux from the far west.

The neutrals, the enemies, the French allies were, at long last, all congregated together; and in the next summer, after long days of deliberate, solemn formalities and endless floods of highly allusive, highly figurative Indian oratory, the first great general Indian peace was accepted. For the French it was, in its way, an even greater diplomatic triumph than the Peace of Ryswick itself. The two parts of the settlement—the Indian peace and the European treaty—had confirmed the French Empire in North America in all the grandeur of its extent. The French held most of Newfoundland. They had recovered Acadia. They occupied all but one of the fur-trading posts on Hudson Bay. And when, in 1699, the incredible ubiquitous Iberville had explored the lower Mississippi and established the post at Biloxi, their inland empire, based on the continent's two greatest river systems, extended all the way from the Gulf of St. Lawrence to the Gulf of Mexico.

This was the high-water mark of French enterprise in North America. From that moment onward, the flood-tide of success gradually receded. But, in the New World at least, it was at first a very gradual recession; and nothing very striking occurred to indicate that a point of no return had been reached and passed. It was true, of course, that New France was not permitted to enjoy the successful settlement of 1697–1701 very long. The brief interval of peace which the Treaty of Ryswick had brought ended all too swiftly in the opening of that even greater conflict, the War of the Spanish Succession; and the new war, though its main actions were to be fought in Europe and the Mediterranean, was much more a colonial war than its predecessor, the War of the League of Augsburg, had been. To prevent France from enjoying a monopoly of the Spanish trade in the New World was one of the principal reasons for England's entrance into the Grand Alliance against Louis XIV. The English at home were determined to stop the expansion of French interests in the Western Hemisphere; and the English in the Seaboard Colonies were increasingly anxious to put an end to a power which offered a continual threat to their growth in North America. The War of the Spanish Succession might plunge New France into an ordeal far worse than any she had experienced before. It might; but New France showed no sign of undue apprehension. She had been supremely successful in the past. Why should not her success continue in the future?

And yet what were the resources of which she could dispose? In what strategical and tactical terms could she plan the campaigns of the future? Iberville, whose grasp of the grand strategy of the continent equalled his brilliant skill in manœuvre, was full of grandiose plans for concerted attacks on Boston or other key centres of English power on the Atlantic Seaboard. He might, if he had been properly supported, have performed prodigies for France in North America; but from a nation whose eyes were focused upon a rapidly deteriorating cause in Europe, what real chances were there of adequate support? In 1704, two years after the war began, the battle of Blenheim brought the first of a string of ruinous defeats on

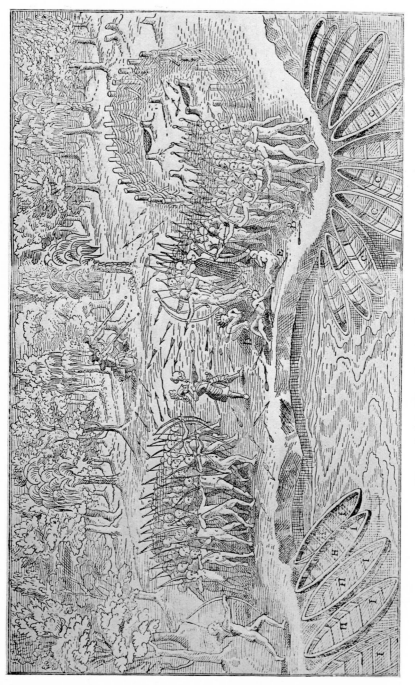

1. Champlain's First Battle with the Iroquois, 1609

2. The Siege of Louisbourg, 1758

land; and at sea the plan of eating away England's naval strength by an organized, widespread system of privateering attacks upon her commerce was obviously failing to achieve its object. English shipping losses were heavy. But fundamentally England's resources had not been seriously strained. Her ships still rode in triumph in home waters and dominated the vital sea lanes to the Western Hemisphere. In these circumstances what could France do but persistingly continue a strategy of raids and surprises which, though ineffective, was the only strategy open to her in North America? She would not—or could not—spare any substantial part of her splendid European army for the New World. Even if she had been willing to send it, could it have been got in safety across the Atlantic?

If France's options were unreal, New France had no choice at all. Without support from the Motherland, she was quite incapable of maintaining a major offensive against New York or Boston. All she could do was to carry out a series of raids and border forays which would mask her own deficiencies, keep the English off balance and preoccupied, and possibly prevent them from launching a serious invasion to the north. It was the kind of strategy and the type of warfare which best suited the fur-trading colony's genius; and this time New France was able to carry on its favourite form of combat with a new economy, for now there was only one enemy and one main strategic area that really counted. The fighting on Hudson Bay was not resumed. The Indian peace continued unbroken. The long, open south-western flank of the French inland empire, which stretched from Lake Ontario to the Mississippi, was never troubled. The French could concentrate upon the islands and the seaboard of the North Atlantic. The privateers of Port Royal preyed on English commerce, the garrison at Placentia sacked St. John's, Newfoundland, the Acadians and the Abenaki Indians harried the frontier settlements at Wells and Casco Bay. And from Montreal, typical guerrilla war-parties, composed of regulars, militia volunteers, and Indians, descended upon the New England villages of

D

Deerfield and Haverhill, and repeated the massacre, the pillage, and the flaming destruction of Frontenac's raids.

Would the French border forays achieve their objective? Or would they simply goad the English into a determined effort to end the everlasting menace of French power in North America? And if England decided that she could afford to undertake a large-scale combined operation against New France, how well would the English and the North Americans solve the inevitable problems of co-operation and co-ordination? In 1707, when New England tried on its own account to take Port Royal, the results were singularly unimpressive; and two years later, when an ambitious joint attack was planned for the reduction of the whole of New France, only Port Royal, a solitary conquest, finally fell to Anglo-American arms. It was not until 1711, when the war in Europe was virtually over, that a full-dress invasion of the fur-trading colony by land and sea at last got under way. That summer, Colonel Francis Nicholson marched his colonial army through the forest as far north as Lake George; but in the meantime Sir Hovenden Walker, ascending the St. Lawrence with the fleet, was encountering tragic difficulties. The ships, badly piloted through a difficult navigation, sailed too close to the reefs and submerged islets of the north shore; and eight transports and nearly a thousand man were lost in the breakers pounding over Egg Island. The expedition was abandoned. The army at Lake George was recalled; and Colonel Nicholson, denouncing the fleet and its commander with ejaculations of 'Roguery', 'Treachery', threw his wig on the ground in a rage and stamped on it.

II

New France had given a good account of herself. Through her own courage and enterprise, as well as through the misfortunes and the incompetence of the enemy, she had been enabled to hold her own. If the war had been concluded in

North America, on the basis of its North American results, New France might have kept its possessions, including Port Royal. But, of course, the peace was not made in North America. It was made in Europe; and in Europe the war and the reign of Louis XIV were drawing to an end together in defeat and discouragement. Concessions would have to be made in the peace negotiations; and for a variety of good and substantial reasons, commercial England was bound to insist that some of these concessions must be made in North America. France struggled to retain her colonial empire intact. She was compelled to yield. Yet she managed, in two regions at least, to qualify the gravity of her losses. Though Newfoundland had to be surrendered, the right to dry fish was retained for French fishermen, on the northern shores of the island; and while Acadia had to be given up, its boundaries were defined with deliberate ambiguity, and the islands in the gulf which were closest to it were kept in French control. In the maritime region, the bitterness of defeat was tempered; but in the interior there was no mitigation of the losses which New France was forced to suffer. She renounced her claim to sovereignty over the Iroquois and she surrendered the forts and territories which she had won from her commercial rival on Hudson Bay.

The Treaty of Utrecht vitally affected the alignment of powers in the New World. It settled the lines on which the struggle for North America was to be fought. But it did not decide the issue. It postponed the outcome for another generation. There was, of course, no doubt at all by this time as to who the great antagonists were. Spain and Holland, though they both still ranked as rich colonial and commercial powers, had dropped out of this great imperial struggle; and in both the West and the Far East it was France and England who now confronted each other alone. The first round had been a draw. In the second, France had been undeniably worsted. But, although the War of the Spanish Succession had exhausted her, it had not weakened her ambition or robbed her of her marvellous recuperative powers. She had, as it turned out, thirty years of peace in which to effect a complete recovery. Her army was one of the greatest fighting machines in Europe; her navy was gradually rebuilt in accordance with the best precepts of naval science. And out in North America she still possessed an empire whose vast extent and infinite possibilities challenged the imagination. Nothing of real importance had been lost. Everything might be repaired. All that was needed was to strengthen and reorganize these scattered northern possessions in preparation for the decisive conflict of the future.

The French set to work energetically, purposefully. There was a great deal to do. New France possessed three main fronts—the maritime, the north-western, and the south-western—which must be defended at all costs, which must be pushed forward if possible. The first, the maritime front, was perhaps the most important of the three. It guarded the entrance to the St. Lawrence. It was the key to the French inland empire. And, since the enforced concessions of the Treaty of Utrecht, it was unquestionably weaker, and more precariously held, than it had been before. Acadia, in accordance with its ancient boundaries, and Newfoundland had gone. The good harbours of Placentia and Port Royal had been surrendered. But the French still held Cape Breton which they called Isle Royale, and Isle St. Jean, the present Prince Edward Island; and here, on this inner ring of island defences, they proposed to establish a new Acadia—an Acadia which would be not only populous and prosperous, but also aggressively competitive.

The ink was scarcely dry on the Treaty of Utrecht when a small exploring party set out from France to select suitable centres for the restored Acadia. Isle Royale was a wild, lonely, almost empty island; and on its south-eastern coast, where low sullen hills and sombre marsh and moorland sloped slowly down to a rocky, desolate shore, the planners found a site for the future seaward fortress of New France. It was a fine harbour, almost enclosed by a protecting arm of land which was extended into the sea by submerged reefs and islands; and on the crown of this jutting peninsula the French built the elaborate fortifications of Louisbourg, 'the Dunkirk of America'. On the landward side, a glacis, a ditch eighty feet in width, and stone walls which, with their four great bastions, rose thirty feet into the air, provided impressive protection; the harbour was guarded by batteries established on one of the islands as well as on shore; and inside the town, some five hundred regular soldiers together with the militia furnished by the settlers and the fishermen provided, on paper at least, a stout defence. The artificial fortifications raised on this drear and deserted corner of Cape Breton were the most imposing in North America. Everything proclaimed the importance which the French attached to the position they had chosen. Louisbourg was to act as a protecting centre for the fishery, a focus for future settlement, and a guardian of French interests in the strategically vital maritime region.

It was a powerful establishment. And yet, behind its formidable exterior, there were serious weaknesses. The arrangement of the batteries protecting the harbour was, in places, highly questionable; and these defects in Louisbourg's prime function of defence were an unhappy indication of still more fundamental deficiencies in its character. The fortress, conceived as the active focus of a prosperous French maritime empire, continued to repose on a narrow, artificial, and impermanent base. It attracted few settlers; it never became a thriving commercial centre. The great French fishery in the North Atlantic was an extremely dispersed enterprise, mainly carried on by the fleets of large fishing ships which came out annually from old France. A resident fishery did develop about Louisbourg, but it was a relatively small one; and the Acadians, who, it had been hoped, at the time of the signing of the Treaty of Utrecht, would agree to migrate from Nova Scotia to the French islands, Isle St. Jean and Isle Royale, refused sullenly to follow the flag. Louisbourg was as strong only as brick and stone could make it. Its towers and battlements, rising through fog against the dun background of empty moorland, were an incongruous expression of artificial grandeur.

And yet, if the French remained weak in the maritime region, it could certainly not be said that the English were becoming strong. During the last two wars, England and New England had repeatedly attempted to end French rule in Acadia. At Utrecht, the British diplomatists had insisted upon the surrender of the region. And yet, once they were put in possession of it, the English seemed to lose all interest in its present and future. The French pursued the restoration of their fortunes in the maritime region with an anxious and purposeful determination; but the British treated their new territorial acquisition, Nova Scotia, with serene indifference or only slightly embarrassed neglect. At Port Royal, renamed Annapolis Royal in honour of Queen Anne, the signs of parsimony and disregard were obvious. In and about the decaying fort, there were only a few officials, a handful of traders, and a discontented and undisciplined garrison. At Canso and at other places along the south shore of the peninsula, hundreds of fishermen from New England used to congregate every summer for the season's catch. But these migratory enterprisers had not yet made permanent settlements of any size; after the Treaty of Utrecht as well as before it, the Acadians formed the real population of Nova Scotia.

The Acadians had certainly not shown themselves devoted followers of the French Crown; but they were equally unwilling to become faithful subjects of His Britannic Majesty. They spoke of themselves as 'the neutral French'; they refused to take the oath of allegiance which the British officials kept pressing upon them. And the ambiguous, equivocal legal position in which they stubbornly remained was an all too accurate indication of the state of political suspense in which Acadia still rested. It was an area of the highest strategic importance, in which the final issue was yet to be determined. Without question the French had suffered an initial reverse; but it was also becoming increasingly apparent that they had regained a definite moral initiative.

Out west, in the region which the French called the *pays*

d'en haut, the political state of affairs bore much the same
appearances of uneasiness and uncertainty. Here, in an inland
commercial empire which was the greatest achievement of
French power in North America, New France had of necessity
to do battle on two fronts; and in the first decades after the
Treaty of Utrecht she managed, through courage and enterprise, to show at least the semblance of the initiative in both.
The south-western front, for commercial as well as political
reasons, was vital to her continued existence. Preponderance
on the long line of communication which stretched from the
lower St. Lawrence to the upper Mississippi was necessary both
to link Canada and Louisiana, the two divisions of her continental empire, and to defend the fur trade from the competition of New York, Pennsylvania, and Virginia. The Treaty
of Utrecht had dealt that commercial and military superiority
a hard blow. It had recognized British suzerainty over the
Iroquois; and in 1722 the Governor of New York, making a
very literal interpretation of his new authority, had caused a
blockhouse and a trading post to be erected on the south shore
of Lake Ontario at the mouth of the Oswego River.

This was an aggressive advance post which bit deep into the
heart of the French fur-trading and military system. Already
the authorities at Quebec had set themselves vigorously to undo
the evil effects of the Treaty of Utrecht; and now the establishment of Fort Oswego provoked them to intensify their efforts.
They used all the experience they had gained in over a century
of contacts with the Indians to cultivate their increasingly
friendly relations with their old enemies, the Iroquois. They
busied themselves, so far as the straitened finances of the colony
would permit, in extending the system of defences, half-military
forts and half-trading posts, which had been begun by the
building of Fort Frontenac and Fort Detroit. The fort at
Niagara, which had begun life as a flimsy wooden affair five
years before, was stoutly rebuilt in stone in 1725; and in the
debatable frontier territory south-west of Lake Erie, Fort
Miami was erected on the Maumee River and Vincennes on

the Wabash. All these outposts, it could be argued plausibly enough, were for trade; but the French scarcely bothered to offer this explanation for the structure which they raised during the 1730's at the head of Lake Champlain, close to the spot where Champlain had had his first famous encounter with the Iroquois over a hundred years before. Fort St. Frédéric—or Crown Point as the Anglo-Americans called it—was not a fur-trade post. Its function was essentially military. It was intended to dominate the Hudson River—Lake Champlain valley, and to threaten Albany, while it protected Three Rivers and Montreal.

On the north-western front, in the region beyond Lake Superior, the French were forced, even more obviously, to take the initiative against their triumphant rival, the Hudson's Bay Company. By the terms of the Treaty of Utrecht, the posts on Hudson and James bays were returned to their English proprietors; and henceforward the French made no attempt to destroy their opponents' trade by capturing the bases from which it was conducted. The strenuous overland expeditions to the bay, the sudden attacks by sea on the English company's stations, which had been such a dramatic feature of the War of the League of Augsburg, were never resumed again; and the fur traders of Montreal were compelled to rely solely upon their second competitive method, which was to intercept and divert the Hudson's Bay Company's source of supplies.

It was a method which was growing more toilsome and difficult all the time, for the fur trade, in obedience to its own nature, was travelling inevitably westward across the continent. The richest Hudson's Bay Company's fur cargoes were coming now from the drainage basin of Lake Winnipeg and the Saskatchewan River valley. The far-off Nelson and Churchill rivers carried these cargoes down to posts on the west side of Hudson Bay; and to circumvent this remote and lucrative trade, the French were forced to advance from the head of the Great Lakes, across the height of land and out into the central plains of the continent. This, which was the last great achievement of French exploring enterprise in North America, was the work of the trader-explorer Pierre Gaultier de Varennes, Sieur de La Vérendrye. During the decade of the 1730's Vérendrye, his sons, and his nephew, Sieur de la Jemeraye, pushed the French fur trade systematically north-westward, in efficient stages, from Grand Portage at the head of Lake Superior. Forts were erected on Rainy Lake, at Lake of the Woods, and on the Red River a few miles up from Lake Winnipeg. And finally, with the building of Fort Bourbon in 1739, the French reached the Saskatchewan, and the trade of the Assiniboine and Saskatchewan rivers was incorporated in the continental trading system of the St. Lawrence.

III

In 1739, when Fort Bourbon was founded, the thirty years' peace, which had followed the Treaty of Utrecht, was drawing rapidly to a close. The War of the League of Augsburg and the War of the Spanish Succession were fading memories; peace had become the natural, normal state. But between eighteenth-century France and eighteenth-century Great Britain any peaceful settlement was basically impermanent; and when the fifth decade of the century opened, the final round of the Anglo-French struggle for empire was close at hand. How well pre-pared was New France for this last and greatest ordeal? Out-wardly everything must have seemed reassuringly prosperous. With the strengthening of the south-west commercial system and the extension of the trade to the valleys of the Assiniboine and the Saskatchewan, there had come a definite period of economic well-being and social ease. The last fifteen years of the peace were good years for New France. And yet had its character altered for the better in any really significant way? Was it not—despite its growth and increasing prosperity—a fur-trading colony still, with all a fur-trading colony's incur-able deficiencies and weaknesses?

It had grown; but it had grown in the curious, lopsided

fashion which the fur trade seemed to dictate. In territorial extent, New France was truly magnificent. The English colonies had not penetrated westward beyond the Appalachian Highlands, but New France, through its occupation of the river systems of the Mississippi and the St. Lawrence, had daringly pre-empted the whole interior of the continent. It was, on the map, an enormous, grandiose empire; but it was occupied and defended not by thriving communities of people, but by a few forts, a few trading posts, a small company of extremely able fur traders, and a fragile network of Indian alliances. In the St. Lawrence valley settlement was concentrated mainly between Quebec and Montreal; but it extended, virtually unbroken, all the way up the Atlantic Seaboard; and while the population of the English colonies was now getting close to a million five hundred thousand, there were only about fifty thousand Frenchmen in the two provinces of Canada and Louisiana. The days when the government of Louis XIV had promoted and assisted settlement were long past now; and, in the main, the population grew by means of the large families of its own natural increase. It was a small company—poor in numbers and resources—with which to defend a vast and showy empire.

Its main occupation was still the fur trade; and the fur trade had stamped the colony deeply with its strong, crude impress. New France had begun life as a fur-trade outpost and a mission station; and now, after nearly a hundred and fifty years of existence, it had continued to maintain much of its original character. Colbert and the seventeenth-century planners, disturbed by these social distortions, had endeavoured to reproduce something of the complexity and balance of the society of the motherland; and in their endeavour literally to create a 'New France' overseas, they had instinctively relied upon the feudal land-holding system which was the original property basis of the French social order. It was sensibly realized, of course, that French feudalism, with the preposterous privileges and appalling burdens which had come to characterize it in the seventeenth and eighteenth centuries, could not be literally transported to the New World with any hope of success; and the land-holding system which actually developed in New France, called the seigniorial system, was a modification of the original which had been definitely liberalized both in the interests of the state and to the advantage of the tenantry. The landlord or seigneur, whose duties to the colony and the local community were carefully prescribed and whose rents could not be raised at will, was, to a large extent, a government agent for land settlement. The tenant, who was usually called a *habitant* or *censitaire*, from the *cens* or rent he paid, was protected from the possible exactions of his lord and bore not a tithe of the brutalizing burdens of his prototype in old France.

Along the St. Lawrence, the water boulevard which flowed in a north-easterly direction towards the sea, the entire existence of the colony was focused. Every landlord and every tenant wanted access to the stream which was the life-blood of the settlement; and the dividing lines of the long, narrow, rectangular seigniories, running from north-west to south-east, were drawn perpendicularly to the course of the river. The *habitant* holdings into which the seigniories were divided were ribbon-like farms each of which had likewise its frontage on the St. Lawrence; and along the river between Quebec and Montreal, and up the Richelieu, settlement extended in a thin but unbroken fashion, as if along the single street of a sparsely populated but interminable village. Here, in the unpretentious manor-houses, and the white-washed stone *habitant* cottages, with their high-pitched roofs and small dormer windows, a little rural society worked and played in ways which, a generation or so later, Nicholas Krieghoff was to capture for all time in his lively pictures. The rude plenty, the gaiety, the contentment and the unquestioning faith of the small community were real enough; but they were based upon a rather narrow subsistence agriculture, which never succeeded in discovering a good outlet overseas, and sometimes could not even supply its own domestic urban market. Farming was inevitably a depressed business in a colony where the fur trade was the only real source of wealth; and the ex-army officers and sons of good but untitled families who became seigneurs were incapable of attaining the positions of economic importance and social leadership which Colbert and the imperial planners had assumed would be theirs.

The places which the seigneurs had left vacant were occupied by the clergy and the fur traders. These two strangely contrasted groups, the 'black robes' and the *coureurs-de-bois*, stood for the colony's twin dominant activities, missionary enterprise and western trade; and the prominence and influence which they acquired in the affairs of New France were the inevitable rewards of the key parts they had played in its development. After 1663, the efficiency experts of Louis XIV's centralized monarchy, who hoped to broaden and diversify the social structure of the colony, tried their best to change this state of affairs. They succeeded, to some extent, in reducing the power of the clergy in the politics of the colony; but they utterly failed to provide new skills and trades on the lower St. Lawrence and to prevent the fur trade from draining away the colony's best man-power into the interior. They tried to reduce the number of the *coureurs-de-bois* by a licensing system; but the *coureurs-de-bois* burst through these paper defences into the west. Picturesque, prodigal, reckless, resentful of authority and calloused to hardship and danger, they quickened the drab life of the seigniories with the adventure, the violence, and the ambition of their western commercial empire. They supplied New France with its economic drive and its military tactics, just as the priests and the members of the religious orders provided the colony's schools and hospitals, imposed its moral standards, and maintained its spiritual values. The fur traders became increasingly solid and respectable citizens as the province grew in prosperity during the eighteenth century; the clergy lost a little of their political power; but to the end these two social groups remained the poles around which the active life of New France centred. It was a curious distinctive little society, small, tough, and enduring, well adjusted to its new environment and filled with an invincible determination to survive.

Its government was, on the whole, perhaps as well fitted as any could have been to the genius of the people and the needs of the community. The French monarchy was a centralized, authoritarian government; and the French Empire had as its main principle the subordination of the colonies to the control of the Mother Country. When New France became a royal province, the chief officials and institutions of a typical province of old France, the governor, the intendant, the small nominated council, and the troop of subordinate officials were duly installed at Quebec, Montreal, and Three Rivers. This paternally despotic system had its obvious defects. It made little attempt to secure the formal approval and consent of a resident population which was freer in spirit than that of the old world; and the swift efficiency, which was potentially its greatest asset, depended upon the amicable co-operation of the chief officials at Quebec and was often sacrificed to the minute and time-consuming supervision of Paris.

Centralized, authoritarian government had been established almost automatically in New France; but, on the whole, it was encouraged, rather than resisted, by the natural tendencies of the region. The St. Lawrence, which gathered and focused the far-flung activities of the French Empire, had always seemed to prosper most satisfactorily under monopoly and centralization. The affairs of an unbalanced and precarious economy, which was dependent upon a single luxury staple, could best be administered at a single centre; and from a single centre the expansion and defence of its continually enlarging hinterland could be most efficiently directed. New France was a small, poor province. It bore the crushing burden of western empire. It could be overwhelmed by the vastly superior numbers of its enemies. Yet, in the final ordeal that lay before it, it could, if all went well, make the best use of its small resources. It could maximize its brave but limited strength.

4

MONTCALM AND WOLFE

I

On a day late in April 1745, in the coastal waters off Canso, at the north-eastern tip of Nova Scotia, an impressively large company of ships and men was assembling. Four British men-of-war commanded by Commodore Peter Warren of the West Indies station, rode at anchor in the tumbling waves. A large number of fishing ships and schooners, of all rigs and sizes, waited respectfully near by; and in these rough transports was crowded a volunteer colonial army of four thousand artisans, farmers, and fishermen who had sailed north-east from New England under the command of their own amateur general, the colonial merchant, William Pepperell, of Kittery, Maine. The New Englanders, most of whom came from Massachusetts, had reached the Canso rendezvous early in April. Warren, with his warships, arrived in the last week of the month. And in the early morning of April 30th the vanguard of this undisciplined but vigorous expeditionary force began to disembark in Gabarus Bay, less than two miles to the west of the fortress of Louisbourg.

The war—the War of the Austrian Succession, which ended the long, thirty-years' truce between France and England—had begun only a year before. Already the French in North America had obviously lost the initiative. They had begun quickly enough, in the traditional French-Canadian style of 'la petite guerre'. Privateers started immediately in their accustomed efficient fashion to prey upon New England commerce; the blockhouse at Canso was overwhelmed in a surprise attack. But the expedition which set out overland for the capture of Annapolis Royal was tamely abandoned when the expected naval support from Louisbourg failed to appear; and in the meantime William Shirley, the Governor of Massachusetts, was rousing the whole of New England by his popular appeal to end the menace of the 'Dunkirk of America'.

During the early months of 1745 an eighteenth-century Puritan Crusade, inspired both by New England moral indignation and New England commercial greed, began to get enthusiastically under way. The Methodist George Whitefield supplied a pious motto, *Nil Desperandum Christo Duce*, for the militant Protestant host; its senior chaplain, Parson Moody, carried an axe with which to hew down 'the altars of Antichrist' at Louisbourg. The unprofessional New England volunteers violated most of the regulations and all of the etiquette of the formal eighteenth-century armies; but they showed skill and dash, as well as dogged endurance, in their conduct of the siege. The isolated Royal Battery, whose position was one of the principal weaknesses in the outward defences of Louisbourg, was quickly seized; the Island Battery, which guarded the entrance to the harbour, was pounded into silence with well-directed gun-fire. The time had arrived for a final combined assault by land and sea upon the fortress. The attack was about to be delivered; and then, on June 16th, after a siege which had lasted only a little over six weeks, Chambon, the French commandant, surrendered Louisbourg with all the honours of war.

It was a desperately serious loss. It meant the destruction of the French position in the maritime region. It meant the serious embarrassment of their main stronghold in the St. Lawrence valley; and these were consequences which, in the first year of the war, the French were completely unwilling to accept. A great, an immediate, effort at recovery was necessary; and in

June 1746, just a year after Chambon's tragic surrender, it was made. From Quebec, Ramezay set out with a little army of nearly seven hundred militia for Acadia; and—what was infinitely more important—a splendid French fleet—ten ships of the line, half a dozen smaller vessels, and some sixty transports carrying three thousand five hundred troops—sailed from Rochefort under the command of De Roye de Rochefoucauld, Duc d'Anville, for the rendezvous at Chebucto, on the south shore of Nova Scotia. Never before—even counting Tracy's expedition of 1665 and the arrival of the Carignan-Salières regiment—had France put forward such a stupendous effort on behalf of its North American possessions. Never before had any French armament in North America been given a more ambitious programme of recovery and reprisal than that which the Comte de Maurepas had conceived for D'Anville's amphibious force. The French were to recapture Louisbourg, take Annapolis Royal, destroy Boston, and harry the whole New England coast.

It was possible, of course, for Ramezay to bring his little force down in safety to the Isthmus of Chignecto, for this was a traditional French-Canadian raiding operation. But the reconquest of Acadia depended really upon the success of D'Anville's great expedition; and D'Anville's fleet had sailed away from Rochefort into an uninterrupted succession of appalling disasters. Dead, glassy calms at first delayed the progress of the armada; the violent electrical storms and gales which followed scattered the men-of-war and sank several of the transports. It was over four months before the fleet was finally able to anchor in Chebucto harbour; and by that time a terrible pestilence, bred in the contaminated holds of the neglected ships, had begun to run through the helpless company on board with virulent swiftness. By October, three thousand sailors and soldiers had died of plague. D'Anville, worn out with fever and anxiety, died also. His successor, the impetuous D'Estourmelles, attempted to commit suicide. And it was the third in command, La Jonquière, who brought the

3. Loyalists' Settlement on the St. Lawrence, 1784

battered and diseased remnants of the doomed expedition back in humiliation to France.

The macabre horror of these accumulated disasters might have paralysed the fighting arm of any nation; but the French, with the fate of their North American possessions at stake, were not finished yet. Ramezay, with his small army of experts in forest warfare, was still in Nova Scotia, waiting and hoping. In February 1747 a raiding party of militiamen and Indians set out from the French base in the Isthmus of Chignecto, fought its way on snowshoes through the piled drifts of a bitter winter, and overwhelmed the Anglo-American garrison at the outpost of Grand Pré. In May, despite the sinister omens of the calamities of the preceding summer, a fresh fleet of war-ships and transports, under the command of La Jonquière, now appointed Governor of New France, set sail for the St. Lawrence. If La Jonquière had been able to bring his substan-tial reinforcements safely to Quebec he might, with Ramezay's help, have renewed the attempt to retake Louisbourg and capture Annapolis Royal. But before it even got clear of Europe, the French fleet was set upon and badly outfought by an English squadron under Admiral Anson. When, finally, La Jonquière limped up the St. Lawrence to Quebec with less than half of his convoy, he was in no state, and had no spirit, to begin offensive operations; and Ramezay, without naval sup-port, could take neither Louisbourg nor Annapolis Royal.

Ths misfortunes of the French at sea had their compensa-tions in the land exploits of the crack professional army of the day. The war may have been lost in North America, but it was very nearly won in Europe and the Far East; and the Peace of Aix-la-Chapelle, which closed the conflict in 1748, recognized this fairly even balance of good fortune. Louis-bourg, despite the resentment and indignation of the Americans, was restored to France; and when the fleur-de-lis floated once more over the great fortress on Cape Breton Island, it might well have seemed that Acadia had lapsed once more into its old apathetic state of indecision and ambiguity. Yet it was not

E

so. The old familiar appearances masked a completely different state of affairs. Both sides evidently regarded the Peace of Aix-la-Chapelle as a mere truce. Both sides were intent upon dominating a region which, they realized, was of crucial strategic importance for their respective North American empires; and both were determined—peace or no peace—to prepare for the decisive encounter of the near future.

In 1749, by that very harbour where D'Anville's wretched men had died in their hundreds three years before, the British established the fortress and settlement of Halifax. It was the only colony which ever came into existence in North America as a direct result of the action of the British government. It was the obvious and admitted rival of Louisbourg; and it had been founded as a direct consequence of Louisbourg's restoration. The challenge of Halifax demanded an immediate and emphatic rejoinder; and the French hastened to make it. The Chevalier de La Corne, arriving with a force of six hundred men, laid claim to the north shore of the Bay of Fundy; and Charles Lawrence, dispatched from Halifax by Governor Cornwallis, hastened north-west to defend the Isthmus of Chignecto from invasion. Both sides sought immediately to occupy and fortify the most advanced positions possible. And soon, from opposite sides of the little river, which now forms the boundary of Nova Scotia and New Brunswick, the English Fort Lawrence and the French Fort Beauséjour confronted each other ominously.

II

Meanwhile, in the centre of the continent, on the frontiers of the vast inland empire of the French, there was the same electric atmosphere of impending storm. With every year that passed, the task which the fur-trading colony of the St. Lawrence had set itself grew more hugely difficult and exacting. In the north-west, it was true, the Canadian position was not unfavourable, for the great forced march to Lake Winnipeg and the Saskatchewan valley had put the French in a strongly competitive position. North-west of Lake Superior, they had some cause to be content; but below the Great Lakes, on their south-western front, there were only too many reasons for the gravest apprehension. Here, in the region of the Ohio River and its tributaries, was a territory which, from every point of view, was crucially important to New France; and here equally was a land into which the colonies of the Atlantic Seaboard, and in particular New York, Virginia, and Pennsylvania, were destined inevitably to expand. The few score American traders now competing for the south-west fur trade were simply the advance guard of the far greater oncoming army of agricultural frontiersmen who would replace the ephemeral dominion of Indian commerce with the enduring occupation of settlement. They could crack the tenuous, long-drawn-out line of communication between the St. Lawrence and the Mississippi at its most vulnerable joint. They could break and destroy the French Empire in North America.

All this lay in the future, no doubt. But it was a future, the French now began to realize, which was drawing very close. During the War of the Austrian Succession, they had not had to face any direct Anglo-American attacks upon their south-western front; but, for all that, the remote, dramatic events which had occurred in Acadia in the years 1744–7 had had indirect but very definite commercial and political effects in the Ohio valley. The war at sea, the shattered French fleets, and the half-wrecked French convoys had seriously interrupted the vitally necessary flow of trade goods to the interior; and the disasters which had overtaken D'Anville and his successors had gravely injured French prestige with their savage allies. A sullen murmur of resentment, contempt, and disaffection began to echo from tribe to tribe down the valley of the Ohio. There were Indians who were quite prepared to intrigue with the English; there were other, more numerous Indians who were ready enough to barter furs with them. Traders like George Croghan and Conrad Weiser busied themselves in proffering superior English trade goods and anti-French political counsel; and in 1749 a syndicate of Anglo-American land speculators took the name of the Ohio Company and secured from the Crown a grant of five hundred thousand acres on the Ohio for settlement.

The French were alarmed. It was 1749, the year of the founding of Halifax. Obviously, in both east and west, the struggle for the continent was gaining in intensity; and just as the establishment of the great English fortress in Nova Scotia was followed by vigorous counter-moves, so now the French began with energy and determination to repair the damage which their cause had suffered in the Ohio valley. A typical French-Canadian army of regulars, militia, and Indians under the command of the veteran fur trader, Céloron de Blainville, set out on a great circular tour of the Ohio—'la Belle Rivière'— and its tributaries, and Lake Erie. At regular intervals on his journey, Blainville planted leaden plates asserting the sovereignty of the King of France; and, at almost every point on his long perambulation, he found evidence of Indian indifference and English hostility which seemed to mock the claims he had preferred. A show of force on the Ohio was not enough! And in the year that followed, the French struggled to tighten their hold upon the region, and to shorten and protect vital lines of communication with the south-west. In 1753, a blockhouse was erected at Presqu'isle, on the south shore of Lake Erie; a road was cut through the forest to the Rivière aux Boeufs, a tributary of the Allegheny, the headwaters of the Ohio; and here a second protecting fort, Fort Le Boeuf, was built.

It was at this point that the English colonials officially intervened. A young Virginian gentleman named George Washington appeared unexpectedly at Fort Le Boeuf as the representative of the Governor of his Province and politely requested the French to remove themselves from territory which Virginia claimed as its own. The French officers in the blockhouse at Le Boeuf were equally polite. They agreeably entertained the young Virginian emissary; but they made it perfectly clear that they were determined to remain in the Ohio region. 'They told me', Washington reported later, 'that it was their absolute design to take possession of the Ohio, and by God they would do it.' This unambiguous message left Robert Dinwiddie, the Governor of Virginia, unimpressed; and in 1754 he dispatched a small force of colonials westward to clear the region of its presumptuous French trespassers and to build an English fort where the Allegheny and the Monongahela rivers unite to form the Ohio. The fort was only half completed when the indomitable French arrived in force. They appropriated the building, finished it, and defiantly renamed it Fort Duquesne. And when Washington toiled westward with another small colonial contingent to undo this scandalous piece of French effrontery, he was beaten, after a hot fight of several hours, and compelled to retire, leaving his enemies in triumphant possession.

All along the great arc which stretched from Cape Breton Island to the Ohio valley, the colonial subordinates were locked together in a furious and inconclusive struggle. It was too much for the principals in Europe; and, with sudden violence, they intervened. The Peace of Aix-la-Chapelle, it was true, was still theoretically in operation. England and France were still officially at peace. But this did not prevent each of the giant imperialistic contenders from throwing the full force of his might into a struggle which both realized was rapidly approaching its final paroxysm. In November 1754, George II defiantly announced to Parliament that he intended to defend his North American possessions by force of arms. In January 1755, two British regiments of the line, with Major-General Braddock in command, left England for Virginia; and in the following May a great fleet of eighteen French vessels, carrying the new Governor, the Canadian-born Marquis de Vaudreuil, the new commander, Baron Dieskau, and three thousand French regular troops, set sail from Brest. New France stood in desperate need of the heavy reinforcements which Dieskau was bringing, for in the spring of 1755 Braddock was maturing a most ambitious general plan. There were to be concerted attacks against Fort Beauséjour, Fort St. Frédéric, and Fort Niagara. Braddock himself was to strike at Fort Duquesne. And once these primary objectives were gained, the four armies were to move forward together for the final reduction of Canada.

Towards the end of a long day in June, Braddock's force was drawing close to its objective. The deliberate, systematic day's march was nearly over. The little army, with its British regulars in their red coats and colonial militia in their blue uniforms, was marching proudly forward in column behind beating drums and waving banners. The last formidable obstacle, the Monongahela River, had just been crossed, and Fort Duquesne was very close. The newly improvised road narrowed as it climbed upward from the river valley. The dark, dense forest closed in on either side. And then suddenly, without the slightest warning, the Anglo-American column crashed into a small French-Canadian force, under Captain de Beaujeu, which had been sent forward to check Braddock's advance. Both sides recovered almost immediately. A small British cannon, put at once into action, poured grape shot at the enemy. Beaujeu was killed. The French seemed to be yielding. The road ahead of Braddock's force emptied with mysterious rapidity; and the British column surged forward in a clumsy effort to deploy in the cramped space of the defile. It never finished the manœuvre. By now it was almost completely surrounded. Instinctively, swiftly, the little Canadian force—regulars, militia, and Indians—had slipped into the thick woods on either side; and the packed, bewildered redcoats, huddled in disorder on the open road, and firing uncertainly and ineffectually into the green, unrevealing foliage, were shot to pieces by that unseen and murderous force, a typical French-Canadian forest army. Braddock's advance was abandoned. Braddock himself died of wounds; and the Anglo-Americans lost no fewer than nine hundred men.

The first year of a war, which was now open and declared in

everything but name, was ending not unfavourably for the French. It was true that the brilliant success over Braddock was not elsewhere repeated; but it was also true that the four-pronged British attack had failed to penetrate to the quick of the French system. Shirley made no serious progress against Niagara. Johnson scored a tactical victory over Dieskau's regulars in the Lake George district; but at the end of the campaign Fort St. Frédéric remained securely in French hands. It was only in Acadia that the British really succeeded in achieving their objectives. Here Fort Beauséjour and Fort Gaspereau were surrendered in a spiritless fashion; and here also the British found a summary and severe solution of the Acadian problem in the wholesale transportation of this adamantly neutral people to other parts of British America.

The campaign of 1755 was over. It had brought the French one smashing triumph and much general satisfaction; but it was full of sinister significance for the future of French Canada none the less. The bungling ineffectuality of the English attack was obvious; but so also were the growing strength and purpose with which the Anglo-Americans were mustering their forces for the final phase of the continental struggle. How could the French best meet this onslaught? The swift, secret tactics of forest warfare could achieve much; but Braddock's defeat had led the native French-Canadians to exaggerate the value of 'la petite guerre' just as Johnson's tactical victory at Lake George had encouraged them to underestimate the fighting qualities of the French regulars. There was division in the high command and dissension in the ranks; and this at a time when, above all else, New France needed the strength of unity. She was a weak, poor, under-populated colony, about to enter the last round of a struggle for existence against overwhelming odds.

III

In May 1756 Great Britain declared war on France. In June France responded with her own defiant declaration. And in

December William Pitt seized control of English affairs in an imperious and purposeful grasp. A completely new phase of the conflict had opened. For over a year, it was true, the principals on both sides had been engaged; but the principals had been fighting an unorthodox half-acknowledged war in an uninspired and ineffective fashion. All this was now changed. Great Britain assumed the initiative with imagination and daring; she was determined to hit with all the strength she possessed; and the theatre in which she sought a final decision was North America and the North Atlantic Ocean. All the conflicts of the past—the War of the League of Augsburg, the War of the Spanish Succession, the War of the Austrian Succession—had been really lost and won on the battlefields of Europe; but this time the fate of New France was to be settled in North America. It was to be settled, moreover, by the trained professional armies and navies of the two greatest imperial powers of the time. The day of the swift raid, the daring foray, the successful ambuscade was over or nearly over; and the wild scenery of North America became a theatrical backdrop against which the crack troops and the best military science of Europe were to be displayed.

In the spring of that fateful year, 1756, Louis Joseph, Marquis de Montcalm, arrived at Quebec. He was in all probability the greatest field general of the Seven Years' War; but in New France he faced a situation which was desperately, almost irremediably, serious. He had, in the seven splendid regiments of La Reine, Guienne, Béarn, La Sarre, Languedoc, Royal Roussillon, and Berry, a total of only a few thousand regulars; he could count upon an effective strength of perhaps eight or nine thousand Canadian militia. It was a pitifully small number with which to meet the far vaster potential resources of England and English America; and Montcalm knew—it was an inescapably gloomy fact in all his calculations—that the force at his disposal could not be regularly and certainly reinforced. The convoys still occasionally got through—the arrival of Montcalm himself and of the new battalions which came with him was sufficient proof of that; and even yet there were fortunate occasions when French warships managed to obtain a temporary mastery in Canadian waters. But these spacious moments of freedom were transitory, almost accidental. The British were slowly but relentlessly establishing their command of the Atlantic. It was only a question of time before they would attempt to bottle up the French fleets in their Atlantic ports, seal the St. Lawrence from all relief, and settle Quebec with a knock-out blow.

Inevitably, the one possible strategy for Montcalm was the strategy of defence. Almost certainly he could not win in North America; he could only play for time in the hope that the great military power of continental France would be strong enough to wrest a decision in Europe. He could play for time; but it was a desperate game in which, in the end, he would have to fall back upon the resources of New France; and New France, in this supreme crisis of its existence, displayed all its characteristic weaknesses and limitations to the full. As the months went by, as the state of war gradually became a virtual state of siege, the fur-trading colony relapsed into a condition of chronic distress. There were bad harvests, food shortages, constant inflation. There was something else—something far more lamentable—as well. Upon the misfortunes of economic and political weakness were piled the mistakes and crimes of blind ill-will and corrupt self-interest. Vaudreuil, the Canadian-born Governor, who was jealous of Montcalm and sensitively resentful of French prestige and patronage, paralysed the high command with his constant interference. Bigot, the Intendant, battened upon the miserable colony with his light-hearted, swindling depredations. 'What a country, what a country,' Montcalm lamented 'where knaves grow rich and honest men are ruined.'

Yet he struggled to defend it. There were, he knew only too well, three possible invasion routes. One, by the St. Lawrence, was from the sea; the second was the well-worn, obvious inland gateway by Lake Champlain and the Richelieu River; the third and last was the remote western approach through the headwaters of the Ohio and the Lower Lakes. The two routes from the interior were, of course, protected by forts; but Montcalm had no intention of waiting tamely for the enemy within these defences. For the first two years of the war, he successfully masked the essentially defensive nature of his strategy with vigorous offensive operations. In 1756, Oswego, the important British western base on the south side of Lake Ontario, was taken; and a year later Montcalm pushed resolutely down the Richelieu valley to capture Fort William Henry, the British stronghold at the head of Lake George.

It was only in 1758, the third year of the war, when the Anglo-Americans sought to thrust their way simultaneously and in force up the three approaches to the heart of New France, that Montcalm failed to preserve his system intact. At Fort Ticonderoga, it was true, he repulsed the inept Abercromby's frontal assault with coolly efficient slaughter. But, for sheer lack of manpower, the western outposts—Fort Oswego, Fort Duquesne, even Fort Frontenac—were all abandoned; and, what was infinitely worse, an overwhelming British land and naval force brought about the second and final capitulation of Louisbourg. The seaway to New France was open. Most of the western defences were down. In the spring of 1759 the Anglo-Americans mustered in overwhelming numbers for the renewal of their threefold attack; and General James Wolfe and Admiral Charles Saunders sailed up the St. Lawrence to Quebec.

Without hope of reinforcements, with a command which was torn by dissension and riddled by profiteers, Montcalm took his last stand on the rock which Champlain had chosen for his 'habitation' a century and a half before. Quebec was not a scientifically constructed fortress like Louisbourg; it was at best a fortified town. The great cliffs about Cape Diamond gave the place superb natural protection; but further up the river, above Cap Rouge, the approaches were more open; and below the town nearly as far as the Montmorency River, the low

Beauport flats invited attack. Montcalm, with his limited resources, could not be everywhere. He lost control of the whole
south shore of the St. Lawrence. His defensive line—perhaps
over-extended as it was—stretched the whole length of the
Beauport shore, nearly six miles in all, between the rivers St.
Charles and Montmorency. Here he dug himself in systematically, and waited. He had not long to wait. On the last day of
July, Wolfe launched an attack on the left of his position,
where the low ground rose towards the Montmorency heights,
and was beaten back with serious loss. It was Montcalm's
fourth victory against the British. Oswego, William Henry,
Ticonderoga, and now Montmorency—surely these were auspi-
cious omens! The 'old fox', as Wolfe called him, had never
been beaten yet. If only he could hold out until the autumn!
Autumn would mean the inevitable withdrawal of Saunders's
fleet and the abandonment of the whole expedition. And
slowly, painfully, autumn was drawing close. July had already
gone. August was going. It was September!

And then a mysterious thing happened. Wolfe broke his
camp on the north shore, immediately below Montmorency,
and moved up the river on the south side. What was he doing?
Where was he going to strike? Montcalm's intelligence was bad.
The constant passage of ships and men up and down the river
in front of Quebec was all part of an elaborate game of mysti-
fication in which the British navy and army zealously joined to
deceive him. A break-through up river at some place such as
Pointe aux Trembles was a distinct and dangerous possibility;
but so also was a renewal of the attack on Beauport, under
cover of the feint which these misleading activities above the
town would supply. There were dangers everywhere. Even the
great serene heights immediately above the town did not seem
entirely secure.

It was perhaps possible for a man to clamber up one of the
few breaks in the cliffs, such as the Anse au Foulon, to the
Plains of Abraham above; but could an attack in any strength
be mounted in this way? Was Wolfe, having drawn the French

forces successfully to both wings, preparing, with incredible audacity, to make his main thrust in the centre, through the cove of the Anse au Foulon, up to the heights themselves? Montcalm began rapidly to strengthen his centre and right wing; and on September 5th he ordered the Guienne Regiment up to the high rolling plateau immediately above Quebec. One day later Vaudreuil sent it back to the Beauport lines. The Plains of Abraham were left virtually defenceless. Only the culpable Vergor, Bigot's friend, who had surrendered Beauséjour in 1755 without a shot, was stationed there with a small company of Canadian militia. And yet, four days later, on September 10th, a French officer stationed close to the Anse au Foulon, saw through his telescope a small group of British officers carefully surveying the heights about him from the opposite shore. Perhaps Montcalm and Vaudreuil underestimated the possibility of a successful ascent of the cliffs. Perhaps they disagreed about the urgency of guarding against it. They were, at any rate, bewildered by a multiplicity of dangers, and they made no further special efforts to defend the Plains of Abraham. The early autumn days slipped by. Tomorrow would be September 13th.

At about four in the morning of that day, a sentry at the French post of Point Sillery, a short distance above the Anse au Foulon, heard a curious sound from the river below.

'Qui vive?' he challenged.

'France.' The reply was low but distinct.

'A quel régiment?' snapped the sentry.

'De la Reine.'

The sentry hesitated. He was still curious. The voice was authoritative and confident—clearly an officer's voice. Yet there was something odd about it. Was it the accent or simply the low tone in which the words were uttered?

'Pourquoi est-ce que vous ne parlez pas plus haut?' he persisted.

The reply was impatient and brusquely commanding:

'Tais-toi! Nous serions entendus.'

Montcalm and Wolfe

The sentry subsided in doubtful silence. He expected a convoy from upstream, bearing badly needed provisions for Quebec, that very night. He might have feared a surprise attack by the British; but he could hardly have imagined that a Highland officer named Simon Fraser, who spoke excellent French, would have taken his place in the leading boat. Down below in the darkness there was silence. The British held their breath in painful expectancy. Then the boats moved softly on and a few minutes later they grounded on the shingle of the Anse au Foulon.

Wolfe was the first on shore. During much of the summer he had been seriously ill and depressed; but now, at the point of crisis, every ounce of his daring genius was flung into the execution of his 'desperate plan'. 'I know perfectly well you cannot cure my complaint,' he had told his surgeon only a little while before, 'but patch me up so that I may be able to do my duty for the next few days and I shall be content.' Now the crucial moment, for which he had tried to prepare himself, was at hand. Swiftly, silently he led the way to the spot he had chosen for the first ascent.

'I don't think', he said anxiously to his leading soldiers, 'we can by any possible means get up here, but however we must use our best endeavour.'

Only a few minutes later, most of de Vergor's miserable guard was overpowered in its sleep. Vaudreuil slept soundly. They all slept; and it was not until after six o'clock that Montcalm, riding up from the Beauport lines, learnt the full enormity of what had happened. Hurriedly he collected his men. Almost the whole of the army's left wing, by Vaudreuil's express instructions, remained inactive in the Beauport entrenchments; and the five regiments which assembled that morning a little west of the town were a sadly mixed company which had been reinforced, not with regulars from France—for none had reached the St. Lawrence—but with drafts of Canadians. The rolling plain ahead of them was not the forested road leading to Fort Duquesne nor the heights above the Montmorency River.

It was almost a parade ground. And everything might depend upon the disciplined fighting cohesion which Montcalm's force so tragically lacked. He hesitated. And yet, he realized, it might be fatal to delay. Delay would enable the enemy to entrench, to bring up cannon, and consolidate his position. If Montcalm attacked now, he might catch the British off balance. He might, at one stroke, convert the complete surprise into an overwhelming disaster.

It was ten o'clock. The rain, which had been falling earlier, now slackened, and the sun broke magnificently through the clouds. Montcalm signalled the advance, and the whole array of white- and blue-clad soldiers surged forward. The troops started with a shout of confidence; but soon the long lines began ominously to lose both their symmetry and their resolution. The Canadians fired, dropped to the ground to reload, or scurried to cover on either side of the battlefield. The French regulars, unnerved by the increasing disorderliness of their formation, halted, fired, moved forward again uncertainly and repeated their ragged fusillade. And then, at the forty paces Wolfe had specified, the two long lines of redcoats broke their unnerving silence with a crashing volley. The French charge was stopped dead. The French lines began to waver. Wolfe, in his moment of triumph, was shot and dying. Montcalm was mortally wounded while he tried in vain to rally his men. There was no rallying them. They broke, turned, and fled. And Montcalm's black horse walked his dying master slowly back into the city through the St. Louis gate.

5

THE PARTING OF THE WAYS

I

In 1763, when by the Peace of Paris France ceded all her North American possessions, with the exception of Louisiana west of the Mississippi, to Great Britain, it seemed certain that a new and very different future had opened up for Canada and Acadia. Canada and Acadia had now lost their separateness. Surely they would soon lose their curious personalities. They were now British colonies, ordinary members of a larger company of British colonies, in a continental empire which stretched all the way from Hudson Bay to the Gulf of Mexico; and in 1763 the systematic reorganization of this continental empire seemed imminent. In the past, the British provinces had been treated with a generous laxity and had been permitted to develop much in their own free fashion. But the war had brought up a number of important colonial problems, of which the acquisition of the French possessions presented only one; and it seemed obvious that Great Britain herself should attempt to find common solutions in the interest of all. The triumphant conclusion of a great colonial war was the obvious point of departure for this administrative enterprise; and Great Britain embarked upon a belated, clumsy, and tragic attempt to systematize and standardize her North American Empire.

The Royal Proclamation of October 1763 was the first major instalment of this reforming imperial programme. It made several important general provisions for all the colonies, as well as a number of equally important particular arrangements for the new provinces, including Quebec. The western boundary of the Province of Quebec—the new name which Great Britain had given Canada—was to run just a little west of the Ottawa River; and a purely temporary limit, drawn along the watershed of the Allegheny Mountains, was placed on western expansion from the Seaboard colonies. Pontiac's Indian rising, which broke out in the spring of 1763, after the terms of the Treaty of Paris had become known in North America, had proved only too clearly with what murderous intensity the Anglo-Americans were hated by many of the tribes of the interior; and British officials were determined to establish a temporary Indian reserve, in which, without any interference from troublesome frontier settlers, they could seek a peaceful solution of their Indian problems. For some time, at least, settlement was not to be permitted west of the so-called Proclamation Line; but in generous compensation, it was to be encouraged to expand laterally up and down the seaboard and into the new colonies which had been acquired from the French.

This, of course, was the cue at which the provinces of Quebec and Nova Scotia were to begin to play the humble parts which had been assigned to them in the great scheme of British imperial reorganization. In the past they had always been rather strange colonies—strategically important, no doubt, but unpeopled, under-developed—mere primitive outposts for the fisheries or the fur trade. Now they must develop into healthy British normality. They must become solid, prosperous agricultural settlements, occupied by British colonists in the respectable fashion which obtained along the Atlantic Seaboard. And since British colonists would unquestionably expect British institutions in any part of the Crown's dominions, Nova Scotia and Quebec must be immediately supplied with these constitutional inducements to immigration. Nova Scotia had already been granted a representative assembly in 1758, the

The Parting of the Ways

year before the capture of Quebec; and now, it was assumed, Quebec itself should be treated in the same generous fashion. The Royal Proclamation of 1763 made two important promises respecting the constitutional future of Quebec. It offered a general assembly 'in such Manner and Form as is used and directed in those Colonies and Provinces in America which are under our immediate Government'; and it assured prospective colonists that they could count upon 'the Enjoyment of the Benefit of the Laws of our Realm of England'.

If there was any part of the new northern dominions in which this programme of settlement and anglicization might have seemed assured of real success, it was unquestionably Nova Scotia. As the British had reconstituted it, it was a large, scattered, broken province, which included the newly con-quered French islands of Cape Breton and St. Jean and ex-tended as far into the continent as the Gaspé highlands. The forcible removal of the Acadians in 1755 had left it virtually empty and ready for occupation; and it lay directly in the path of the northern migration movement from New England, which was already peopling Vermont, New Hampshire, and Maine. Before the end of the Seven Years' War, immigrants from the New England colonies had begun to take over the abandoned Acadian farms in the Bay of Fundy region, and to establish new fishing settlements on the south shore of the peninsula; and for some years after the peace they continued to enter the province in modest numbers. There were, of course, other small groups—Germans, Irish, Yorkshire English—who helped to settle the empty colony; but unquestionably the New Englanders formed the dominating part of the population. Surely they would mould its character in their own image? New England had simply moved one long stage further up the Atlantic coast to Nova Scotia. Nova Scotia would inevitably become a typical New England colony, indistinguishable from all the others. It would be the newest New England.

And yet, strangely enough, it did not turn out exactly that way. Nova Scotia had always been a debatable, ambiguous

land, a land of conflicting interests and rival loyalties, a bastion
of the St. Lawrence as well as an outpost of New England; and
even the presence of a new population of hard-headed Yankees
could not decisively alter its character or change its destiny.
The Yankees were, in the first place, not sufficiently powerful
in numbers. A dozen years after the Peace of Paris, there were
only about seventeen or eighteen thousand settlers established
in Nova Scotia; and they were distributed widely among the
scattered land masses of a broken, sprawling province, far from
each other, and further still from their relatives and friends in
old New England. They did not find it easy to combine for
political purposes. They never quite succeeded in controlling
the redoubtable Halifax oligarchy, composed of officials, merchants, and army and navy contractors, which was firmly
attached to Great Britain, and gave the province somewhat
corrupt but reasonably efficient government. The New Englanders could stamp Nova Scotia with their social customs and
the moral and religious values imparted by their Congregational Churches; but they were not able to make their historic
'town meeting' the legal form of local government in the
province and they were equally incapable of dominating its
legislative assembly. Constitutionally, politically, Nova Scotia
was an unlikely-looking offspring of the old republic of
Massachusetts.

If the British programme of northern colonization had been
only a qualified success in Nova Scotia, it was a complete
failure in Quebec. The British imperial planners, if they had
been historically minded, might have discovered the existence
of other earlier imperial planners, who had similarly tried to
change the character of the fur-trading colony of the St. Lawrence and who had dismally failed. The failure of these seventeenth-century French architects of empire had been due, in
large measure, to their inability to maintain large-scale immigration and to promote successful agricultural settlement;
and now the British scheme, as laid down in the Proclamation
of 1763, collapsed as a result of the same defects. The army

veterans and stout civilian settlers, who, it was hoped, could be induced to migrate north from the Seaboard colonies to Quebec, simply failed to come; and the only important body of British immigrants, other than soldiers and officials, which reached the St. Lawrence in the years following the Peace of Paris, was a small but highly important group of merchants, who promptly took over the control and direction of the fur trade. Far from changing—or even wishing to change—the old economy of the fur-trading colony, they devoted themselves, with great energy, to the promotion of its historic enterprise. They identified themselves closely, sympathetically, with an almost unchanged French-Canadian society. The French officials and officers as well as some of the landowners and merchants had, of course, returned to France after the conquest; but the great majority of the sixty-five thousand inhabitants stayed in Quebec and with them stayed their priests.

This failure of the policy of large-scale immigration in effect knocked the bottom out of the whole British scheme for the anglicization of Quebec. The province continued to be largely inhabited by the 'new subjects'—French-speaking Roman Catholics whose main economic activity was still the fur trade; and the attempt to make it conform to the standardized colonial pattern which had been worked out on the Atlantic Seaboard had proved a complete failure. English common law could only have been imposed by brute force in a province where land had been granted *en fief et seigneurie*, and where every will and contract had been drawn up and executed in terms of the old Custom of Paris. English representative political institutions would have been almost equally difficult to establish without either disfranchising the largest part of the population or altering—or evading—the antiquated laws by which Protestant Great Britain still sought to prevent Roman Catholics from taking part in municipal or national government. The 'old subjects'—the British merchants and fur traders who had only recently arrived in Quebec—were, of course, vociferously eager for an assembly. But an assembly was no part of the French-Canadian political tradition; and the first three British governors of Quebec after the conquest—the professional soldiers James Murray, Guy Carleton, and Frederick Haldimand—were disposed to regard the views of the 'new subjects' sympathetically. They started a reaction against the political and legal promises of the Proclamation of 1763 which took form eleven years later in the Quebec Act.

In the meantime, another more general provision of the Proclamation of 1763 was encountering equally serious difficulties. The whole policy of the Indian reserve, the prohibition of western settlement, and the imperial control of the fur trade was breaking down against the resistance of all the colonies, including Quebec. If the fur-trading provinces, New York, Virginia, Pennsylvania, and Quebec, could have agreed among themselves to regulate the fur trade and administer the western region, all would have been well. But Quebec, just as in the days of Talon, Frontenac, and Iberville, was intent not upon western partnership but western monopoly; and the new directors of the northern fur trade, though they were English-speaking Protestants as well as British subjects, struggled to realize the territorial ambitions of the St. Lawrence against the competition of their fellow colonials from the south just as strenuously and pertinaciously as their French predecessors had ever done. Obviously, if the western imperial reserve was to be abandoned, some form of government would have to be put in its place; and the British, with an odd recognition of claims which they had previously denied, decided that Quebec was best fitted for this administrative task. By the Quebec Act of 1774, the old western empire of New France, including the vast triangle of territory south of the lakes between the Ohio and Mississippi rivers, was restored to Quebec.

The Quebec Act not only restored the lost dominions to the fur-trading state. It confirmed its historic character in other ways as well. It reintroduced French civil law, strengthened the position of the Roman Catholic Church, and established government by council in which Roman Catholics might take part through the provision of a special oath. The Quebec Act was the statutory repudiation of the whole policy of the Proclamation of 1763 and the statutory recognition of the enduring vitality and the distinctive personality of the colony of the St. Lawrence.

II

One early spring day in 1775, just after the break-up of the ice on Lake Champlain, there appeared unostentatiously in Montreal a promising young New England lawyer, a graduate of Yale College, named John Brown. Brown had ventured north into this strange, alien world of Quebec as the agent of the Boston Committee of Correspondence. He came armed with a generous stock of revolutionary pamphlets and a sheaf of official letters from the New England revolutionaries. His mission was to second the appeal which the 'Continental' Congress had already addressed to the Canadians, to urge them personally to identify themselves with the cause of resistance against British tyranny, and to send delegates to the great assembly at Philadelphia.

He could hardly have appeared at a time more propitious for his cause. On May 1st, only a few short weeks away, the Quebec Act was to go into operation; and to the British merchants and fur traders of Montreal, a number of whom were old residents of the Thirteen Colonies, the Quebec Act was quite simply an insufferably objectionable statute. It was true, of course, that it had gratified them by restoring the old western empire of the fur-trading colony; but their satisfaction at this territorial enlargement of Canada was lost in their anger at the denial of assembly. They were angry at Governor Carleton. They were furious with his Francophil Council. They were disgusted by the incomprehensible conduct of the imperial Parliament. They crowded surreptitiously into the 'town meetings and nocturnal cabals', as Governor Carleton called them, which Brown addressed with his persuasive revolutionary eloquence. Yet strangely enough, in the light of all the circumstances, they were not to be moved into positive action. 'There is no prospect', John Brown wrote flatly to the Committee of Correspondence in Boston, 'of Canada sending delegates to the Continental Congress.'

This curious reluctance of the Canadian merchants to declare themselves was a significant indication of the role which these unaccountable northern provinces were destined to play in the next crisis in North American affairs. The armed revolutionary struggle had already broken out; within little over a year the Thirteen Colonies would declare their political independence; and on the face of it, it seemed so likely, so logical that Quebec and Nova Scotia would follow them into successful rebellion against imperial authority. Quebec was peopled by a French-speaking population which had been transferred to British sovereignty only a dozen years before and which might reasonably be presumed to welcome the first opportunity of cutting itself loose from its new imperial masters. Nova Scotia was occupied by first-generation New England pioneers who might be expected, with equal justification, to leap at the chance of associating themselves with their rebellious relatives and friends in the Thirteen Colonies.

If, during these critical years when the revolutionary storm was rising rapidly on the Atlantic Seaboard, the two northern colonies had remained in a state of political contentment, there might have been less reason now to expect them to play a positive part. But in fact, of course, they had not remained in a state of political contentment; at that very moment, both of them were violently agitated. The merchant community of Quebec was bitterly opposed to Governor Carleton; the politically active part of Nova Scotia was engaged in a furious controversy with its Governor, Francis Legge. Who would not have expected that these local provincial agitations would become merged in the general American protest movement, and that Quebec and Nova Scotia would join their fellow colonists in the rejection of British authority?

The Parting of the Ways

Yet this was not the way in which events seemed to be shaping. The rhythm of politics in the northern provinces, however vehemently accented, never became perfectly attuned to that of the Atlantic Seaboard. Quebec and Nova Scotia seemed instinctively disposed to reject continentalism in the form of either the standardized continental imperialism which the British had tried to impose or the uniform continental resistance which the Americans were now attempting to promote. The isolated New Englanders in Nova Scotia, busy with the prosaic concerns of pioneer home-building and far away from the brisk currents of agitation in the Thirteen Colonies, never made any positive widespread attempt to join their fellow colonists in resistance. The French-Canadians of Quebec, who had no knowledge of the English parliamentary tradition and no experience of the eighteenth-century French Enlightenment, remained tepidly unresponsive to the liberal catchwords beloved of the American revolutionaries. The legal and ecclesiastical provisions of the Quebec Act had pleased the seigneurs and the priests and inclined them to support the apparently benevolent sovereignty of Great Britain. If, therefore, there was any group which could possibly take the initiative in propelling Quebec and Nova Scotia into the American Revolution, it was the merchants of Halifax, Quebec, and Montreal.

Yet obviously these mercantile Haligonians and Montrealers were not going to do it. They showed no enthusiasm for the political leadership which the American merchants had exercised with such astonishing results. To join the movement of resistance now developing in the Thirteen Colonies would mean accepting the self-denying provisions of the non-importation agreements; and to accept the non-importation agreements would mean cutting themselves off from their customers and suppliers across the Atlantic and allying themselves with their traditional commercial rivals in North America. Montreal, whether it was directed by French or English, had always struggled with northern and southern American competitors for the control of the commerce of the continental interior; and Halifax, like Louisbourg before it, was already dreaming of a time when its shipping would dominate the Atlantic and oust New England from the West Indies trade.

Both colonies were independent rivals of the Atlantic Seaboard, just as they were dependent partners of Great Britain; and they showed not the slightest inclination of breaking with their friends for the sole advantage of their hereditary enemies. No effort was made by the northern merchants to promote resistance to Great Britain; they frowned on anything but the most discreet criticism of her policies. The Stamp Act, the Townshend Duties, the East India Company's tea monopoly were either accepted passively in Quebec and Nova Scotia or awakened only mild and isolated protests which were in laughable contrast with the deafening furore in the Thirteen Colonies. Even the stentorian appeal of the 'Continental' Congress and John Brown's personal visit aroused little interest or enthusiasm; and by the spring of 1775 it was obvious that the entire continent was not going to unite in a great spontaneous outburst of revolutionary ardour.

There was no great new North American union. There was simply a renewal of the traditional North American war. In May, the 'Green Mountain Boys' captured the British posts at Crown Point and Ticonderoga; and at the end of August, an American revolutionary army, sanctioned by Congress and with General Montgomery in command, started north up the historic Lake Champlain–Richelieu River route for the invasion of Canada. It was merely a fresh instalment of an old but perennially popular serial story. For generations, Great Britain had been attempting to eliminate Canada and Acadia as separate political entities in North America and to impose a unity on the continent. The Thirteen Colonies which were to be the heirs of the original British imperial domain, took over these continental ambitions as an essential part of their inheritance; and the invasion of 1775 was the first phase of an American continental imperialism which later acquired the mystical title of 'Manifest Destiny'. At the beginning, it looked as if this original American attempt to carry out the policy of continentalism by force of arms might possibly be a success. With the aid and comfort of a few French-Canadian 'patriotes' who wavered from one side of the conflict to the other in accordance with its fortunes, Montgomery captured Montreal and pushed on down the river to unite with the forces of General Benedict Arnold, who had managed to reach the St. Lawrence after a journey of incredible hardship and peril up the Kennebec River and down the Chaudière.

Only Quebec remained; and Montgomery boasted that he would eat Christmas dinner inside the fortress or die in the attempt. In reality the position of the combined American armies was extremely grave. Without cannon of sufficient size, with dwindling numbers and inadequate equipment, they could not possibly carry on an effective siege. Their one real chance was the swift surprise of an assault; and very early on the morning of the last day of the year Montgomery and Arnold launched their combined attack against the two sides of the Lower Town. It was a forlorn hope, an almost meaningless gesture of defiance, for even if the Lower Town had been taken, the great walled fortress on the heights would still have resisted capture. The morning was bitterly cold. A stiff wind was blowing from the north; and the darkness was thick with driving snow. At each end of the approaches to the Lower Town, the defendants had erected barricades; and here the Americans, stumbling through drifts and half-blinded in the obscurity, were held and effectively repulsed. Arnold was wounded. Montgomery was killed; and the slain New Yorkers and New Englanders, with 'Liberty or Death' written on the strips of paper pinned to their caps, were found buried in the drifting snow.

The great campaign to enlist the fourteenth and fifteenth colonies in a continental union of resistance to British tyranny was obviously encountering the most unexpected and lamentable obstacles. The sullenly unresponsive northern provinces would not rise of their own accord; and they seemed equally unaffected by revolutionary persuasion or the force of revolutionary arms. These American inducements were visibly failing in Canada; and in Nova Scotia, which had reverted to its old historic role as swiftly as Quebec, they had apparently as little chance of success. With the British in secure possession of the naval base at Halifax and with American privateers plundering every fishing hamlet along the coast, the unhappy province became once more the prey of two imperialist rivals; and the New England frontiersmen, who began in this characteristic Nova Scotian crisis to take on a curious resemblance to the exiled Acadians, sought refuge in the traditional policy of neutrality. Some of them declined to be embodied in the loyal provincial militia; very few were eager to raise the flag of revolt. And in the autumn of 1776, when Jonathan Eddy of Massachusetts led an expedition along the north shore of the Bay of Fundy to the Isthmus of Chignecto in a vain attempt to capture Fort Cumberland, a few score reluctant rebels were all he was able to recruit.

III

It was close enough. When both France and Spain joined the struggle, Great Britain was heavily engaged on all sides, and her strength was extended as it had not been in either the War of the Austrian Succession or the Seven Years' War. France, recovering from the weakness at sea which had cost her her North American empire, had employed the interval since the peace in building a large and powerful navy; and if she had attempted to establish even a brief preponderance in the North Atlantic, as she succeeded in doing with such tremendous results in the Yorktown campaign of 1781, the northern provinces might have faced another and a much more crucial ordeal. But France was no more willing to assist the Thirteen Colonies in the conquest of Nova Scotia and Quebec than the Thirteen Colonies were to help France to the recovery of her lost Empire. After the lamentable failure of Burgoyne's attempt in 1777 to use the Richelieu River–Lake Champlain route for a thrust against the revolting colonies, the northern part of the continent ceased to be a main theatre of the war; and British warships rode unchallenged in the Gulf of St. Lawrence and along the Nova Scotian and Newfoundland coasts.

The policies of the international balance of power, as well as the vital assistance of Great Britain, had thus given strength to that curious capacity for a distinctive, separate existence which the northern colonies had shown for so long. For forty years, ever since the beginning of the War of the Austrian Succession, North America had been convulsed by a series of political and military crises; but during all these tempestuous decades, through war and peace and the rise and fall of empires, Canada and Acadia—Quebec and Nova Scotia—had managed to preserve their identity and maintain their separateness. They had survived two attempts—one by Great Britain and one, an armed attempt, by the Thirteen Colonies—to incorporate them in a single, uniform continental union. The Thirteen Colonies had won their independence from Great Britain; but Quebec and Nova Scotia, relying upon Great Britain, had kept their independence of the Thirteen Colonies.

The St. Lawrence and its outposts on the one hand, and the Atlantic Seaboard on the other, had come once more to the parting of the ways. It was a moment of enormous, yet not conclusive, importance in the history of British North America. Nova Scotia and Quebec had been granted a separate political existence; but the nature and the prospects of that separate political existence still rested in painful obscurity. Would the northern provinces become really viable political entities? Would they be left mere small, mutilated fragments of a broken Empire? Or would it be possible for them to look forward to a great political future in North America? The crucial moment had arrived. The assets, properties, and peoples of the greatest of North American empires were about to be divided; and in the decisive diplomatic encounters in Paris, Quebec and Nova

Scotia could not be directly represented themselves, nor could they count upon Great Britain fighting with real determination and persistence in their interests. Though, at the end of the struggle, she still dominated the Atlantic coast and most of the fur-trading west, Great Britain was weary of the war and ready to conciliate the newly established United States; and in these circumstances it was not difficult for the far-sighted American diplomats to take and keep the initiative in the negotiations. They were prepared to admit—though they made a last stout effort to obtain Canada—that Quebec and Nova Scotia should remain British territory. But they were determined to acquire the lion's share of the unoccupied west and they were eager to secure special privileges for their fishery even in territories which were certain to be on the British side of the new boundary.

For the boundary itself the Americans had two proposals to make. Both were alike in the eastern region, for both began with the St. Croix River, ascended it to its source, struck due north to the height of land between the St. Lawrence system and the rivers draining into the Atlantic Ocean, followed the height of land and the Connecticut River until the forty-fifth parallel of latitude was reached, and then continued along the forty-fifth parallel to its intersection with the St. Lawrence River. From this point westward, the two proposed lines followed radically different courses. One continued straight west along the forty-fifth parallel to the Mississippi River; the other followed the line of the Great Lakes and their connecting rivers to the north-west angle of the Lake of the Woods, from which point it ran due west to the Mississippi. In the end the British agreed to accept the second alternative on the ground simply that the water boundary seemed natural and therefore looked more definite. In reality a line, which was at that time completely artificial and arbitrary, had been drawn through the commercial empire of the St. Lawrence; and, at one stroke, Canada lost the entire south-western half of the vast inland domain which she had discovered, explored, exploited, and to which her historic title had been recognized by the British as late as the Quebec Act of 1774. Thus, in the west, with no concern for the enormous issues involved, Quebec had been despoiled of half its inheritance; and, in the east, where the fisheries were the main resource of the remaining colonies, Nova Scotia and Newfoundland, American fishermen were given the exceptional liberty to fish in British-American waters and to dry and cure their catch on unsettled British-American coasts.

The assets and properties had been divided. The peoples were to separate as well. The American Revolutionary War was a civil war of the English-speaking community; and those who stood for the unity of the Empire—the United Empire Loyalists as they later came to be officially called—were a considerable minority of the population of the Thirteen Colonies. If they had joined one of the over fifty colonial units which were organized during the war to fight for the British cause, their property was usually confiscated; and if they stayed at home, but declined to take the patriotic test which was imposed in most of the states, they were subjected to every kind of civil disability, and to indignity, injury, and spoliation by the mob. At the peace conference, the British tried to obtain justice, if not mercy, for the Loyalists; but all that the American negotiators would do was to promise that Congress would send out earnest recommendations to the various states to cease their confiscations and make generous restitution. The complete refusal of the states to honour these solemn commitments of their representatives in either the letter or the spirit, completed the breach between them and their old citizens; and the Loyalists decided to abandon a state of affairs which both politically and personally had become intolerable to them. Between thirty-five and forty thousand of these first English-speaking displaced persons—there were about a hundred thousand in all—made up their minds to migrate to Quebec and Nova Scotia. They were to be the greatest asset which the surviving North American colonies obtained from the enforced liquidation of the first British Empire.

6

THE STRUGGLE FOR SURVIVAL

I

On our Arrival here,' wrote Richard Cartwright when he had reached Fort George on his journey from Albany up to Montreal, 'it gave me inexpressible Pleasure to think myself at a happy Distance from those Scenes of Outrage, Tumult, and Oppression, which I had long beheld with fruitless Indignation, and to find myself secure from those petty Tyrants who had involved my once happy country in every Species of Distress, & made it feel all the misery that Cruelty joined with Power can cause.'

Cartwright, a man of substance who travelled with several servants, was one of the first of the Loyalists to arrive. It was possible to reach Quebec, even in wartime, by the Hudson River–Lake Champlain route or by its western extension, the Mohawk River. But those who took this western, overland way were mainly frontier settlers from northern New York and Vermont or veterans of the Royal Greens or Butler's Rangers; and the great majority of the Loyalist refugees assembled in New York as the war drew to its close, overflowed the port and its environs, and awaited transportation by sea. In the spring of 1783, the great fleets of transports which the British Government had provided began to bear this large company of the uprooted north-east to Nova Scotia. Some went to Cape Breton, some to Prince Edward Island (Isle St. Jean); almost every point along the jagged meandering coastline of Nova Scotia received its small complement of settlers. But by far the greatest numbers descended at Port Roseway, on the south shore of the peninsula, where the Loyalists built a town called Shelburne which they vainly hoped would rival Halifax, or at the St. John River on the continental mainland. Another town, more permanent than the ephemeral and grandiose Shelburne, sprang into existence at the mouth of the St. John; and the thousands of veterans of the colonial regiments, who occupied the rich intervale lands a hundred miles up the valley to the new village of Fredericton, made the St. John River colony the most important and enduring of the Loyalist settlements in Nova Scotia.

The migration to western Quebec was a good deal smaller than that to Nova Scotia. The fleets of transports which sailed from New York in 1783 carried approximately thirty thousand immigrants to the maritime region; but probably not more than six thousand Loyalists reached the upper St. Lawrence valley, or the shores of the Lower Great Lakes during the years from 1780 to 1784. A few went to far-away Detroit. A number settled at Niagara, which had been the base of Butler's Loyal Rangers during the war. But the great majority were to make their homes in the two long rows of townships, which had been specially surveyed by the provincial government for the purpose and which stretched along the north shore of the St. Lawrence, with one interval, all the way from the seigniory of Longueuil to the peninsula of Prince Edward county. In the spring of 1784, when the largest of the western migrations occurred, the Loyalists with their families, servants, and few belongings, crowded into Durham boats and flat-bottomed French-Canadian *bateaux*, fought their way up the long river, set up their tents and marquees and began to hew down the towering and unbroken forest.

The Loyalists, as a whole, were a fair sample of English-speaking provincial society in North America, a cross-section of rich and poor, literate and uneducated, town and country, seaboard and frontier. The Harvard College graduates who made up the first Executive Council at Fredericton, the veterans of Jessup's Corps and Sir John Johnson King's Royal Regiment of New York who settled along the St. Lawrence, the robust colonists who followed Captain Michael Grass to the first township of Cataraqui west of old Fort Frontenac, and the penniless but gay gentlefolk, the 'dancing beggars', who made merry in the odd, artificial little city of Shelburne, were all in their very different ways representative of the Loyalist migration. It was a movement inspired not by class hatreds, or economic motives, but by political principles. The Loyalists, whatever their social order, occupation, or place of residence, had stood for constitutional government as against rebellion, for the unity of the Empire as opposed to its disruption, and for monarchy instead of republicanism. They were, in the mass, as good democrats, in both the political and social sense, as the fellow colonists whom they had left behind them in the United States. They had grown up in the same egalitarian atmosphere; they were equal heirs of the British tradition of representative parliamentary government; and from the start they showed that they would accept no nonsense from the political authoritarians and the economic monopolists among their own number.

The Loyalists—there can be no doubt of the fact—were the making of the colonies which remained within the British Empire, the provinces which now alone could be described as British North America. Within two years they had increased the total population of Quebec and Nova Scotia by approximately 50 per cent. They had begun to effect a transformation of these colonies, culturally and socially, as well as economically and politically; and, in so doing, they were making British North America a more solid and durable group of settlements, vastly increasing their chances of survival, and holding out before them the dim but not hopeless prospect of a splendid future in North America. Up to that time, Quebec and Nova Scotia had been, to a large extent, mere outposts of the fur trade and the fisheries, mere unsubstantial claims to territory which had been made good at only a small number of points by a feeble and scattered population. Now all this was changed. The Loyalists brought settlement and agriculture—the things all the northern empire-builders from Colbert on had dreamed of—into the heart of these wild and empty territories. They carried on their backs, as the most important part of their refugees' luggage, the makings of a new economy, a new society, a new political organization. A task of enormous hardship and difficulty lay before them. They might fail. They might achieve only an indifferent or partial success. But they started with more favourable chances and with greater conviction than any of their predecessors had done before.

One thing, it was obvious, would have to be done at once. The economic and social possibilities of the new settlements could only be worked out slowly and painfully by the colonists themselves; but the British Parliament and the British Colonial Office could provide political institutions, and it was evident that some form of political reorganization was immediately required. It had not mattered much that Quebec and Nova Scotia were vast and sprawling colonies, when only a small fraction of their territories was occupied; but now settlement had been pushed far into the interior of each province; and for colonists on the upper reaches of the St. John River or on the remote shores of Lake Ontario, the governments at Halifax and Quebec must have seemed very far-away institutions which could have no real understanding of their needs and would never provide satisfactorily for their requirements. Mere distance seemed to demand the partition of the new British North America; but in Quebec nationality as well as geography supplied a potent argument in favour of the division of the province.

Though there were, of course, small minorities of English-speaking 'old subjects' in Quebec and Montreal, the great bulk of the Loyalists had settled on the upper St. Lawrence or on the shores of the Lower Lakes; and to divide the colony along the general line of the Ottawa River would be to effect a fairly neat separation of two culturally distinct peoples. It would also, to be sure, introduce an artificial political division in the economic unity of the St. Lawrence, which had already been artificially divided by the international boundary of the Peace Treaty of 1783; and the Montreal merchants were utterly opposed to this further dismemberment of their commercial empire. But division was the easy and obvious solution; and in 1791 the old Province of Quebec became the two new provinces of Upper Canada and Lower Canada. By that time Nova Scotia had been even more thoroughly partitioned. Prince Edward Island had become a separate government as early as 1769; and in 1784, the year after the coming of the Loyalists, the territory north-west of the Isthmus of Chignecto became the Province of New Brunswick.

In the Maritime Provinces it was possible to introduce representative institutions by the simple means of a dispatch from the Colonial Office to the Lieutenant-Governor. In the Canadas, on the other hand, the process was necessarily more complex, for the promises of the Royal Proclamation of 1763 had been formally annulled by statute, and only another statute could undo the provisions of the Quebec Act of 1774. In 1791, by the so-called Constitutional Act, or Canada Act, the imperial Parliament did what had really become inevitable with the coming of the Loyalists. It abolished the conciliar form of government which had existed in Quebec ever since Champlain had founded it nearly two centuries before, and established in both Upper and Lower Canada a new system of representative government. In both provinces there was to be an elected Legislative Assembly and a second chamber called a Legislative Council, a new institution in British American constitutional history which was to be composed of members nominated for life by the Crown and which looked a little as if it were intended to be a colonial substitute for the House of Lords.

Apart from this, there was no major change in the traditional form of English-speaking colonial government, and no effort to alter the institutions beloved by either the 'old' or the 'new' subjects. Land had to be granted in English freehold tenure in Upper Canada and could be so granted in Lower Canada if desired; but the existing seigniorial system and the old custom of Paris were left undisturbed. The privileges which had been granted to the Roman Catholic Church by the Quebec Act were not changed; and a deliberate effort was made to strengthen the position of the Church of England by reserving a portion of the Crown lands in each province for the support of a Protestant clergy. On the whole, throughout British North America, there had been few attempts to put back the clock, few indications that the British were attempting to prevent a repetition of revolution by a salutary dose of authoritarianism. Great Britain had, in fact, left her venerable colonial system relatively unaltered. She had only one kind of institutions that she wanted to give, her own; and she had instinctively given them again to her new colonies, for better or for worse.

II

This was only a beginning. Political institutions were important; but their establishment and management for useful purposes were only a part of the work which the new British North America had to do. The half-dozen northern provinces which had remained within the British Empire must now come to terms with their new environment, must learn to make the very best of an inheritance which in some ways had been drastically, grievously curtailed but which in others still offered enormous possibilities. New staple products, new industries, new markets, and new trade routes would have to be found for the Loyalists and their successors, the American immigrants who still kept coming into Upper Canada. The new international boundary, which at one stroke had lopped off half of Montreal's western empire, must if possible be modified, or some compensation discovered for the huge losses which it would inevitably entail. Settlement, the inveterate and conquering enemy of the fur trade, had now successfully invaded the region of the Lower Lakes; but beyond the Lower Lakes lay a vast empty territory in which economic mastery was still in dispute, in which the final political decisions were yet to be taken, and where the fur trade still had work of enormous importance to accomplish for the future of British North America.

In the south-west, for a while, the fur traders even had cause to hope that, with Great Britain's help, they could undo the abject and gratuitous capitulation of 1783. All the western fur-trading posts—Niagara, Detroit, Michilimackinac, and Grand Portage—and the region south of the lakes which they controlled, were still in British hands when the Revolutionary War ended. The posts were, of course, to be transferred to the United States, for, by the astonishing terms of the Peace of 1783, they were all on the American side of the boundary. But Great Britain found an ample excuse for their retention in the republic's repudiation of its promises concerning the Loyalists and British pre-revolutionary debts; and once the fatal moment of transfer had been postponed, the fur traders and the Indians at last succeeded in awakening the British to some appreciation of the serious consequences which would follow the total abandonment of the old south-west. For a while the British even hoped that, with the help of the Indians, they might succeed in modifying the boundary of 1783. But the western tribes failed in their vain attempt to defend their hunting grounds from the Americans; and in 1796, in accordance with the terms of Jay's Treaty, the posts were surrendered and the last redcoats marched out of the territory of the United States.

Even yet, the Montreal fur traders were not quite finished. Their adversaries, the Americans, had not won the south-west by force during the Revolutionary War; they were not winning it by commercial competition during the peace. All they had succeeded in doing so far was to extort a diplomatic title to the region from a fatigued and uninterested opponent; and for a while yet the Canadians were able to prevent them converting this formal right into an effective exploitation. Gradually, however, the Americans grew stronger both politically and commercially in the region. Gradually, systematically, as the republic's relations with Great Britain worsened after the resumption of the war in Europe in 1803, they impeded and harassed the Canadian traders south of the lakes with every species of obstruction and vexation. The trade in the south-west was gone, or going. Much of it was already being abandoned to John Jacob Astor, who had revived the old competition from New York. All the Canadian traders could do was to look forward to the day when, if war with the United States came—and, to their lively satisfaction, it looked more probable every year—Great Britain and British North America together would erase the abominable boundary of 1783 by force of arms. That was for the future. For the present Montreal was already winning another fur-trading empire, vastly greater than that which was now slipping from her grasp, in the remote north-west.

Early in the summer of 1784, when the iniquitous treaty was only a year old, and long before the posts had been surrendered to the United States, a half-dozen of Montreal's greatest fur traders had assembled at Grand Portage for a meeting which was to be of crucial importance for British North America's future in the north-west. Five years earlier, in 1779, these merchants had for the first time formed a loose association of partnerships—it was never a formally incorporated joint-stock company—for the prosecution of the trade beyond Lake Superior in competition with the Hudson's Bay Company. In January of 1784 the association had been confirmed and extended in a new agreement; and now Simon McTavish and his nephew, young William McGillivray, had come west with the spring brigades to seek the approval of their western associates. The 'wintering partners' were already there. Grand Portage, with its great dining-hall, its powder magazine, its storehouses, and living-quarters, was crowded like the rallying-place of a Scottish clan. The 'bourgeois' from Montreal in their tall hats and fawn and grey dress coats, the 'winterers' in buckskins and moccasins, the pipe-smoking 'mangeurs du lard' who had paddled the great 'canôts du maître' up the Ottawa and across Lakes Huron and Superior, the real 'hommes du nord' who would drive and carry the smaller 'canôts du nord' across the height of land and into the prairie country, the Indians who stood about watching the movement and bustle with impassive and scrutinizing gravity—they had all assembled for the great annual conclave of the fur trade. The North West Company's agreement was ratified. The company stood forth as Montreal's supreme achievement in that co-operation which, since the days of Champlain, had been the one real salvation of western commerce. And before McGillivray left for the north-west and Simon McTavish returned to Montreal, the new organization was celebrated with a dinner and toasts and dancing in the great hall at Grand Portage.

It was the men of the North West Company who realized the fur trade's destiny to cross the continent. It was the 'winterers', the real westerners, the members of the Beaver Club whose motto was 'Fortitude in Distress' who resolutely staked out a claim to a quarter of a continent for the future Dominion of Canada. They were only just in time. The struggle for the possession of the Pacific north-west had already begun. Spain, that venerable American monopolist, was still attempting feebly to defend its vast south-western claims; the Russians were shouldering their way down the coastline from the north in pursuit of the valuable Alaska seal and sea otter; and Captain James Cook and Captain George Vancouver had come by sea to explore and to assert Great Britain's title to the region. But it was not from the Pacific Ocean or by enterprises and claims such as these that the political fate of the Pacific coast was to be decided. It was to be decided rather by expansion across the continent from the Atlantic coast; and in this race for the western sea it was the United States which was British

North America's real rival. In 1803, the Louisiana Purchase put the republic in possession of an enormous, vaguely defined territory west of the Mississippi; in 1805 the Lewis and Clark overland expedition reached the Pacific as far north as the Columbia River; and in 1811 the ambitious Astor, who in 1810 had founded a new American organization, the Pacific Fur Company, established Fort Astoria at the mouth of the Columbia.

The climax of this transcontinental competition came in the first decade of the century. The North West Company, goaded by the Hudson's Bay Company to the north and paced by its American rivals in the south, struggled to extend its organization to the disputed Pacific. Already, years before the eighteenth century ended, perhaps the greatest of the Company's explorers had paused beside a flat face of rock in Dean Channel, had 'mixed up some vermilion in melted grease, and inscribed, in large characters . . . this brief memorial: Alexander Mackenzie, from Canada, by land, the twenty-second of July, one thousand seven hundred and ninety-three'. From Canada, by land, in the first years of the nineteenth century, came the indefatigable successors who were to complete Mackenzie's work. In 1808 Simon Fraser reached the Pacific by the violent and tortuous river that bears his name; and in 1811 David Thompson, who had discovered the Athabasca Pass, a vital link in the Company's connections with the east, travelled down the Columbia River to its mouth. The North West Company had become literally an organization which stretched from ocean to ocean. Montreal was a fur-trading outpost which had become a small provincial town; but it had fulfilled the destiny which Jacques Cartier had glimpsed dimly from the top of the high hill by Hochelaga. It had staked the limits and laid the bases of the transcontinental nation that Canada was to become.

III

In the meantime, while these spectacular achievements were

being made in the far west, the new settlements in the maritime region and on the shores of the Lower Lakes faced a much more prosaic but equally difficult task. They had to hold fast to the landfall which they had made in northern North America. They had to prove that a satisfactory existence could be lived in the surviving colonies of the British Empire. They had to develop the communities which, in the still distant future, would take over and exploit British North America's enormous inheritance in the north-west. Even after the coming of the Loyalists, they remained only tiny, scattered settlements; but their own colonial leaders and commercial theorists in Great Britain held out high, almost extravagant, hopes for their progress. The Maritime Provinces, with the help of Great Britain, would take over the network of trade routes and markets which New England had built up on the Atlantic Ocean. The St. Lawrence, with Britain's aid, would become the trunk-line of a second commercial empire in which British manufactures would be exchanged for the new natural products of an agricultural west. British assistance was necessary to second the still puny efforts of the north; and for a while it seemed that British assistance would be solidly available. After only a brief consideration of the possibility of mutual free trade and free navigation between the British Empire and the United States, Great Britain returned to the ancient commercial verities of the Old Colonial System. Empire trade was to remain the monopoly of Great Britain and her colonies. The United States would be obliged to accept the economic disadvantages of independence; and the faithful northern provinces would receive the economic benefits of loyalty.

And yet it did not work out quite as had been hoped and expected. The Atlantic trade routes failed to rearrange themselves obediently in accordance with the dictates of the Old Colonial System; and while Upper Canada flourished in a fairly prosperous fashion, Nova Scotia inexplicably lagged behind. After the coming of the Loyalists, the chief population movements passed the Maritime Provinces by, whilst Upper

The Struggle for Survival

Canada, which lay athwart one of the natural routes to the west, was being slowly but steadily peopled by a stream of immigrants from the United States. The pioneer settlements on the shores of the Lower Lakes, emerging fairly rapidly from their state of primitive self-sufficiency, had begun to ship their wheat and flour down the St. Lawrence for export before the end of the eighteenth century; but Nova Scotia, which had hoped by this time to take over New England's triangular trade route, was obviously failing in its attempt to become the West Indies' chief supplier of lumber, flour, fish and provisions. The province's lack of an agricultural surplus for export, its distance from the islands, and its want of experience in their market, all contributed to an increasingly obvious failure; and in 1793, when the war with France began and British American insurance rates rose sharply, the Governors of the British West Indies were permitted, if necessary, to open their ports to American shipping.

Yet it was the war, strangely enough, which in the end brought salvation to British North America. In its final stages, during the ascendancy of Napoleon, when the conflict extended to North America as well as over the whole of western Europe, both sides—and their neutral victims—resorted to economic warfare on a scale unknown before. Napoleon imposed the Continental Blockade; in 1807 Great Britain retorted with the Orders-in-Council; and the United States, attempting in an exceedingly misguided fashion to enforce respect for its rights as the principal neutral carrier, retaliated with the Embargo Act of 1807 and the Nonintercourse Act of 1809. These ponderous economic strokes and counter-strokes, with the scarcities, the widespread smuggling, and the commercial dislocation which naturally accompanied them, did two things of inestimable value for the northern colonies. They forced Great Britain to a new appreciation of the value of British North America as a source of supply; and they offered British North America a delectable opportunity of profiting by the fatuous mistakes of her rivals.

The self-imposed restrictions, which kept the great American merchant marine idle in American ports, gave the northern provinces their great chance to take over much of the carrying trade of the Atlantic and the coveted market of the West Indies. Napoleon's Berlin Decrees, which closed the Baltic and thereby intensified the crisis in the British supply of timber, compelled Great Britain to look with vastly more interested concern on the resources of her forested northern provinces in America. Up to that time, the cost of transporting a bulky commodity like wood across the Atlantic, had made it impossible for British North America to compete with the prices offered by nearby Baltic countries. But now important English firms were persuaded to risk their capital in the British North American timber trade by the grant of a colonial tariff preference high enough to protect their investment and to ensure a profitable continuation of the business after the war was over. The British hastened to enter the trade on a grand scale. Red and white pine timber, the inexhaustible material of both the Precambrian Shield and the Appalachian Highland, became, in short order, the second great staple product in the history of northern North America.

Thus the bitter struggle for existence seemed to be ending, as the first decade of the century drew towards its conclusion, in a burst of real prosperity. Once again, by luck as well as by its own effort, by initiative and perseverance as well as because of the fortunate accidents of the power politics of its allies and rivals, British North America had managed, in its accustomed fashion, to find a way through most of its difficulties. Yet the struggle for survival was not over; and its worst ordeal lay still ahead. Relations with the United States, which had improved at the time of Jay's Treaty, had been steadily worsening again for several years. The old half-unresolved conflict in the centre of the continent, as well as the new contentions at sea which the war with Napoleon had produced, gave the United States ample pretext for the display of that animosity which even the Revolutionary War had not exhausted. The old fearful resentment against Great Britain and British North America still lingered. So also did the imperialistic ambition to complete the work which Montgomery and Arnold had left unfinished, and to make the continent of North America one great political whole.

IV

'What a change an additional regiment would make in this part of the Province,' wrote Major-General Isaac Brock, the Lieutenant-Governor of Upper Canada in July 1812. 'Most of the people have lost all confidence—I, however, speak loud and look big.' How could he possibly look very big? Was it not extremely natural that most of the British North Americans should have lost all confidence? A month before, the United States had declared war against Great Britain. British North America was certain to be the main theatre of the war—was, indeed, the United States' declared political objective. There were fewer than five thousand British regulars in the whole of British North America; and, with Great Britain locked in the final round of a life-and-death struggle with Napoleon, how could these small numbers possibly be reinforced? There were fewer than five hundred thousand British Americans confronting a population of nearly eight millions in the United States; and although the Loyalists and their descendants could be counted on to fight with conviction, the loyalty of the French Canadians was thought to be doubtful, and it was believed that the thousands of recent American immigrants would be only too likely to make common cause with the invaders from the south. It was true, of course, that the United States was not of one mind about the war, and that New England in particular was bitterly opposed to it. It was also true that British North America would have the very real benefit of Great Britain's general preponderance at sea, as well as the somewhat doubtful asset of Indian support in the interior of the continent. But these were only mitigating circumstances. Great Britain fought, not with one arm tied behind her back, but with both hands busy with the weight of another conflict; and the United States, as against British North America, possessed a vast superiority in both manpower and financial and industrial strength.

It might have been decisive superiority; but the Americans could not seem to bring it to bear effectively upon the issue. At sea, of course, they were at a decided disadvantage; and despite the brilliant initial successes of a few of their frigates and the toll taken by their privateers, the British blockade gradually hemmed them in. Inland, in the region of the upper St. Lawrence and the Lower Lakes, it was very different; but here the preponderance of power which the United States undoubtedly possessed, was never concentrated and delivered in a single knock-out blow. The offensive in overwhelming force up the traditional pathway of Lake Champlain and the Richelieu River, which would have menaced the bases of British North American power and left Upper Canada to its fate, was never seriously undertaken. Instead, American strength was frittered away in isolated and uncoordinated attacks upon the outworks, rather than the inner defences, of the St. Lawrence system. The American navy diverted strength from the vitally important Lake Ontario in order to gain a decision on Lake Erie; and American armies spent themselves in attacks on the strategically unimportant Niagara frontier.

Even so, it was close enough. During the three campaigning seasons in which the United States kept the initiative, the Canadas were repeatedly invaded and by vastly superior numbers. American armies hammered at the Niagara frontier, pushed up the Thames valley from the west, struggled down the St. Lawrence towards Montreal in the east, and raided and sacked York, the capital of Upper Canada. Yet somehow Upper and Lower Canada managed to hang on. In the first months of the war they were lifted from their state of apathetic defeatism by the impetuous resolution of General Brock and by the utterly unexpected victories of Detroit and Queenston Heights. Suddenly it became apparent that the war was not necessarily going to go as the Americans had so boastfully predicted. It might even have a totally different ending. The provinces endured and waited. For three seasons the small armies of British regulars and Canadian militia flung back the invasions. The pillage and destruction wrought by the American forces bred in the civilian population a settled hatred of the United States. And then, with the defeat of Napoleon in 1814 and the release of the veteran British armies, the situation was suddenly and completely reversed. For the first time Great Britain acquired the initiative.

This was what British North America had been waiting for from the beginning. For the northern provinces the War of 1812 was potentially a war for the undoing of the abominable Treaty of 1783, for the recovery of lost territories in both east and west. Already, with the occupation of Fort Astoria and the capture of Michilimackinac, their aims had been partly realized in the west. Now, in the last campaign of the war, a fur-traders' offensive on the upper Mississippi resulted in the taking of Prairie du Chien; and, on the Atlantic coast, Bangor and Castine surrendered to Sir John Sherbrooke, and all the territory north of the Penobscot River was annexed to New Brunswick. It was true that the complete and lamentable failure of Sir George Prevost's operations in the Lake Champlain region during the same campaign heavily detracted from these successes. Yet in the few months of a single season, British North America had taken more territory than the United States had been able to in three years of war.

It might have been the justification of a revision of the boundary; but the British diplomats at the peace conference made no serious attempt to insist on the force of the argument. The Treaty of Ghent ended the war on the basis of the mutual return of conquests; and the Convention of 1818, which three years later settled the issues outstanding between British North America and the United States in more detail, made no important territorial changes. The boundary of 1783, unaltered in the east and continued along the forty-ninth parallel west from

The Struggle for Survival

the Lake of the Woods to the Rocky Mountains, was to remain the permanent dividing line between the two countries. British North America had lost a large part of its inheritance in the west; but it had successfully resisted two armed attempts by the United States to force it into a continental union. It had preserved its separateness and its individuality. It was still the potential proprietor of a vast domain in North America. And it faced the future with more confidence and more conviction than it had ever been able to do in the past.

7

GROWING PAINS

I

'I have been at this place since the 1st inst: settling a most important Business,' wrote William McGillivray from Fort William to the Reverend John Strachan on the 26th of July 1821, '... the carrying into effect of the various Deeds and Covenants entered into on the part of the North West Company in London with the Hudson's Bay Company. These arrangements are happily completed, and I part with my *old troops*—to meet with them no more in discussion on the Indian trade. . . . Thus the fur trade is for ever lost to Canada! The Treaty of Ghent destroyed the Southern trade; still the capital and exertion of a few individuals supported the Northern trade, under many disadvantages, against a Chartered Company, who brought their goods to the Indian Country at less than one half the Expence that ours cost us. But it would have been worse than folly to have continued the contest further . . . I was the first English clerk engaged in the service of the North West Company, on its first establishment in 1784, and I have put my Hand and Seal to the Instrument which closes its *career* and *name* in 1821.'

The fur trade, which for over two centuries had been the glory and folly of the St. Lawrence, was at last done and ended; and nothing could have better symbolized the passing of the old Canada and the emergence of the new British North

America than the two successive and conclusive defeats of the old fur-trading city of Montreal. The War of 1812 had been over for only a year, when the American Congress, adopting a policy of rigidly exclusive economic nationalism, decreed that nobody but American citizens could pursue the fur trade in the territories of the United States; and there was nothing that the Canadians could do but surrender the wreck of their once great business to John Jacob Astor. The defeat of the South West Company in 1817 was perhaps not entirely unexpected, for it had been a declining and precarious enterprise for some time; but the collapse of the great North West Company, which occurred only four years later, in 1821, awakened both consternation and dismay. Up until almost the end, the Company had seemed its old self—enterprising, intrepid, and resourceful. In 1815, it had begun a vigorous defence of its interests against the claims of the colony of Assiniboia which the Earl of Selkirk had established on the Red River in the very centre of the principal North West Company supply district. But the costs, the losses, the defeats, and the humiliations of this savage and vindictive private war exhausted an organization which had already overtaxed its strength in an unequal competitive struggle. And now, in the early summer of 1821, McGillivray had gone west to Fort William to explain to the 'winterers' the terms of the union of the North West Company and the Hudson's Bay Company. Henceforth the trade was to be carried on from Hudson Bay. At one stroke Montreal had lost its western dominion. The fur trade had travelled westward across the continent in pursuit of the retreating beaver; and the long, tenuous connection which bound it to Montreal had snapped at last.

The northern provinces forgot the old hazardous staple, fur. For a generation they almost forgot the north-west, which the Hudson's Bay Company was guarding for the future. They had other, more immediate and rather more prosaic things to think of. They were busy laying the economic foundations of the new communities in the maritime region and along the

5. Clearing the Town Plot, Stanley, New Brunswick, 1834

6. King Street, Toronto, about 1825

Growing Pains

shores of the upper St. Lawrence and the Lower Lakes; and they had discovered two new commodities, timber and wheat, which, in addition to fish, the oldest staple of all, could be produced in large quantities in their north-temperate climate. All across British North America, the little provincial economies which were in process of development relied, with varying degrees of emphasis, upon these three staples, fish, timber, and wheat.

Newfoundland, which lay like a great ship moored close to the fishing banks, had always devoted itself exclusively to the fishery; but in that other island, Prince Edward Island, the settlers had almost completely deserted the sea and had come to gain their livelihood from the rich agricultural land of their tiny province. Nova Scotia, though its agriculture had always been weak, and though its timber supplies had already been seriously depleted, possessed a more mixed economy than those of the other Maritime Provinces; but it placed its main reliance upon the sea, and its ships, and fisheries and trade routes, just as New Brunswick found its chief resource in the forest. The magnificent stands of pine which covered New Brunswick attracted such a concentration of effort upon the one staple that at times it almost seemed as if the entire Province had become one enormous timber concession. In Lower Canada and in eastern Upper Canada, along the St. Lawrence and up the Ottawa rivers, the trade in the great squared sticks of red and white pine timber was the dominant economic activity in much the same way as it was in the valleys of the St. John, the Miramichi, and the Restigouche rivers in New Brunswick. West of the Ottawa, the valley of the St. Lawrence-Great Lakes system gradually broadened out into rich and fertile lowlands; and here, though the forest gave men jobs and kept mills busy, it was the trade in wheat and flour which supported the existence of the army of colonists which was swarming into the western peninsular country between Lake Erie and Lake Huron.

The British North American provinces as a group were

H 113

simple, primary-producing provinces; and their secondary industries were all closely related to the basic occupations of their staple trades. A flourishing network of flour mills developed slowly in Upper Canada; and along the lower St. Lawrence and the jagged, irregular coasts of the Maritime Provinces were a number of little ports where men made their living in the construction of wooden ships. The big shipyards at Quebec produced large square-rigged vessels; Pictou, Yarmouth, Lunenburg, and other Nova Scotian ports built schooners, brigs, and brigantines for the coastal carrying-trade; and New Brunswick turned out quantities of the big, clumsily constructed vessels which carried the great loads of timber over to England. An age in which wood was still the main material of construction, wind and water the main sources of power, and ocean, lake and river the main avenues of transport, suited the capacities of the northern provinces in many ways and brought out the value of their assets.

It also—and this was particularly true of the Canadas—revealed some of their basic weaknesses and liabilities. The Maritime Provinces had learnt to live within their limitations and carried on much in their old ways; but in the St. Lawrence valley the abrupt disappearance of the fur trade and the rise of agriculture for export had together brought on an economic revolution. A network of rivers and lakes, which had admirably served the fur trade, was suddenly found to be seriously deficient for the traffic of a growing, settled agricultural community. Without question, the St. Lawrence was the greatest natural communication system leading from the Atlantic Seaboard to the heart of the continent. But for six months of the year it was sealed in ice. Its continuity was completely broken by the falls of Niagara; and its navigation was impeded and endangered by a series of violent and destructive rapids.

All these defects and weaknesses were glaringly emphasized by the completion of the American Erie Canal—a barge canal which linked Buffalo on Lake Erie with the port of New York —in 1825. If the St. Lawrence was to capture a second commercial empire in the interior, if it was to become the main transport route for the traffic of the new agricultural west as it had been for the fur trade, then it must successfully meet this suddenly revived competition of its old rival, the Hudson River. The Lachine Canal, which avoided the rapids south of the island of Montreal, was completed in 1825; the Welland Canal, which by-passed the formidable obstruction of Niagara, was opened for traffic late in 1829. The obstacles at the eastern and western extremities of the system had been overcome; but this left untouched the heart of the problem, which was the series of tremendous rapids on the upper St. Lawrence. And the onerous task of freeing the river from these obstructions was made all the more difficult by the political division of the territory of the valley into two provinces, by the apathy of the French-Canadian majority in Lower Canada, and by the opposition of the agrarian Reformers in the Upper Province.

For both the Maritime Provinces and the Canadas, the preferred, the hoped-for destinations of these new staple products were the markets of Great Britain and her other colonies. To attain these markets British North America had to struggle against its traditional commercial rivals and particularly the United States; and for success it still looked unquestioningly to the benefits—the shipping monopolies and the tariff preferences—of the Old Colonial System. For some time now, the northern provinces had rejoiced in the possession of the timber preference; they kept on hoping for what for them would be a satisfactory preference on wheat and flour; and in their unending struggle for the supply of the West Indies, they relied heavily upon the prohibitions of the imperial navigation laws. This reliance, for small but growing provinces, which desperately needed all the assistance they could get, was natural, inevitable; but in the first decades after the establishment of the general peace in Europe and North America in 1815, the stout support of the Old Colonial System became increasingly more doubtful and uncertain. There were still large numbers of people in Great Britain who regarded the principles of the

Navigation Acts with nearly the reverence accorded to divine revelation; but, as the nineteenth century went on, the whole ancient and venerable mercantile system was being gradually undermined both by the retaliatory policies of that powerful commercial rival, the United States, and by the rapid growth of free-trade sentiment in the United Kingdom. The rise of industrialism in Great Britain offered an opportunity and posed a problem for British North America. Industrialism created vastly increased markets for the natural products of the northern colonies; but industrialism also brought an end to the benefits of the Old Colonial System through the establishment of free trade.

II

Upon the substantial foundation of these new economic ventures and activities, the provincial societies of British North America were slowly taking form and character. They grew. They changed. And the main reason for both developments was the large immigration which was the principal feature of their history from the end of the War of 1812 to the middle of the century. Up to this time, the northern provinces had been peopled very largely by the original colonists from old France and by the migrants from the Thirteen Colonies on the English-speaking seaboard of North America. The coming of the Loyalists had been followed by a fairly steady stream of colonists from the new United States, which settled the Eastern Townships in Lower Canada and gradually spread over the whole south-western section of the Upper Province. At the time of the signing of the Treaty of Ghent, British North America was occupied by a population which had one or more genera-tions of experience on the North American continent.

Now all this was to be changed. Since the great migrations of the seventeenth century, there had been no very large-scale exodus from Great Britain to North America; but now, once again, the westward movement of the British peoples began.

Growing Pains

The depressions, which in the decades after Waterloo returned periodically to distress the United Kingdom, provided the main compulsion for an emigration which began to get under way in the early 1820's; and for the next thirty years British North America was to enjoy the first of the two great periods in which it has been the favourite land of opportunity for colonists from the British Isles. All the provinces benefited, though in varying degrees, from the great influx. Presbyterian and Roman Catholic Scots from the Highlands and the Western Isles occupied Cape Breton and the north-eastern section of Nova Scotia. Scots and southern Irish settled the upper St. John and Miramichi river valleys and swelled the roving population of the lumber camps and shipbuilding ports in New Brunswick. English, Lowland and Highland Scots, Ulster and Southern Irish—by far the largest army of the British migration—pressed up the St. Lawrence River, and, leaving only small detachments of its main body in the Lower Province, swarmed over the lush, green, unoccupied lands of southern Upper Canada. In the quarter-century from 1825 to 1850, the population of Nova Scotia increased from 104,000 to 277,000 and that of New Brunswick from 74,000 to 194,000. These were very respectable increases, indeed, of over 100 per cent each; but Upper Canada bettered them. In the same twenty-five years its population rose from 158,000 to 791,000.

It was a long time before these small provincial societies escaped from the turmoil of the colonization period and acquired a formed and distinctive character. The rapid arrival and settlement of scores of thousands of relatively poor immigrants was an agitating and painful as well as a rewarding process. Inevitably it involved a great deal of social disorganization, cultural impoverishment, and moral disturbance; and its immense ultimate gains were purchased at the cost of much personal heartache, degradation, and total failure. The task of making a new home was easiest 'out front', in the first row of townships from the lake or the river, where half-pay English officers and others with some capital could purchase a cleared and improved farm. It was hardest in the backwoods, 'roughing it in the bush', where the loneliness, the stark primitiveness, and the brutalizing toil brought premature age to many and total shipwreck to some. It was most carefree, exciting and demoralizing in the lumber camps, the canal construction gangs, the hard-drinking uproarious shipbuilding ports which drew the adventurous, or the incurably urban-minded, away from the prosaic, back-breaking task of carving a farm out of the wilderness.

By slow degrees, organized provincial communities began to emerge out of the chaos of colonization. Each had its own distinctive qualities and characteristics; but all were built along the same general structural lines. Throughout British North America there developed small provincial oligarchies, little governing groups of educated civil servants, well-born officers, substantial landowners, comfortable merchants, and cultivated clergymen, who ran the governments of the different provinces, directed their economic energies and aspired to control their social tone and cultural standards. In the newer colonies the Loyalists formed the original nucleus of the oligarchies, and in Fredericton, the sleepy capital of New Brunswick, they still possessed the majority; but, of necessity, the governing class in each province was a fluid, adaptable body, which welcomed the talented among later immigrants, and which, despite the title 'The Family Compact' which was popularly applied to the oligarchy of Upper Canada, was not too tightly connected by intermarriage. In Lower Canada, even more than in the other provinces, the governing class, because of its large admixture of prosperous Scots and English merchants, was easily and invidiously distinguished from the great French-speaking mass of the population; but throughout British North America, as society took firmer shape and class distinctions hardened, the provincial oligarchies began to arouse a more conscious social obloquy and political opposition. The complacent 'Family Compacts' or 'Chateau Cliques' of Halifax, Fredericton, Quebec, and Toronto (York) were criticized and opposed; and nowhere was their leadership more vigorously challenged than in the sphere of religious establishments and educational institutions.

British North America, like every other part of the nineteenth-century English-speaking world, was an intensely sectarian, if not intensely religious, community. The fundamental division between Protestant and Roman Catholic was here unhappily exacerbated; for the French-Canadians, a very considerable part of those who swore allegiance to the old faith, were also clearly marked off from their fellow citizens by their different language and social heritage. The basic dichotomy of these two ways of life was to cause infinite misunderstanding and conflict in the future; but, in the early nineteenth century the divisions in the great Protestant body itself—the breach between the Churches of England and Scotland on the one hand and the evangelical sects on the other—awakened even more contention and animosity. Throughout British North America there were no established churches in the English sense of establishment; but the Church of England and, to a much lesser extent, the Church of Scotland, obviously enjoyed the patronage of government and the support of the quality; and, in Upper Canada at least, this superior social station was strongly buttressed by the lavish endowment of the public lands reserved for 'the support of a Protestant Clergy'—an endowment which the Church of England at first claimed as exclusively its own. If the Anglican Church had been able to retain the allegiance of the great majority of the population, as in England, its claims and privileges would not have been so objectionable or so quickly questioned; but in fact its assumed primacy was unreal. Despite the devotion of many Church of England clergymen to the needs of their enormous, primitive, backwoods parishes, the evangelical sects proved more successful on the frontier; and the Methodists, the Baptists, and the ministers of the Free Church gained from the two older communions.

The opposition to the position, the influence, and the pretensions of the Church of England ranged fairly widely across British North America. It raised everywhere the general question of the relations of church and state; and in Upper Canada it took the very intractable form of an acrimonious controversy over the disposition of that unlucky Pandora's box of troubles, the Clergy Reserves. A substantial number of people—members of the Church of Scotland, for example, and some Wesleyan Methodists—would have been eager or prepared for a division of the proceeds of the Reserves, on some reasonable basis, among the different Protestant communions. But the disputes and heart-burnings which would almost certainly be provoked by any conceivable method of division, prejudiced many people against this solution from the start; and there was a still larger number of Protestants who emphatically disapproved in principle of any state support, however equitable, for organized religion. The 'voluntary principle', as it was called—the principle that churches and sects should be supported by the contributions of their own adherents and without assistance from the secular state—was a principle which always had the endorsement of the Baptists and increasingly won approval from the Methodists and members of the Free Church.

The quarrel between the governing class and the frontier society over the religious and cultural institutions of the new British North America did not end here. The Church of England's exclusive claims to ecclesiastical endowment were hotly denied and attacked; but so also was the leadership which it had instinctively assumed in the field of public education. If British North America was inclined to a bitter sectarianism in religion, it was also passionately concerned about education; and in every province the establishment of a good primary and secondary school system and the founding of suitable institutions of higher learning were subjects which inspired a great deal of lively debate. The evangelical Protestants were just as convinced as the Anglicans and the Roman Catholics of the indissoluble connection between religion and education; but they bitterly resented the dominating authority which the Church of England had acquired in the first provincial universities—the King's Colleges at Halifax, Fredericton and Toronto. The founding of rival denominational colleges—the Baptist Acadia College in Nova Scotia, the Presbyterian Queen's College and the Methodist Victoria College in Upper Canada —was one answer to the problem as the evangelicals saw it. But it was an answer which profoundly dissatisfied many; and the pressure for large provincial non-sectarian universities, such as Dalhousie University in Nova Scotia and the future University of Toronto in Canada, grew steadily stronger.

In the early 1830's the long process of growth and adjustment in British North America, which had begun with the Peace of 1783, was reaching the climax of its difficulties. Ever since the end of the War of 1812, and particularly during the past decade, the pace of change had been disturbingly swift. The collapse of the fur trade, the rise of the new staples, and the huge influx of immigrants from Great Britain had brought about nothing short of an economic and social revolution in the provinces. There were unresolved conflicts between their different important groups and interests; there were unrelieved tensions between British North America as a whole, the outside world in general, and Great Britain in particular. In the Canadas, where the conflicts of rival cultures and the agitations of settlement had been most serious, these strains, for some people at least, were becoming unbearable.

III

In the early 1830's, as the political disputes in Upper and Lower Canada became more acrimonious and uncompromising, two curiously contrasted personalities began to acquire a common political prominence, if not a common notoriety. One was the French-Canadian lawyer, Louis-Joseph Papineau, who had been a recognized political leader in the Lower Province since 1815, and the other was a temperamental and belligerent

Scottish-Canadian journalist, William Lyon Mackenzie, who more than a decade later burst suddenly into the front rank of Upper Canadian Reformers. Papineau was the seigneur of Montebello, a cultivated and distinguished man of fine presence and genuine oratorical powers, who came from a good professional family and had been well educated at the Quebec Seminary. Mackenzie was a diminutive excitable man, with a flaming red wig and a temper that went with it, who had taught himself almost all he knew and whose mind, with its ragbag of ill-assorted and undigested information, was inspired by a passionate hatred of privilege and injustice. Both were men of imitative rather than creative mind, who shared a common emotional instability, and whose leadership was marred by incapacity or irresolution. But in the middle 1830's their popularity was growing as rapidly as the radicalism of their policies. They had broken with their old associates, the moderate Reformers, men like John Neilson in Lower Canada, and Robert Baldwin, Egerton Ryerson, and Marshall Spring Bidwell in the Upper Province. An ultra reform party had, in fact, taken shape; and its appearance in both provinces was a sign that the politics of the Canadas were rushing rapidly to a crisis.

The same state of angry frustration existed in both provinces; but it had been reached from different origins and by different paths. French Canada's fundamental purpose was the defence of a distinctive culture whose continuance seemed threatened, as never before, by the mass immigration from the British Isles; and this essentially conservative position lent a curious ambiguity to the radicalism of the Lower Province. The French-Canadian *Patriotes'* uncritical devotion to their old laws, their old institutions, and their feudal landholding system seemed incomprehensible to English Canadians, whether Liberal or Conservative; and the Upper-Canadian Reformers' passionate preoccupation with the disposition of the Clergy Reserves and the problem of religion and education could have no parallel in the staunchly Roman Catholic Province of Lower Canada.

Growing Pains

The two groups of Reformers were obviously divided by the basic differences of their cultural heritage; but, at the same time, they lived in the same environment and they were concerned of necessity with much the same material problems. Radicals in both provinces could cheerfully unite to attack big corporations such as banks and land companies, though, in Lower Canada, the fact that these suspect institutions were largely controlled by English-speaking Canadians gave an extra vehemence to the denunciations. French-Canadian and English-Canadian farmers, both concerned with local roads and high prices for produce, were apt to be equally unenthusiastic about the merchants' commercial policies and canal-building programme for the improvement of the St. Lawrence transport system. Above all, the Constitutional Act of 1791 had supplied both provinces with the same set of political institutions. In each colony there was the same obstructive Legislative Council. There was the same irresponsible Executive.

By 1837 public affairs in both provinces had reached what, in the eyes of the radicals, was a condition of absolute and infuriating impasse. *Patriotes* and Reformers had alike been driven, by a long succession of disappointments, reverses, and denials, into a permanent state of angry frustration. The Lower-Canadian *Patriotes*, though their majority in the assembly was consistently overwhelming, had been locked for years in an unavailing struggle with the executive over the provincial finances. The Upper-Canadian Reformers, who were by no means so sure of popular favour, had won the election of 1834, only to find that all their pet measures were summarily rejected by the appointed Legislative Council. They credulously put their trust in the new Lieutenant-Governor, the theatrical Sir Francis Bond Head, just as the *Patriotes* at first hoped for great things from the Gosford commission of inquiry in Lower Canada. But Head led the rejuvenated Conservatives to a smashing victory in the new general election of 1836; the Gosford report was temperately unfavourable to the *Patriote* cause; and Lord John Russell, in the Ten Resolutions of 1837, replied to the intransigent demands of the Lower Canadian assembly with a series of categorical denials. If a general state of economic and social well-being had prevailed in the Canadas at the time, these political reverses might have been a good deal less violently disturbing. But the provinces had been socially agitated for years, there had been bad harvests or crop failures, and in 1837 British North America, along with the rest of the Western World, was plunged deep into the distress of a general depression.

The two provincial agitations, with their great mass meetings and threatening demonstrations of force, were drifting irrevocably but aimlessly towards rebellion. The political aims of the movement, particularly in Lower Canada, were vague and undefined; its course was erratic and unplanned to the last degree; but, in general, the extremists took their revolutionary theory and practice from the fashionable model of the American Revolution, and the institutions which they hoped to establish were congressional rather than parliamentary in character. The *Patriotes* founded 'Fils de la Liberté' associations and went about ostentatiously in shapeless garments of *étoffe du pays* as a protest against British imports. Mackenzie inserted large, unrevised chunks of the American Declaration of Independence in his Declaration of the Toronto Reformers. Both he and Papineau placed great reliance upon an elected Legislative Council—or Senate—as the grand cure for their political miseries; and Mackenzie's Draft Constitution for the State of Upper Canada, which was published on the eve of the rebellion in the Upper Province, was obviously based upon the constitutions of the new western American states. In effect, the Rebellions of 1837 were the armed attempts of a small minority to persuade the Canadians to alter the course of their history and to accept the American Revolution which their fathers and grandfathers had rejected sixty years before.

On Monday, November the 6th, a brawl between the 'Fils de la Liberté' and the members of the British Doric Club broke out in Montreal. It was this battle, which swayed all day up and down the city streets, which hastened affairs to their crisis. The alarmed government prohibited armed processions and mass assemblies; on November 16th it issued warrants for the arrest of a number of the principal *Patriote* leaders. Then the countryside resisted; and the armed resistance swelled confusedly into an open insurrection. At St. Denis, in the Richelieu valley, the *habitants* stood their ground bravely against the tiny force of redcoats sent against them; they fought with desperation in the savage little affray at St. Eustache, north of the Island of Montreal. But they were badly armed, their leadership was, in general, incompetent or cowardly—Papineau fled the scene of action with remarkable celerity—and the rebellion was little more than a series of armed riots, unplanned, purposeless, hopeless.

It was very late on the night of Monday, December 4th, when Alderman John Powell burst breathlessly into the bedchamber of Lieutenant-Governor Head, and waking Sir Francis from his complacent slumbers, informed him, in stuttering, almost incoherent phrases, of the outbreak of rebellion in Upper Canada. Without professional military defenders— for Sir Francis had confidently dispatched all the troops down to the Lower Province—the citizens of Toronto frantically prepared for the hourly expected rebel onslaught; but in reality the few hundred untrained, inexperienced and dispirited farmers who were assembling at Montgomery's Tavern, a little north of the city, could only have taken the capital by surprise, and that chance was rapidly slipping away from them. For two days, while a series of tragic accidents, comic terrors, and fatal debates over grand strategy paralysed the rebel movements, the provincial militia was pouring into the capital from all sides; and on December 7th, seizing the initiative which Mackenzie had forfeited, the loyalist army, under Colonel Fitzgibbon, marched up Yonge Street in the midday sunshine to scatter the enemy. It was all over in less than half an hour. The disheartened rebels waited apprehensively in a little wood. The cannon roared over their heads; a ball crashed into Montgomery's Tavern behind them; their right flank was turned by one of Fitzgibbon's supporting columns; and they broke and fled.

The rebellions, as internal disturbances, as risings of native Canadians, were completely over in a matter of days or weeks. But the armed agitation, of which they were only the first manifestation, continued for another year as an undeclared, guerrilla warfare between the Canadians and the citizens of the northern United States. The radical leaders had drawn much of their inspiration, their theory, and their practice from the American Revolution; and now the American Revolution, responding eagerly to this unwitting invitation, made its third armed attempt to force the Canadas into a continental political union. The members of the American Patriot Societies and Hunters' Lodges, together with a few Canadian 'fellow travellers', attempted to do unofficially what the invasion of 1775–6 and the War of 1812 had failed to accomplish. While the authorities of the northern states looked on with benevolent detachment, they openly organized half a dozen raids on Canadian territory during the course of 1838; and although these small invasions were all stopped at the border, the casualties at one of them, the American attack on Prescott, were heavier than those at the Battle of Queenston Heights in 1812. Thus, in the end, the rebellions were linked with the foreigner, with the reassertion of American imperialism; and the Loyalist cause was identified with the defence of British North America's separateness and autonomy.

8

THE END OF THE OLD ORDER

I

On a day late in May, 1838, in the full flush of the brief northern springtime, John George Lambton, first Earl of Durham, rode up to the old Castle of St. Louis in the port of Quebec. Seldom, if ever, had the citizens of British North America beheld a personage who combined political prominence and social grandeur in such an astonishing degree. He was mounted on a white horse and clad in a brilliant uniform. His luggage took two days to land. The buffet at his lavish receptions and supper parties was resplendent with family plate and racing trophies. His Byronic moods, his imperious yet gracious manner, the carelessly baroque magnificence of his style of life soon became almost legendary in the Canadas. He had once confided to Creevey that he could 'jog along' on forty thousand pounds a year. He was known privately as 'King Jog'; but his political sobriquet was 'Radical Jack'. Of all the Whig grandees who had put through the Reform Bill of 1832, he was reputed to be one of the most democratically inclined; and now, clothed with exceptional power and accompanied by a brilliant staff, he had come out to Canada as the High Commissioner of the young Queen Victoria, to undertake a thorough investigation of the troubled affairs of British North America.

Nine months later, in the winter of 1839 the *Report on the*

The End of the Old Order

Affairs of British North America was presented to the imperial Parliament. The Durham *Report* is a deservedly famous document, one of the greatest state papers in the history of the British Empire; and perhaps its most important function was to help the British North Americans to recover their belief in their own chosen destiny, to assist them in regaining confidence in the political methods which they instinctively preferred. The northern provinces had decided, in the end, that they wished to maintain their separateness in North America and to continue their membership in the British Empire. Naturally enough, the rapid development which they had recently experienced in that Empire would necessitate—had already necessitated—changes in its Old Colonial System; but these changes, in the opinion of most British North Americans, were matters for piecemeal reform and mutual concessions between colonies and Mother Country. It was this deliberate procedure which the rebels of 1837 had sought to change. They had attempted to substitute the American Revolution for British North America's peaceful change. And they had failed. Even with the covert help of the American revolutionaries themselves they had failed dismally. And American institutions and American practices had sunk once more into extreme disrepute.

Lord Durham represented the shift back from the politics which had wrecked the first Empire to the politics which were to save the second. He expressed British North America's reversion to character, its return from the aberration of 1837. He gave the support of his position and his eloquent prose to historical tendencies which had already shown their strength in the northern provinces and to political ideas which provincial politicians had already been trying to formulate. One of these was the idea of union, which the St. Lawrence had always encouraged, and which all those who had worked with and for the river system had always tried to realize; the second was the idea of self-government through a colonial variant of that latest development of the parliamentary system, the cabinet. The form in which Durham originally cast the idea of union

7. The Charlottetown Conference, September 1864

8. The New Houses of Parliament at Ottawa at the time of Confederation

was the prematurely ambitious project of a federation of the whole of British North America. That, he came reluctantly to realize, was for the future; and he substituted for it, as an essential preliminary, the unification of the whole St. Lawrence valley through the political union of Upper and Lower Canada. This was the scheme for which the British commercial community of Montreal had been clamouring for two generations. Durham accepted their plan. He also took over the scheme of colonial responsible government which the Toronto Reformer, Robert Baldwin, had been advocating for more than a decade.

Baldwin was a cautious moderate whose temperament and political theory were in equally sharp contrast with those of the defeated Mackenzie. Mackenzie had relied upon Jeffersonian principles and congressional practices; Baldwin took his stand on British parliamentary traditions and cabinet procedures. 'I now come to the consideration of the fourth remedy,' he had written to the Colonial Secretary two years before Durham's arrival, in an elaborate review of the various proposed solutions of the colonial problem, 'which consists of nothing more than having the provincial Government as far as regards the internal affairs of the Province, conducted by the Lieutenant-Governor . . . with the advice and assistance of the Executive Council, acting as a Provincial Cabinet, and composed of Men possessed of the public confidence, whose opinions and policy would be in harmony with the opinions and policy of the Representatives of the People.' It was this cumbrously expressed, but expansively vital principle which Durham took over and made the central recommendation of his *Report*. Like Baldwin, he stressed the fact that this was essentially an 'English' remedy, and that 'no change in the principles of government, no invention of a new constitutional theory' was necessary. Like Baldwin again, but more forcefully, he drove home the point that if the Crown 'has to carry on the Government in unison with a representative body, it must consent to carry it on by means of those in whom that representative body has confidence'.

This central political recommendation of the *Report*, though Durham had qualified it expressly and by implication, was too much for the Whig government in Great Britain. The Colonial Secretary, Lord John Russell, carefully analysed the logical contradictions and absurdities which, in his view, made the proposed scheme quite inadmissible. Obviously, executive power throughout the British Empire was the power of the Crown; and how could the Crown have responsible advisers in a colony when it had 'other advisers, for the same functions, and with superior authority' in England? 'It may happen, therefore,' Russell continued, 'that the Governor receives at one and the same time instructions from the Queen, and advice from his executive council, totally at variance with each other. If he is to obey his instructions from England, the parallel of constitutional responsibility entirely fails; if, on the other hand, he is to follow the advice of his council, he is no longer a subordinate officer, but an independent sovereign.' The logic seemed unanswerable; and, given Russell's premises, it was, in fact, irrefutable. The impregnable constitutional position which the Colonial Secretary had occupied could not be taken by a frontal assault. But could it not be turned, as Baldwin and Durham had already hinted, by a flanking movement?

At the moment, neither the Whig cabinet, nor its successor, Peel's Tory government, was at all interested in these devious tactics; but, despite their stiff constitutional orthodoxy, they were benevolently aware of the fact that British North America stood very badly in need of economic assistance and administrative reform. A major job of reconstruction, carried out along generous and liberal, if not exactly Durhamite lines, was obviously necessary; and in 1839 Charles Poulett Thomson, who was later raised to the peerage as Baron Sydenham, was sent out to undertake the task. Sydenham, the former President of the Board of Trade in Melbourne's Cabinet, was an engaging, cocksure little man, with the drive and plausibility of a company promoter, the tough aggressive realism of a captain of industry, and all the benevolent despot's contemptuous impatience with the labouring processes of democracy. He came out to British North America with a large programme of practical reforms, and he completed it with a breezy, nonchalant dexterity which seemed almost magical. He obtained the approval of both provinces for their legislative union. He laid the bases of a system of municipal government. He even succeeded in getting legislative approval of a division of the proceeds of the Clergy Reserves among the different Protestant communions. And at the opening of the first session of the Legislature of the united Province of Canada, in a speech which confidently sounded the note of constructive planning and material improvement, he publicly announced the inspiring news of a £1,500,000 imperial guaranteed loan.

Yet, though he showered material benefits with a lavish hand, he held tightly to Lord John Russell's strict theory of colonial government. 'I have told the people plainly', he wrote in his brusque, confident fashion, 'that, as I cannot get rid of my responsibility to the home government, I will place no responsibility on the council; that they are *a council* for the governor to consult, but no more.' The Governor, in Sydenham's opinion, was to be his own prime minister, with rows of obedient back-benchers at his command; and for parties, other than the coalitions which he promoted himself, he had nothing but impatience and contempt. In 1840, on a visit to Halifax in his capacity as Governor-in-Chief of British North America, he persuaded Joseph Howe and other Reformers to enter a union government in Nova Scotia; and in the first session of the legislature of united Canada, he dexterously divided the Reform party and secured the allegiance of an important section of its members. He was a company chairman who was able to report successful operations and to announce good dividends. And under him and his immediate successors the Old Colonial System had its last measures of success and its final burst of prosperity.

The End of the Old Order

II

Yet, in the meantime, the forces which were to accomplish its downfall had been rapidly gaining in strength. The growth of new communities in British North America had led to the development of a political maturity which had found vigorous expression in the demand for Lord Durham's plan of responsible government. The rise of industrialism in the United Kingdom had created a new and assertive national interest which had discovered an appropriate economic philosophy in the doctrine of free trade. The two movements—the fiscal revolution in the Mother Country and the political revolution in the North American colonies—reached their climax at almost exactly the same moment of time; and it was the force of their united impact which broke the Old Colonial System.

In Great Britain the stupendous conquests of industrialism had never permitted a complete recovery of that faith in Empire which had been half lost in the tragedy of the American Revolution. For the masters of the new manufacturing machine, the men who sought world markets and the traffic of the Seven Seas, the material benefits of the surviving Empire could, in fact, be contemptuously disregarded. The protected markets and shipping monopolies of the few, small, underpopulated colonies which remained were relatively inconsiderable in themselves; and—what was equally important—they totally failed to offset the very large, direct charges which Great Britain had to defray for their defence and administration, as well as the heavy indirect costs which the whole protective system laid upon British production. This detailed, realistic cost-accounting of the Empire, which had begun as the academic exercise of Adam Smith and the classical economists and had continued as the fashionable doctrine of *avant-garde* intellectuals such as the Utilitarians and the Philosophic Radicals, now acquired a new popularity, and a far greater political potency, in the propaganda of the Anti-Corn Law

The End of the Old Order

League. Free trade had become an important political issue.
The political parties showed obvious indications of a perplexed
interest; and the long and painful conversion of Sir Robert
Peel began. In 1842 Peel introduced the first of his reforming
budgets; and although the new regulations made the import of
Canadian wheat into the British market easier, the twenty-five
shilling decrease in the duty on foreign timber was an ominous
portent of the trouble that was approaching for the Canadian
timber trade.

In the meantime, while those two pious demagogues,
Richard Cobden and John Bright, were earnestly sapping the
economic foundations of the Old Colonial System, the British
North American provinces were undermining its political bases
with equal zeal and success. It was Nova Scotia and the new
'empire' Province of Canada which took the lead in the movement. Prince Edward Island was too small and Newfoundland
had too recently received the grant of representative institutions for them to play a prominent part; and New Brunswick,
whose assembly had been recently granted the control of the
large crown revenues arising from the timber royalties, was
rejoicing in a high state of political gratification. Canada and
Nova Scotia were older provinces, of obviously greater political importance, more complex interests, and a depth and
variety of experience which the other colonies had not yet been
able to acquire. Above all, Canada and Nova Scotia were
already developing the fairly well defined and organized
parties which were the indispensable requisite of the colonial
cabinet government which Lord Durham had recommended.

Nova Scotia, though it was much smaller in size and population than its sister province, played just as active a role as
Canada in the struggle for responsible government. Nova
Scotia's political tradition, which had begun with the founding
of its assembly in 1758, was the oldest by a good margin in the
whole of British North America. A maritime, trading province,
seriously regarded in an age when empire was supposed to
consist of ships, colonies, and commerce, it had already done

much, through the fight for the West Indies trade, to liberalize the Old Colonial System; and the solid weight of its political influence, unlike that of Canada's, had never been divided and impaired by the sorry mess of an abortive rebellion. The Province's Reform party, firmly united by the clear, single goal of responsible government, was well served by the sober leadership of Herbert Huntington and J. B. Uniacke and galvanized by the exuberant energy and creative ability of Joseph Howe. Howe, who had already made perhaps the most dignified statement of the colonial case for responsible government in his *Letters to Lord John Russell*, was just as effective in the rough and tumble of the Assembly's debates and in the boisterously vulgar battles of the contemporary press. In the autumn of 1843 he retired, along with his principal Reform associates, from the coalition government which he had been persuaded to enter under Lord Falkland; and then, using all his abundant and brilliant talents as politician and journalist to the full, he entered joyously into the party battle for responsible government.

In comparison with the versatile and imaginative Howe, Robert Baldwin and Louis Hippolyte Lafontaine were very sober, solid politicians; and the making of a political party in Canada was a much more complex and difficult business than it was in the more culturally united Nova Scotia. It was hard enough to get English-speaking and French-speaking Canadians to work together amicably in any case and it was particularly difficult when the French had only too good reasons for believing that the union was designed to swamp them and submerge their culture. The Reform party organized by Baldwin, Lafontaine, and Francis Hincks was the first party which frankly recognized the cultural duality of Canadian life and the political partnership of the two Canadian peoples. But there still remained an irresistible tendency to form nationalist blocs and to divide sectionally along the old interprovincial boundary line. Any opposition party, in the early years of the united Province, was bound to rely heavily upon the solid phalanx of Lafontaine's French-Canadian supporters; and when, in the autumn of 1843, Baldwin and Lafontaine resigned from the Executive Council in protest against Governor Metcalfe's refusal to accept their advice in the disposal of the patronage of the Crown, it was fairly easy for the Conservatives to capture the support of the greater part of Canada West, the Old Upper Canada, in defence of the Governor's position. But the Conservatives, though still, in a special sense, a Governor's party—a 'King's party'—were obviously determining government policy in much the same way as their rivals had sought to do; and, like their rivals also, they were soon endeavouring to gain the allegiance of a section of the French-Canadians.

III

The full, open acceptance of responsible government—within the limits of domestic provincial affairs, as Durham and Baldwin had advocated—was drawing rapidly closer. But the formal admission had not yet been made; and it was not on the side of politics, but of economics, that the Old Colonial System received its first really shattering blow. In 1846 Peel finally did the deed of abolishing the Corn Laws: and, to their consternation and horror, the merchants of Montreal learnt that all protective duties—and consequently all colonial preferences—on the import of grain into Great Britain would come immediately to an end. The Repeal of the Corn Laws had, of course, relatively little effect on the Maritime Provinces; it did not do much injury to the farmers of Canada West, for there were alternative routes by which they could ship their grain, prices kept up fairly well for a few years, and new markets were opening up in the United States. For all these complacent people, the Repeal of the Corn Laws meant little; but for the millers of Canada West, the Montreal merchants, and all those who had a vital interest in the transportation system of the St. Lawrence, the repeal was nothing short of a paralysing disaster. The new canal system, in which Canada had invested so much, was just being completed; and the Canada Corn Act of 1843—by which the British Parliament had at last admitted Canadian wheat at the merely nominal duty of a shilling a quarter—had attracted an immense traffic in cereals down the St. Lawrence. Now a large part of this was gone; and, at a stroke, Montreal lost one of its greatest competitive advantages in the struggle for the western trade.

The Repeal of the Corn Laws, and the sharp reduction of the timber duties which accompanied it, were visibly hastening the end of the economic foundations of the Old Colonial System. And, at the same time, the final renunciation of its political principles was being formally announced. The break-up of Peel's party in the battle over the Corn Laws had brought the Whigs back to office; and Lord John Russell's government —with the third Earl Grey, Lord Durham's brother-in-law, as its Colonial Secretary—decided to accept the revolutionary change in colonial government which 'Radical Jack' had recommended seven years before. In the key dispatches of 1846–7, which were written to Sir John Harvey in Nova Scotia and circulated to the other governors, Grey pronounced in favour of 'the immediate adoption of that system of parliamentary government which has long prevailed in the Mother Country, and which seems to be a necessary part of representative institutions in a certain stage of their progress'.

The full consequences were soon revealed. In 1847 there were general elections in both Nova Scotia and Canada. In both provinces the Reform parties secured a majority; and the two governors, acting in their new capacity as the benevolently impartial 'mediators and moderators' among all parties, invited the two successful party leaders to form provincial governments. The practical way around the obstacles of Lord John Russell's irrefutable constitutional logic had been found. In genuinely imperial matters, such as defence and foreign policy, the Governor was still an imperial officer, responsible to the British Government; but in purely colonial affairs, he had become a local representative of the sovereign, acting

The End of the Old Order

normally on the advice of his provincial ministry. The Earl of Elgin, the new Governor of Canada, was prepared fearlessly to play the part assigned to him; and the full implications of the new order were dramatically revealed in 1849 when a highly controversial measure of the new Reform government, the Rebellion Losses Bill, was presented to the Legislature. For the old 'British party' in Montreal, the Rebellion Losses Bill was an abominable bill which awarded compensation to rebels as well as loyalists. They expected the Governor to veto or reserve the Bill; but he did not. And this, for merchants who were already shattered by the collapse of the Old Colonial System and the ruin of their trade, was the final unforgivable blow. 'Elginism' had completed the hideous work of destruction which 'Cobdenism' had begun. The old British Empire, political and economic, was in ruins.

On the night of the 25th April 1849 a vast crowd was gathering on the Champ de Mars in Montreal. It was an unquiet city, full of defiant anger and unconcealed excitement. That afternoon Lord Elgin had come down from Monklands and had given his approval to the Rebellion Losses Bill; and that afternoon as he had emerged from the Legislative Building, he had been mocked with groans and hisses and pelted with volleys of refuse. Broadsheets had been quickly struck off announcing a protest meeting of the citizens. The bells were rung, men hurried through the streets informing everybody of the approaching assembly; and by eight o'clock there was a crowd of thousands at the Champ de Mars. The sky was bright with stars. It was a clear, cool night, with a high wind; and the red torches waved and sputtered angrily in the darkness. Resolutions denouncing the Rebellion Losses Bill and demanding the recall of the Governor were voted with thunderous unanimity. But by this time resolutions, however violent, were not enough. The crowd was restless, unappeased, ugly with ungovernable fury; and suddenly it turned, moved, and began to race through the city streets towards that prime source of its injuries, the Parliament Buildings.

The End of the Old Order

A rain of stones shattered the windows. The great front door burst open. In the assembly hall somebody carried off the mace; and from the speaker's chair a stentorian voice could be heard dissolving Parliament in the Queen's name. People were breaking lights; they were smashing furniture; and, at last, at the west end of the building a group of rioters fired the papers in a storage room for stationery. In a minute the room and its contents were ablaze; in a few minutes more the flames were bursting from the gaping doors and broken windows. And the shouting crowd drew back admiringly and fearfully as the whole fiery scene rose bright out of the obscurity and the sky was reddened overhead.

IV

On the 25th of July 1849, exactly three months after the burning of the Parliament Buildings in Montreal, a new association, called the British American League, met for a seven-day convention at Kingston, Canada West. Nothing could have revealed more clearly the anxious, speculative mood of 1849 than this highly talkative assembly, with its few independents and Reformers, and its many worried Conservatives. For the most unbending Tories, the passage of the Rebellion Losses Bill and the Repeal of the Corn Laws had really meant the end of British rule in Canada and the end of Canada's membership in the Empire; and even for those who were not prepared to rush to these catastrophic conclusions, the events of 1849 inevitably raised the most painful doubts and uncertainties about the future. For seventy-five years, ever since the American Revolution had first broken out, British North America had sought with increasing conviction to preserve a separate, independent political existence in North America; and for seventy-five years she had based her best hopes of material success upon the economic benefits of British mercantilism. Now these hopes appeared to be blasted. Great Britain had made the second American Revolution herself. She had declared herself economically independent of the northern colonies. And, without her help, was it possible for them to build a viable economy of their own? Over a thousand responsible merchants and politicians in Montreal said that it was not. In the autumn of 1849 they signed the Annexation Manifesto, advocating the political union of Canada with the United States. Would it not be better to accept their gloomy conclusions and to admit that the whole attempt to found a separate British North America had been a huge, presumptuous mistake?

The Canadians—except for a very small minority—showed no signs of making this abject admission. Three months before the annexationists of Montreal announced their despairing remedy, the British American League had already examined and rejected it. There was no abandonment of the enterprise which the northern colonies had half-unwittingly begun seventy-five years before. There was simply a determined effort on the part of the Canadians to think their way through the problems of the strange new order which had come into being between 1846 and 1849. The triumph of free trade meant the search for new markets as well as a persevering attempt to retain the old. The introduction of responsible government meant the end of the old British governance, the end of oligarchical rule, and the absolute necessity of accepting the cultural duality of Canada and the political comradeship of French-speaking and English-speaking Canadians. Major adjustments would have to be made; but there was still continuity with the past and hope for the future. The old political connection with Great Britain remained, with all the benefits of its diplomatic and military support. The St. Lawrence trading system remained, with all its natural advantages and commercial possibilities. There were old assets upon which reliance could still be placed and fresh prospects to which the provinces could look forward. The year 1849 marked the conclusion of a campaign, not the end of a war. What was needed was not a treaty of capitulation, but a new strategy.

In the first half-dozen years after 1848 the northern provinces made their initial efforts to accommodate themselves to the facts of their new situation. The task of adjustment was harder for Canada than for any of the other colonies. It was hardest of all for the Canadian Tories who at a stroke had lost their political influence as well as their economic and social privileges. John A. Macdonald, the progressive and attractive Kingston lawyer, played the main part in transforming the Toryism of the past into the Liberal-Conservatism of the future; and his rival, the journalist George Brown, rapidly emerged as the leader of a new moderate Reform party. Between them, they succeeded in winding up the still exasperatingly unsettled affairs of the Province's colonial past. In 1854 the Clergy Reserves were finally secularized, and the commutation of the seigniorial tenure system was carried through. These overdue colonial debts were paid off, the old and bankrupt colonialism itself was liquidated; and Canada, which had felt the agitations of this second American Revolution most acutely, passed, like the rest of British North America, into a new age in its domestic affairs.

Obviously also, it was entering a new era in its external relations. A fresh strategy was just as necessary in foreign trade as it was in domestic politics; and it was natural for provinces which had thrived on the preferences of the Old Colonial System to seek a comparable commercial relationship with England's only possible trade substitute, the United States. A liberal reciprocal trade agreement would carry with it none of those frightening annexationist implications which British North America dreaded so much; it would simply widen the markets for British American lumber and cereals which were already opening up in the United States. Canada, which, with Great Britain's help, took the lead in the struggle for a reciprocity treaty, would probably not have been able to offer sufficient commercial inducements herself to overcome the indifference of the United States. But by the Convention of 1818 the American fishing vessels were permitted to enter British American coastal waters only for wood, water, shelter, and repairs; and Great Britain's announced determination to defend the three-mile limit against interlopers decided the United States to seek a commercial agreement which would give her citizens free entry into the inshore fisheries of the Maritime Provinces. In 1854 the ponderously complicated wards of the American political system yielded at last, and the door swung slowly open for the passage of a Reciprocity Treaty which established free trade in natural products between the northern provinces and the United States. The Treaty gave a southern direction and a continental significance to British North American trade; but it did not divert interest from the old east-west traffic of the St. Lawrence, and it did not end Montreal's old dream of a western commercial empire. Obviously the new orientation and the new strategy of British North America had yet to be determined.

9

BRITISH NORTH AMERICA UNITES

I

The struggle for the Reciprocity Treaty was British North America's first instinctive effort for survival in the panic bewilderment which followed the collapse of the Old Colonial System. It was an effort prompted by the habits of the old colonial dependence; but it was not the only response to the crisis of 1849; and there were other actions and speculations which revealed equally clearly the first stirrings of a new self-sufficient nationality. British North America had, in fact, been launched upon its bracing career of home rule and economic competition at a time which was singularly favourable for heroic experiments in nation-building. It was an age of industrialism and nationality; an age when wood, wind, and water were yielding primacy to steam and steel; when the little provinces, small states, loose federations, and great sprawling, decentralized empires of the past were being vigorously reorganized into a new group of powerful nation states. The appearance of Italy and Germany, the rise of a new United States from the ordeal of the Civil War, and of a new industrial Great Britain from the disintegration of the second British Empire, were all imposing portents of a new state of affairs, both economic and political. They supplied British North America with precept and example. But they did more than this. The break-up of the Old Colonial System, a characteristic episode in the age of industrialism and nationality, had provided the northern provinces with the two indispensable instruments of their future career of nation-building. Industrialism had brought the railway, the successful tool of national expansion and integration. Responsible government implied fiscal autonomy and the use of the tariff as a device for national self-sufficiency. These were the weapons appropriate to the new age; and on them British North America built her strategy for the future.

Late in 1853 a small, squat engine, with a spreading funnel, the property of the St. Lawrence and Atlantic Railway Company, started off, with a little string of carriages attached to it, from the south shore of the St. Lawrence, opposite Montreal, on its long journey south-east to the Atlantic port of Portland, in Maine. The St. Lawrence and Atlantic was intended to break the winter stillness which reigned over Montreal, like the ice which bound the river, by giving it a salt-water port on the Atlantic Seaboard; and it was only one of the many determined attempts made by the northern provinces to protect their territories from the spreading encroachments of the American railway system and to strengthen the attractions of their cities, Halifax, St. John, Montreal, and Toronto, as focal points of transoceanic and transcontinental trade. The Grand Trunk Railway, of which the St. Lawrence and Atlantic soon became a part, stretched westward all the way from Portland on the Atlantic coast to Sarnia, at the foot of Lake Huron. It was designed to reassert Montreal's historic claims to the trade of the international North American west, just as that grandiose Maritime enterprise, the European and North American Railway, was planned to draw the traffic of the whole north-eastern Seaboard to the closest port to England, Halifax.

All these early railways were separate Canadian or Maritime undertakings, which sought traffic in the United States and made no effort to link British North America as a whole together. In effect, the new power of iron and steam had been used to reach old commercial goals. But there were other, new, purely British North American objectives which the railway had made possible of realization for the first time; and from the beginning both Maritimers and Canadians were well aware of these opportunities. The European and North American Railway and the Grand Trunk Railway were, in fact, simply separate divisions of the original grand design for an Intercolonial Railway which would connect Montreal and the ice-free port of Halifax through British-American territory. The plan of strengthening the east-west transport system of the St. Lawrence by an extension to the Maritime Provinces, which had been one of the first projects of the railway age, had fallen through for a time. But it remained stubbornly, hopefully, in men's minds; and behind it, in hazily grandiose outlines, was the still vaster conception of a railway which would traverse both the Precambrian Shield and the Rocky Mountains and find its appointed terminus on the Pacific slope.

The northern provinces had discovered the enormous potential value of railways. They soon began to discover the crucially important uses of the tariff. When, in 1846, by the British Possessions Act, the imperial Parliament had permitted the colonies to regulate their own customs duties, it had unquestionably expected them to follow its own wise example and establish free trade. But free trade, which was admirably suited to an economically mature country with an industrial head start over everybody else, would have been tragically inappropriate for the northern colonies, particularly Canada; and Canada, as it advanced through the early stages of its own industrial revolution, found increasingly good reasons for raising, rather than lowering, its customs duties. There was, in the first place, a small but highly vocal group of manufacturers which now began to press for an increase in tariff protection. The presence of these capitalists, in significant numbers, was in itself a sign of industrial growth; but there were other arguments than those which the manufacturers had advanced for the action which the Canadian legislature soon began to take. The Canadian Government, in order to attract reluctant

British investors, had repeatedly given its guarantee in aid of the financing of Canadian railways; and when the expansive boom of the Crimean War was suddenly followed by a severe depression, both railways and government confronted bankruptcy. More revenue must be found and at once. And where could it be got so easily and painlessly as from customs duties? Customs duties were the historic British North American tax. Other forms of taxation—particularly income tax—were administratively difficult, if not impossible, in a primary-producing colony. In 1858–9, despite outraged protests from Great Britain and the United States, the Canadian tariff was substantially raised. It had been recognized for the first time as an indispensable, a vital, instrument in the economic strategy of nation-building. It had been used—it was to be used again—to build railways. It could also be used to ensure the traffic which the railways would carry from east to west.

II

The means of achieving nationhood lay ready. The will to nationhood was growing rapidly as well. During the 1850's—in part as a result of the break-up of the old imperial organization and the decline of the old imperial faith—both Maritimers and Canadians were becoming more and more conscious of the enormous property which British North America might inherit. They had not, of course, done as well territorially as they had hoped; but, on the paper of treaties at least, a truly imperial domain had been staked out. The Ashburton Treaty of 1842, which left Maine jutting up like a huge wedge between New Brunswick and Canada, still permitted the essential communication between the St. Lawrence valley and the Seaboard. To the north, on the Pacific coast, the limits of Russian penetration had been fixed by the Anglo-Russian Convention of 1825; and to the south, after many years of anxious uncertainty, the Treaty of Washington of 1846 had continued the forty-ninth parallel as the international boundary to the

Pacific Ocean and had given the whole of Vancouver Island to British North America. It was a gigantic inheritance; and for a variety of important reasons, British North Americans were becoming more excitedly aware of its infinite possibilities during the 1850's than they had ever been before. The provinces on the St. Lawrence and the Seaboard were occupied colonies with exploited resources; the north-west, the one great possible area for their future expansion, was obviously growing out of its primitive status as a fur-trading preserve. Great Britain, as well as the whole of British North America, was beginning to realize that some radical reorganization of the British territories in North America was impending and, indeed, inevitable. They were also beginning to realize that if they did not rapidly take action themselves they would be forestalled by the United States.

The pressure for the establishment and extension of the east-west British-American axis grew stronger and stronger. The Maritimers conceived of it largely in terms of the construction of the Intercolonial Railway and the linking up of the St. Lawrence valley and the Seaboard. The Canadians thought of it mainly as the settlement and exploitation of the prairies of the north-west. It was something distinctly new for the Maritimers to consider the traffic of the continental hinterland, for hitherto their fortunes had been pursued at sea; and although Quebec and Montreal, from the day of their foundation, had always instinctively sought expansion westward, the commercial empire for which they had struggled had lain as much south as north of the international boundary. The novelty of the expansionist movement of the 1850's and 1860's lay in the emphatically north-western direction which it took. In effect, the northern provinces were beginning to substitute a British North American for a North American economy, and a national for a continental interest. For over a quarter of a century, ever since the union of the Hudson's Bay Company and the North West Company in 1821, the north-west had dropped out of Canada's concerns and even out of its knowledge. Now suddenly, Rupert's Land and the North-West Territories—the lands which the Hudson's Bay Company had held in trust for the future Dominion of Canada—rushed out of the background through the middle distance and into the very foreground of men's hopes and imaginations.

The lands were prized for themselves. They were prized even more because they were, for the first time, in danger. Settlement had always been the inveterate and invincible enemy of the fur trade; and now settlement was pressing perilously close to the last preserve of the fur trade on the North American continent. It could not, of course, come from central British North America, for the Precambrian Shield interposed its difficult barrier between the Province of Canada and the western prairies. It came, and could only come, as things stood at that time, from the United States. The American frontier was creeping steadily north-west across the prairies; and, on the Pacific coast, it advanced with a bound into British American territory, as soon as gold was discovered on the Fraser River in 1856. In 1858, between twenty-five and thirty thousand miners, mainly Americans, had arrived in the new colony of British Columbia; and in the same year, Minnesota Territory, with its dangerous proximity to the Red River Colony, became a state. Economically the settlements on the Fraser River were dependent upon San Francisco, and even the Hudson's Bay Company had begun to bring in its supplies and mails from Minneapolis and St. Paul.

For years, ever since the opening of the diplomatic duel over the Oregon country, the future of the British north-west had remained enveloped in a vague uncertainty. The provinces of the east had watched the varying fortunes and speculated about the future possibilities of the prairies and the Pacific slope with growing interest; but it was not until the 1860's that this concern deepened into a positive anxiety. In 1861 the Civil War broke out in the United States; and for the next decade the relations between the republic and Great Britain and British North America deteriorated threateningly. The *Trent* crisis, which occurred as early as the autumn of 1861, was simply the first of a long series of ugly episodes which repeatedly brought the English-speaking world to the verge of war; and in 1862 the Province of Canada began to make drastic plans for the improvement of its militia.

War was the most terrible of all contingencies; but it was not the only danger against which British North America might have to guard. It was possible that the United States might use the force of its diplomatic pressure to compel Great Britain to cede all or part of British North America as compensation for the huge losses which, the republic alleged, had resulted from British breaches of neutrality during the war. It was more than probable that the rising protectionist forces in the United States would bring about the abrogation of the Reciprocity Treaty at the earliest possible moment. The Treaty dealt exclusively with primary products, not manufactured goods; but it had been under heavy fire from American manufacturing and commercial interests ever since the introduction of the new Canadian tariff in 1858–9; and the repeated Anglo-American controversies of the American Civil War had enabled these critics to intensify their attacks. The Reciprocity Treaty might go the way of the Old Colonial System. And if all external, preferential markets vanished, what could British North America do but fall back upon the resources of its own potential national economy?

But pressure from the United States was not the only influence which was forcing British North America to reach a decision about its collective future. There was also pressure from Great Britain; and since the northern provinces hoped, as an essential condition of their political survival in North America, to remain inside the British Empire, the influence which Great Britain exerted was a prime factor in all their calculations. The public men of England assumed, as a complacently unquestioned article of faith, that the British North American provinces, like all mature colonies, would soon desire their complete and formal independence. Great Britain would, of course, do nothing to hasten a break which the provinces apparently did not yet wish; but if the connection was to remain for a while longer at any rate, it must, British statesmen insisted, be continued on terms which were acceptable to the Mother Country. Colonies which enjoyed the luxury of responsible government and which had the power to establish protective tariffs against British manufacturers, could very well afford to assume a good many more responsibilities. And North American responsibilities, for colonial defence and colonial government, were charges which Great Britain was getting increasingly anxious to drop.

The garrison system of imperial defence was a heavy burden. The Crown colonies, which might have to be set up in place of the Hudson's Bay Company's rule in Rupert's Land, would be an additional and very unwelcome load to carry. Would it not be possible now, at this stage in colonial development, to transfer most of these responsibilities—and opportunities—to the broad shoulders of the British North American provinces? And if the colonies were still too weak, individually, to accept the tasks, could they not be combined in a sufficiently powerful union? During the 1850's and early 1860's British Colonial secretaries and British North American governors were earnestly considering the problem of colonial union. Some advocated a general federation. Some believed that regional unions, either federal or legislative, were a first necessity. In 1864, spurred on largely by the urgings of the Maritime governors and the interest of the Colonial Office, Nova Scotia, New Brunswick and Prince Edward Island decided to hold a conference to consider a proposal for their legislative union.

III

On the 14th June 1864 the Conservative Taché government of Canada, with George E. Cartier and John A. Macdonald as its principal French- and English-speaking ministers, was defeated in the provincial legislature by two votes. It had held

office for less than three months; and the shortness of its tenure
and the closeness of the vote by which it had been defeated
were equally painful evidences of the chronic instability of
Canadian political life. The Province of Canada had admirably
succeeded in solving the problems of its colonial past; but it
had utterly failed to find a way out of the difficulties into which
it had been plunged by the Union Act of 1840. It was true, of
course, that the Union Act had itself helped to make these
difficulties almost insoluble. By its terms, the two sections of the
Province, Canada East and Canada West, which corresponded
with the old colonies of Lower and Upper Canada, had been
given equal representation in the provincial legislature, irrespective of population; and this political equality had tended
to harden the sectional division of the Province and to exacerbate its inevitable cultural misunderstandings.

In form, Canada was a unitary state. In fact, it was an informal federal union, in which most of the important functions
of government were carried on sectionally. The cabinet, the
legislature, and several of the important departments of
government were organized on a sectional basis. Much of the
legislation that was passed had to be sectional in character;
and the political parties, though they tried, of course, to win a
following in both French- and English-speaking Canada, had
an irresistible tendency to become strong in one section of the
Province, and correspondingly weak in the other. They tended
also, as a natural consequence, to reach a level of approximate
political equality; and thus the public affairs of the Province
were characterized both by a permanent state of sectional conflict and a chronic condition of political instability.

Geographically and economically, the two sections were
united by the St. Lawrence River; they were divided socially
by their two different cultural inheritances. They had found it
just as difficult to live together as they had to live apart; and
for over a decade the public men of the Province had been
seeking for some constitutional way out of this constant state of
political deadlock and cultural exasperation. There were people

who wished to break up the union completely; there were other people who were equally determined to make it a real union by introducing representation by population in the legislature. But gradually these radical solutions were forgotten in the instinctive general desire for some kind of settlement which would preserve both the unity and duality of the Province. Obviously this could only be done, as people said at the time, through the application of the 'federal principle'. But how was the 'federal principle' to be applied? In 1858–9 the two political parties made up their minds on the subject. In 1858 the Conservatives had decided in favour of a general federation of the whole of British North America. In the following year the Reformers of Canada West, assembled in convention, had come to the conclusion that it would be best to start with a regional federation of Canada East and Canada West.

Five years later, when on the 14th of June 1864 the Conservative government went down to defeat by two votes, nothing had yet been done to carry out either of these constitutional proposals. Two indecisive general elections had been held. Ministries had come and gone. The Province had staggered on politically for a few years. And the repetition of that familiar event, the downfall of a ministry, might have meant merely that it would stagger on, under slightly different auspices, for a few years more. But this time, at long last, the outcome was miraculously unexpected. The majority of the Reformers of Canada West, led by George Brown, agreed to join with the Liberal-Conservatives in a coalition government which would make a determined effort to end the Province's political deadlock through a fundamental constitutional change. Both the Conservative and the Reform federal schemes were combined in the programme of the coalition; but the Conservative plan was given priority. The new government was committed, in the first place, to an attempt to form a general British North American federation.

It had need for speed. But it had the energy of conviction. And it also had incredible luck. The Maritime Provinces had already agreed to hold a constitutional conference that year; and although the union in which they were ostensibly interested differed radically from that which Canada was now seeking, the members of the coalition government refused to be intimidated by these differences. They asked permission to send delegates to the projected Maritime Conference; and, in reply, they were courteously invited to be represented 'unofficially'. The limitation could hardly have seemed material to the Canadians. The Maritime Conference gave them a most favourable opportunity to launch their federal scheme. It gave them a pulpit from which they could preach to the whole of British North America. They would use the occasion with all the zeal imparted by their conviction and their sense of urgency.

On the 1st September 1864, when the formidable Canadian delegation of eight Cabinet Ministers arrived at Charlottetown, Prince Edward Island, the Maritime Conference was just about to begin. Colonel J. H. Gray, the Island's Prime Minister, acted as host; Samuel L. Tilley led the New Brunswickers; Charles Tupper headed a non-partisan contingent from Nova Scotia. They were all ready to start, though with many reservations and without much enthusiasm, when the arrival of the Canadian delegation was announced; and then, with curiously significant readiness and unanimity, they agreed to postpone their official business until the Canadians were heard. During the next few days the eight members of the coalition government proceeded literally to take over the sessions; and when the conference moved off from Prince Edward Island on a tour of the other Maritime Provinces, it was always the Canadian plan of a general federation which was described and extolled at the dinners and public meetings in Halifax, St. John, and Fredericton. The Maritimers utterly failed to reach any decision on the subject of Maritime union; and the only positive result of the conference was an agreement that a new conference should be convened on October 10th at Quebec for the purpose, this time, of taking into formal consideration a general federal union of the whole of British North America.

British North America Unites

At Quebec the Canadians, with the constructive and adroit Macdonald as their principal spokesman, had the chance of presenting their programme formally and in full. They had spent the summer and early autumn in earnest study of it, and the principles and details of the scheme were settled in their minds. Its fundamental basis was the idea of British parliamentary government under the Crown. 'In framing a Constitution for the General Government,' ran the third of the Quebec Resolutions, 'the Conference, with a view to the perpetuation of our connexion with the Mother Country, and to the promotion of the best interests of the people of these Provinces, desire to follow the model of the British Constitution, so far as our circumstances will permit.' The last attempt —the armed attempt of the rebellions of 1837—to introduce American political theory and congressional government into the Canadas—had failed dismally; and the Quebec Conference simply ratified the previous firm decision to maintain the political tradition of Great Britain and British North America.

The new federal union was to be a constitutional British monarchy—the 'Kingdom of Canada' was the title subsequently inserted in one of the early drafts of the British North America Act—and its institutions were all derived from the constitutional history of the British Empire. Executive authority was to be exercised by the Governor-General, in accordance with the well-known principle of responsible government and cabinet rule. Legislative power was vested in a Parliament of two houses, the Senate and the House of Commons. The constitutional ancestors, if not the names, of both these institutions were British, for the Senate, which was first referred to by the familiar British American name of 'Legislative Council', had none of the special powers of the American Senate and occupied approximately the same position in the Canadian system as the House of Lords did in the British.

The second of the two fundamental principles of the federal plan which the Canadians presented at Quebec was the idea of a strong central government. Macdonald and Tupper, as they both frankly avowed, would have preferred a legislative to a federal union, if that had been possible; and there were good reasons why a majority of the delegates should have shared their leaders' aversion for a weak, decentralized federation. The Civil War, which was still raging in the United States, had planted in all of them a deep distrust of the fatal divisive power of states' rights. Their own provincial governments had not yet demanded or acquired sovereign powers; there was no really solid theoretical basis for the assertion of provincial rights at Quebec; and the delegates were not inhibited, by any essential constitutional principle, from attempting to correct what they took to be the vital defect in the American system.

They sought to strengthen the central government of the new Canada both through the distribution of powers, and the organization of the new institutions, federal and local. The membership of the Senate was constituted on the basis of regional, rather than provincial, equality; and the powers of appointing provincial lieutenant-governors and of disallowing provincial legislation—the principal controls over the provinces which the imperial authorities had possessed under the Old Colonial System—were transferred to the federal government. In the American constitution, all powers not specifically assigned to the central government, were reserved to the states or the people. 'They commenced, in fact,' Macdonald argued, 'at the wrong end'; and one of the main purposes of the Fathers of Confederation was to reverse this American constitutional principle by conferring general or residuary powers—'all the great subjects of legislation'—upon the new federal legislature. 'We thereby strengthen the Central Parliament', Macdonald declared, 'and make the Confederation one people and one government, instead of five peoples and five governments with merely a point of authority connecting us to a limited and insufficient extent.'

IV

When, less than three weeks later, the Quebec Conference

broke up, it had completed a task which only six months before might have seemed quite incapable of accomplishment. It had passed a series of seventy-two resolutions—the Quebec Resolutions—which embodied a detailed, carefully worked out plan for a federal union of British North America. And, for a while, everything seemed to foreshadow the rapid, successful translation of the new system into law. The leading delegates were fairly confident that the Quebec scheme would get an enthusiastic reception in their respective provinces. The British Government, which had been waiting for just such a unanimous expression of colonial opinion as the Quebec Conference seemed to supply, hastened to give the Seventy-Two Resolutions a warm and almost unqualified public endorsement. The United States, it was true, did not add its compliments and good wishes; in fact, the only greeting which the new Canadian nation was to receive from its great neighbour was a resolution subsequently passed by Congress expressing outraged disapproval at the very idea of a British North American federation.

It was the threat of American encroachment and the fear of American diplomatic or military aggression which had driven British North Americans to consider union as a measure of defence; and during the autumn of 1864 the pressure of these perils and apprehensions was suddenly renewed and intensified. In October, at the very time when the Quebec Conference was in session, agents of the Confederate States of America launched from Canada a futile raid on the Vermont town of St. Albans; and this episode, which the United States regarded as the climax of a long series of British and British-American breaches of neutrality during the Civil War, produced a violent explosion of temper in the republic. Passports—a thing till then unheard of in North America—were demanded of Canadians travelling to the United States. A threat was made to abrogate the Rush-Bagot agreement limiting naval armaments on the Great Lakes; and the American Congress definitely announced that the Reciprocity Treaty was to come to an end at the earliest possible moment, in 1866.

British North America Unites

Once again, and with frightening emphasis, British North America had been shown the wisdom of falling back upon its own collective resources, both political and economic. The warnings were plain and unmistakable; and yet, despite them, the Confederation movement stumbled and halted for a while in a fashion which seemed inexplicable to its advocates. It had been agreed at Quebec that the different provincial governments would seek to get the Quebec plan ratified in their respective legislatures as a preliminary to its enactment in statute form by the imperial Parliament. In Canada, where the coalition ensured large majorities in favour of the Seventy-Two Resolutions, the federal scheme was ratified without difficulty; but elsewhere throughout British North America its reception was very different. Both Newfoundland and Prince Edward Island eventually rejected the plan. In Nova Scotia a formidable opposition was developing under the leadership of Joseph Howe; and in New Brunswick the Premier, S. L. Tilley, deciding to put the issue of Confederation before the people in a sudden general election, was decisively defeated by an anti-Confederate coalition.

The defection of Newfoundland and Prince Edward Island was regrettable but not too serious. The defeat of the Confederates in New Brunswick was a fatal blow, for 'the Province of the Loyalists' was an essential link between continental Canada and peninsular Nova Scotia, and without its presence Confederation would be quite literally meaningless. For over a year, from the winter of 1865 when Tilley's government was defeated until the spring of the following year, the whole Confederation movement was arrested in a dead stop. Everything which earnest purpose could inspire and ingenuity could devise, was done to reverse the fatal verdict in New Brunswick. The imperial Government lent the force of its grave persuasions. The Canadians lavishly contributed campaign funds to the New Brunswick Confederates. Even the Fenian movement in the United States, that latest manifestation of republican animosity towards Great Britain and British North America, assisted the cause of union by its futile but frightening frontier raids. All these external forces helped; but fundamentally it was the state of affairs in New Brunswick itself which altered the decision against Confederation. The maritime tradition of the seaboard provinces and the rugged particularism which had developed as an essential part of it, made Nova Scotia and New Brunswick deeply suspicious of a continental union in which the populous Canada would obviously be dominant. But the anti-Confederate government in Fredericton could not conceive a valid alternative destiny, either political or economic; and it was this bankruptcy of policy which caused its defeat in the second New Brunswick election in the late spring of 1866.

Once Tilley was back in power again, the Confederation movement briskly resumed its onward course. Nova Scotia and New Brunswick, though their legislatures never accepted the Quebec Resolutions, authorized a renewal of the negotiations for union; and late in the autumn of 1866 delegates of the three provinces met once more in conference at the Westminster Palace Hotel in London, for a final revision of the Quebec scheme. The London Resolutions, embodied in the British North America Act, passed the imperial Parliament in March, 1867; and on July 1st, the first 'Dominion Day', the federal union of Canada, Nova Scotia, and New Brunswick came into being. A nation which had scarcely ceased being a colony; a potentially transcontinental state which only yesterday had been a few patches of settlement on seashore and riverbank; a union which was composed of two sharply contrasted cultures was about to begin one of the most significant modern experiments in nation-building. And on the 1st of July 1867 both French-speaking and English-speaking Canadians set out on their joint adventure with high hopes, and stout hearts, and good will. 'We are of different races', George E. Cartier had said simply, 'not for strife, but to work together for the common welfare.'

10

ACROSS THE CONTINENT

I

The last fireworks blazed in the sky, the bands played *God Save the Queen*, the crowds slowly dispersed, and the first, radiantly beautiful 'Dominion Day' came to an end. Next morning, when the Canadian people awoke, the hopes and aspirations of a thousand prayers, congratulations, good wishes, and prophecies had stiffened into a few columns of print in the morning newspapers; and the members of the Canadian government were at last face to face with the difficult, concrete business at once prosaic and exciting, of nation-building.

It was on the shoulders of the Prime Minister, Sir John Macdonald—he had been knighted at Confederation—that the chief burden rested. At fifty-two, he was in the prime of life and at the height of his powers. There was no sign of portliness in his tall, slight, jaunty figure. The defiant panache of his dark, curly hair had subsided only a little; and the ugly charm of his face, with its big nose and genially sardonic smile, was as attractive as ever. He knew every ruse, device, surprise, and stratagem of politics; he took life easily and enjoyed it to the full, despite the sorrows it had brought him; and not a few critics in the past had deplored the limitations of his boyish 'want of earnestness' or had written him off as an ingenious party hack. They could hardly have been more wrong. At

Confederation he had shown to the full the great resources of creative power which he possessed. Without any question, he had been the principal author of the new union and the new constitution. The first of July was his day; Canada was almost his nation. He was determined to expand it, develop it, promote its interests, and defend its inheritance.

An enormous, continental task awaited him. The four provinces which had been united on the 1st of July 1867— Nova Scotia, New Brunswick, Quebec, and Ontario, the latter two formed out of the old Province of Canada—were only a small fragment of British North America as a whole; and even that small fragment was far from being inspired by a uniform zeal and devotion to the new union. Nova Scotia, in which a strong anti-Confederate movement had developed, was an exceedingly dissatisfied province; and somehow it must be mollified. But the pacification of Nova Scotia was only the beginning of the long labour of completing the nation's political structure. The two island provinces, Newfoundland and Prince Edward Island, remained obstinately outside the union. The great empire in the north-west, Rupert's Land and the North-West Territories, was still the property of the Hudson's Bay Company; and until the Hudson's Bay Company's lands were secured, there was little prospect of the new Pacific province, British Columbia, entering Confederation. There was not even any real certainty that Confederation could be completed on a continental scale without serious loss of territory to the United States. The evil legacy of the American Civil War still poisoned the relations of the United Kingdom and Canada on the one hand and the republic on the other. In 1867 the United States purchased Alaska from Russia; and there were not a few people—including President Grant and his Secretary of State, Hamilton Fish—who still indulged the hope that the imperialistic designs of 'Manifest Destiny' might be fulfilled by the annexation of all or part of British North America.

This was the complex, interrelated set of problems which Macdonald set out to solve in 1867. He had been the chief

architect of the transcontinental federal plan. He was to become
the principal builder of the national structure. His first success
—the pacification of Nova Scotia—seemed superficially the
easiest. Joseph Howe, the leader of the anti-Confederate cause,
whose great powers and exuberant energies had met with so
many disappointments and reverses, had lost the last great
battle of his career to his junior rival, Charles Tupper. Once
the British Government had, for the second time, rejected the
plea for Nova Scotia's secession from the union, it was obvious
that the settlement of the Province's grievances could only be
found constitutionally within the framework of Confederation.
Macdonald sought to make it as generous and tactful a settlement as he possibly could. Advantage was taken of a disparity
in the original financial arrangements to grant Nova Scotia
larger subsidies; and Howe was offered, and accepted, a post
in the Dominion Cabinet. The leaderless anti-Confederate
movement subsided. On the surface, the pacification was complete; but a faint after-taste of resentment and bitterness lingered.

In the west, the task of nation-building seemed to bristle
with greater difficulties and more intimidating dangers; but the
first steps in the incorporation of the Hudson's Bay Company's
territories were taken with deceptively reassuring ease. 'We
hope to close our session this week,' Macdonald wrote to the
Lieutenant-Governor of Nova Scotia in June 1869, 'and a very
momentous session it has been. We have quietly and almost
without observation annexed all the territory between here and
the Rocky Mountains. . . .' The calm boast was very nearly
true. The Hudson's Bay Company, yielding to persuasive
pressure, had finally agreed to cede to the Crown its territorial
rights in Rupert's Land in return for three hundred thousand
pounds to be provided by Canada; and Rupert's Land, together with the North-West Territories over which the Company had enjoyed a monopoly of trade, was to be transferred
by Great Britain to Canadian jurisdiction. Canada established
a provisional form of territorial government for the north-west
and appointed its first Lieutenant-Governor, William Mc-

Dougall. The transfer of the territory was to take place formally on the 1st December 1869. Outwardly everything seemed to promise extremely well. And yet, all the while, a determined and truculent opposition was rapidly gathering strength.

The only considerable settlement in Canada's new north-western empire was the Red River settlement, which clustered about the Hudson's Bay Company's post, Fort Garry, at the junction of the Red and Assiniboine rivers. It was a remote, inaccessible fur-trade colony, which had been built up over the years by the servants and settlers of the North West Company and the Hudson's Bay Company; and of the various groups which in 1869 formed its population—Hudson's Bay Company officers, English, Canadian, and American traders, Scots and English settlers, and French and English half-breeds—only one element, the Canadian traders, was very eager for the approaching union with Canada. The *Métis*, the French half-breeds, who made up the most politically conscious and organized part of the community, were strongly opposed to the unconditional transfer of the territory. They feared—and with good reason—that the onrush of white settlement into the north-west would mean the end of their own distinctive, half-nomadic way of life. And it was they, under the shrewd guidance of their leader Louis Riel, who first took decisive action. They stopped William McDougall as he was about to cross the border into his new government. They seized Fort Garry. And with the passive or active support of the many people at Red River who resented a transfer, which had taken place without the colony's concurrence and almost without its knowledge, they set up a provisional government.

The Canadian Government—and Sir John Macdonald in particular—were extremely worried. The great programme of western expansion had received a serious if not fatal check, at the very moment of its commencement. The rising at Red River was grave enough in itself. Its first repercussions in both Canada and the United States were highly disturbing; and its ultimate consequences might be disastrous. The resistance of the French-speaking *Métis* of the north-west awakened a sympathetic echo in the Province of Quebec and aroused the old cultural animosities between French-speaking and English-speaking Canadians. The successful opposition at Red River instantly attracted the interested attention of American annexationists and the American Government; and any serious increase or prolongation of the unhappy disturbance might invite American intervention and conceivably rob Canada of its western dominion. The stakes of the game were huge. Macdonald had to act decisively yet circumspectly, with both a show of force and the solid reality of concession. A military expedition, in which imperial troops were conspicuous, was sent to Red River in the spring of 1870 in order to prove to the world in general and the United States in particular that Great Britain and Canada were united and in earnest in support of Canadian claims to the north-west. In the meantime, the Dominion had been busy negotiating with the convention of Red River citizens and with the agents of the provisional government; and in 1870 the district entered Confederation as a province, the first western province, with the usual provincial rights and functions.

The creation of Manitoba, the acquisition of the whole of Rupert's Land and the North-West Territories, had brought Canada, as Macdonald had said, to the Rocky Mountains. Beyond lay the Province of British Columbia; and union with British Columbia had now become a timely and feasible project. The Dominion was eager to acquire its frontage on the Pacific; and British Columbia's small population of roughly ten thousand people was overwhelmingly in favour of entrance into Confederation. In 1870 delegates journeyed down to Ottawa to discuss terms of union with the federal government; and the Dominion accepted the formidable engagement to begin a railway to the Pacific within two years and to finish it within ten. In July 1871 British Columbia became the second of the new western provinces; and Canada's future heraldic device— *a mari usque ad mare*—was already justified.

The 'Dominion from sea to sea' had become an accomplished fact; and—what was perhaps equally important—the accomplished fact had been accepted by the two nations that counted most for Canada, the two English-speaking nations, the United Kingdom and the United States. On a brilliant May morning, just two months before British Columbia was to join the union, this tacit acceptance became almost a formal act of recognition. The American and British plenipotentiaries—including Sir John Macdonald of Canada—had assembled in a room in the Department of State to put their signatures to the completed Treaty of Washington. The room was bright and sweet with masses of spring flowers; and a relaxed and friendly feeling of accomplishment and goodwill was in the air. Only Macdonald did not share it. He had come down to Washington hoping to persuade the United States to accept a broad reciprocal trade agreement, comparable to the Reciprocity Treaty which the Republic had abrogated in 1866; and he had utterly failed. He had been compelled to surrender the navigation of the St. Lawrence and the liberty of the inshore Canadian fisheries for what he thought were completely inadequate returns; and fish alone was to enjoy the free entry into the American market which he had hoped to obtain for all Canadian natural products. He was bitterly disappointed. He knew that the Canadian people would be bitterly disappointed. And yet, as he himself argued later, there was much in the Treaty for which Canada could be profoundly grateful. The perilous disagreements which had arisen between Great Britain and the United States during the American Civil War had been peaceably settled. And the danger that American force or American diplomacy would be used to rob Canada of its continental inheritance was apparently over.

II

Two years later, in 1873, when Prince Edward Island entered Confederation, the design of a united British North

America, with the solitary exception of the absent Newfoundland, had been realized. The political framework of the union was complete. It was much. It was much more than, only a few years before, Macdonald had expected could conceivably be accomplished in so short a time. But obviously, as he and the wisest of his fellow citizens realized, it was only the first stage of a huge, protracted, and difficult task. Confederation was a claim which had been staked but not worked or exploited. It was a scaffolding within which the solid and imposing structure of the future would take long laborious years to construct. The little nation of a few million people needed a vast increase in population, which only immigration on a large scale could supply. The virtually empty north-west must be settled and developed; a new national industrial machine, far stronger and more diversified than in the old days of wood, wind, and water, would have to be built up in the east to sustain the business of nation-building; and the whole transcontinental economy must be linked together and integrated by means of all-Canadian railways. These were the generally recognized and accepted goals. But how were they to be achieved? The Canadian people and its governments spent the next few years in working out an interrelated set of policies—the 'national policies'—by which the design for the future could be realized.

About one of these policies—perhaps the most fundamental of all—there was no real doubt or disagreement from the beginning. The settlement of the west was the first essential. Its lands must be made swiftly and attractively available to a huge army of migrants. Canada would have to present itself to the peoples of Great Britain and Western Europe as a land of opportunity; and obviously she would fail to awaken their imaginations and gain their preferences if she could not offer them terms of settlement which equalled or bettered those of the United States. More than two generations before, in the days of the Loyalists and their followers, British North America had granted land free to settlers; and now that the United States had abandoned land sales and introduced the Free

Homestead system, it was easy, as well as necessary, for Canada to return to the original British North American practice. The lands of the Canadian north-west were to be surveyed on the familiar rectangular North American system, in sections of six hundred and forty acres; and the quarter-section of one hundred and sixty acres was to become the Free Homestead farm which would be open to every bona-fide settler on competitively attractive terms. In the early autumn of 1869, the federal surveyors drew their principal meridian—the 'Winnipeg Meridian' —north from the international boundary; and, within the next fifteen years the Indians had withdrawn by Treaty into reservations, the survey had been completed with both accuracy and astonishing speed, and the north-west quarter of the North American continent was open for settlement.

Yet even this was obviously only a beginning. The migrants would need transport to reach the north-west. Transport would be equally necessary to get their produce out to its destined markets; and until an all-Canadian railway had linked them effectively together, the three main sections of the country— the North-West, central Canada, and the Maritime Provinces —would remain almost as divided as if they had been in separate continents. The first division of the national transcontinental, the line from Halifax on the Seaboard to Quebec and Montreal on the St. Lawrence, had been pledged unconditionally in the British North America Act; and this, the Intercolonial Railway, was built by the Canadian Government as a public work in the years immediately after Confederation. The second great stage, the railway between the St. Lawrence valley and the Pacific Ocean, would obviously be a vastly more difficult and costly undertaking; and at Confederation it had simply been declared that the line would be built as soon as the state of the finances would permit. The terms of union with British Columbia converted this highly conditional promise into an unqualified commitment. The railway must be begun within two years, and finished within ten, of British Columbia's entrance into Confederation. How was it to be built? Should it be undertaken as a public work or a private enterprise? And if as a private enterprise, what company was to get the charter for its construction and where was the necessary capital to be secured?

It was at this point, at the crucial moment of beginnings, that a sinister figure first entered the affair of the Pacific Railway. It was Sir Hugh Allan, the wealthy Montreal shipowner; and outwardly nobody could have seemed less likely to bring scandal or failure to the scheme. Allan's seniority among Canadian financiers, his great commercial successes, the knighthood he had earned for his services to transatlantic transport, all seemed to ensure respectability and inspire confidence. Yet, as soon as he began the struggle for the Pacific Charter, his whole character and conduct began to alter. The very immensity of the enterprise seemed to rouse in him a strange ambition and an even stranger recklessness; and he plunged abruptly into a course of dissimulation and intrigue.

Very early in the formation of his plans, he had associated himself with a group of American capitalists, directors in the American Northern Pacific Railroad; and their prominence in his syndicate inevitably prompted anxious questions. The Canadian Government and Canadian public opinion were utterly opposed to the dominance of American capital in this national venture; but Allan was determined secretly to maintain his connection with his American friends. He was even more determined to defeat his Canadian rivals, to obtain the Pacific Charter, and to become president of the company. His scheming, gambling efforts to attain his ends multiplied the number of his enemies and put into their hands the means of his undoing. The highly compromising letters which he had written to his American associates, the proofs of the lavish money contributions which he had made to the Conservative campaign fund in the general election of 1872, found their way into the possession of the Reform Opposition in Parliament; and the result was that notorious and dramatic revelation, the 'Pacific Scandal' of 1873. The Pacific Scandal involved everyone connected with this first attempt to build the transcontinental railway in a common ruin. It broke Allan and his company. It brought about the downfall of the Conservative Government. It nearly ended the career of Sir John Macdonald. It postponed for almost a decade the completion of the railway and the integration of the Canadian economy.

The late autumn of 1873 saw the dramatic culmination of the Pacific Scandal, the resignation of Sir John Macdonald, and the formation of a new Liberal or Reform government, under Alexander Mackenzie. It also witnessed the drear beginnings of an economic phenomenon of much more lasting importance, the Great Depression of the last quarter of the nineteenth century. The first six years of Confederation had been years of prosperity, years which encouraged national hopes and favoured national accomplishments; but in the autumn of 1873 the country began to slip slowly into a long period of economic adversity. And it was during the first phase of this slump, while the slow attrition of bad times was wearing away extravagant hopes and sharpening anxieties, that a new and important debate over the national policies of the future began. Up to this time, the nation had been solidly united in its support of the plans for transcontinental development. People had agreed that the west should be settled and the Pacific Railway built. People had tended to assume, in the first enthusiasm of union and the flush of early prosperity, that the policies of western settlement and all-Canadian transport would succeed of themselves. The depression now proved the contrary. The depression sharply raised the question of whether Canada should take other steps—very positive steps—to hasten the lagging process of national expansion.

What, above all, should be done with that instrument—already recognized as a key instrument—of national well-being, commercial policy? Ever since the downfall of the Old Colonial System, British North America had hesitated to declare itself too emphatically in favour of any one fiscal theory; and the combination of a low revenue tariff and preferential markets abroad was a safe mixture well suited to this transitional period in Canadian economic development. The Reciprocity Treaty with the United States, which had coincided with a series of foreign wars and booming markets for Canadian staple exports, had come to seem almost a synonym for prosperity. If it could have been renewed, on equally generous terms, it might have remained a popular foundation stone of Canadian fiscal policy. But by the middle 1870's, just when the incidence of the depression was becoming really serious, all hope of its renewal had completely vanished. Sir John Macdonald had tried in vain to negotiate a new agreement at the Washington Conference of 1871. George Brown, the agent of Mackenzie's new Liberal government, tried again in 1874; and although Canadian manufacturers were horrified by the tariff concessions he was prepared to make, the draft treaty which resulted from his visit to Washington was summarily rejected by the American Senate. Great Britain had wiped out Canada's preferential markets by flinging her gates wide open to the produce of the world. The United States had destroyed those markets equally effectively by slamming shut the door of her protective tariff. Canada's old dependent career as a favoured producer of staple products for more mature metropolitan economies was ended.

A change of plan was necessary. Negative reasons alone would have dictated it. Yet negative reasons were very far from being solely responsible for the great and fundamental change in commercial policy which was impending. Something much more positive, much more purposeful, much more faithfully a reflection of the new mood of confident and constructive nationalism was now influencing men's thoughts about their country's economic future. A transcontinental economy which would be strong enough and diversified enough to support the burdens of nation-building seemed absolutely essential to both public men and private enterprisers; and both fixed upon the protective tariff as the effective means by which their purposes could be achieved. The state needed revenue for its great national public-works programme. Industry wanted protection from foreign dumping and an opportunity to fill the needs of its own domestic market. The protective tariff was not merely a depression measure or a second-best alternative to reciprocity. It was also a nationalist cause. In 1876, the Conservatives adopted protection as the main economic plank in their political platform. With it they fought a rousing electoral campaign through three strenuous summers; and with it they triumphantly won the general election of September, 1878.

III

In midwinter of 1879 the new Parliament opened for its first session. The weather was extremely cold but extremely beautiful; and Ottawa was buried in gleaming heaps of snow and canopied with intensely blue skies. The incoming trains were stuck for hours in snow-drifts; but the capital was crowded with visitors, for everybody of any consequence wanted to be present to greet the new Governor-General, the Marquis of Lorne, and his royal consort, the Princess Louise, the daughter of Queen Victoria. The blue, bright weather, which the journalists tactfully insisted was 'royal weather', almost came to seem, in the months and years that followed, like a blessing which the Queen's new representative had brought with him. Lord Lorne and his Princess came inevitably to stand for the radiant blue skies and the warm, encouraging sunshine of prosperity. Suddenly, everything began to look up. It was true that no new group of capitalists had yet presented itself eagerly with an offer to build the Pacific Railway; but by an enormous stroke of good luck, which the grateful Conservatives could only regard as clearly providential, the passage of the new tariff was quickly followed by a real economic recovery. The harvest of 1879 was bountiful. Prices were buoyant. The volume of Canadian exports was steadily increasing.

And then, nearly seven long years after the shame and failure of the Pacific Scandal, there came the real miracle, the supreme manifestation of good fortune. A tall, thin, bearded man, with a pair of deep-set, brooding eyes and an air of watchful and determined purpose, presented the government with an offer to build the Pacific Railway. It was George Stephen, a Scotsman who came of Highland stock, who had been made president of the Bank of Montreal and who had, more recently, acquired a good deal of experience, and won a large measure of success, in a railway enterprise in the north-western United States. The Montreal financiers and western enterprisers whom Stephen gathered about him for this new venture formed a group utterly different from the notorious directorate of Sir Hugh Allan's Canada Pacific Railway Company of 1872. The dominating personalities in the Stephen syndicate of 1880 were not Americans who wished to control the Canadian national transport system for their own purposes, but Canadians who had gained useful experience in the United States.

From the first the government was obviously attracted by the Stephen offer; but, with the awful memory of the Pacific Scandal ringing a warning, Macdonald hesitated to make a rapid decision; and it was not until a committee of the Cabinet had gone to England in the summer of 1880 and carefully investigated all rival proposals, that an agreement was finally reached with George Stephen and his associates. On the 21st October 1880, at Ottawa, they put pens to paper of the most important contract in Canadian economic history. The new Canadian Pacific Railway Company, in return for government assistance which was substantial but not nearly so generous as that offered to Allan, committed itself to construct a line from the St. Lawrence valley to the Pacific Ocean. The sections of the railway already built as public works were transferred to the Company without charge; and in addition it was given a land grant of twenty-five million acres and a cash subsidy of twenty-five million dollars.

George Stephen, who became the Company's first president, and his cousin Donald Smith, a Highlander like himself who came from the same district of Speyside, were the railway's principal capitalists and strategists; and early in 1882, the effective inner triumvirate was completed by the addition of that genius of railway construction, the American-born William Cornelius Van Horne. Under these three men the line was driven westward past mountains, over prairies, and through forests at spectacular speed. The national character of the undertaking grew more defiantly emphatic all the time. In order to fulfil the government's basic condition and to create an all-Canadian system, the company accepted the heavy and costly burden of building north of Lake Superior; and in the far west, with the double purpose of protecting its own territory and competing for American traffic, it adopted a much more southerly route than that originally intended. In those first prosperous, confident years of the 1880's, the Canadian Pacific Railway seemed to assume success and to command it at will. Despite the frigid inhospitality of the London and New York money markets, George Stephen succeeded in disposing of a great block of stock. Van Horne worked out a system of rapid track-laying which seemed a marvel even to experienced observers; and Major Rogers discovered the essential pass through the mountains, which bears his name, only when the railway had already been irrevocably committed to the southern route. The Canadian people watched and thrilled with a new and strange sense of accomplishment. The whole country seemed to be whirled away up the tracks of the Pacific Railway towards national success.

Prosperity had come. The railway would soon be finished. And what the nation needed now was the great army of enterprising and resourceful settlers who would occupy and exploit the now available north-west. Already, with the coming of good times, the inert prairie country had suddenly quickened. The census of 1881 revealed that the population of the tiny province of Manitoba had nearly quadrupled in the first ten years of its existence. Migrants were swarming into the north-west; and a veritable mania of speculation in land—something strangely new in the history of the region—reigned at Winnipeg. The

Canadian Government, with its Free Homestead system, and the Canadian Pacific Railway, with its millions of acres of land, were eager to swell this incoming tide of humanity; and, during the early 1880's, Canada was hopefully attempting to persuade the British Government to support an assisted immigration scheme which would transfer the victims of industrial overcrowding in the United Kingdom to the open spaces of the Canadian north-west. For this and other governmental purposes—arranging loans and assisting in the negotiation of treaties in which Canada was interested—a permanent Canadian agent in Great Britain could be very useful; and in 1880 the Canadian Parliament established an important new officer, the Canadian High Commissioner in London.

It was a significant move, for the future as well as for the present. Up to that point, Canada had made no serious attempt to claim the high sovereign powers of foreign policy and defence. British military and diplomatic support had been, and remained, absolutely essential for Canada's survival on the North American continent; and a unified imperial system of defence and diplomacy was the historic—and still seemed the best—method of providing this protection. Sir John Macdonald agreed with the Governor-General, Lord Lorne, that it would be possible 'to stave off for a very long time to come any wish on the part of Canada for a separate set of representatives in foreign countries'. The diplomatic unity of the empire was to remain; but henceforth Canada and its representatives—of whom the High Commissioner in London was the most important—must have a voice and play a part in the formation of its policies. 'The sooner the Dominion is treated as an auxiliary power rather than as a dependency,' Macdonald wrote, 'the sooner will it assume all the responsibilities of the position including the settlement of its contribution to the defence of the Empire whenever and wherever assailed.'

In 1882 the Conservatives won another general election. For the next eighteen months, the success of the national plan and the prestige of Macdonald's government were at their height.

11

THE LONG ORDEAL

I

O n a night in early September, 1883, a black and
killing frost descended out of a still, autumnal sky on
the wheat crop of the north-west. For the few, widely
scattered settlers of the new prairie country, it was an unqualified disaster. But it was more than a single disaster; it was
the precursor of a long and dismal succession of calamities. The
boom, which had given work and hope to so many Canadians,
dwindled rapidly and remorselessly away; and before the
autumn was out, the depression, like a sinister grey familiar,
had returned to haunt the Dominion. Within a few months, all
the national projects had run into discouragements or difficulties; all the national policies were vulnerable once more to
criticism and attack. In the east, the industrial machine ground
down gradually into slow motion; and in the north-west, which
was the crucial popular test of the success of the national
experiment, there were ominous signs of discontent. The
deepening of the depression, the growth of a really serious
protest movement on the prairies, would both take time; but
the calamity which overtook the Canadian Pacific Railway was
sudden and almost overwhelming. In the autumn of 1883 the
company was just over three years old; but already it was in
serious trouble. By the end of the year it had drawn close to
bankruptcy.

The Long Ordeal

The defiant energy of the triumvirate, Stephen, Smith, and Van Horne, had brought about its own undoing. The railway had been driven westward with efficient but headlong speed; and the galloping pace of the construction had hastened the exhaustion of the Company's funds and compelled it abruptly to seek fresh financing. Stephen had worked out a complicated financial plan for purchasing a Dominion guarantee of interest on the hundred million dollars of his authorized capitalization; and he hoped, once Canadian Pacific securities had thus been converted into a gilt-edged, 5 per cent investment, to dispose, at a good price, of the whole of the huge remaining block of the Company's stock. A year before the operation might have been possible and profitable; but now it was fatally too late. Railway shares moved uneasily, uncertainly, and then plunged downward. Before the end of the year the Northern Pacific Railroad, the Canadian Pacific's great American rival, had become bankrupt; and it was only too obvious that the watching ring of George Stephen's enemies in London and New York were waiting gleefully for his own financial collapse. In a few weeks he was at the end of his tether. His short-term creditors were yapping like a pack of curs at his heels; there was no more money for construction; and in desperation he turned back to the Canadian Government which, he knew very well, regarded the railway as a national undertaking which was absolutely essential for national success. His requirements were enormous. A government assurance was immediately necessary before the frightened Bank of Montreal would produce a copper more; but the advance which paid off the loans maturing early in the New Year was only the first of the Canadian Pacific Railway's colossal necessities. Before the end of January, 1884, Stephen had presented the stupendous total of his needs. He wanted a government loan of twenty-two and a half million dollars. It was very nearly as much as the Company's original cash subsidy!

The moment was crucial—perhaps fatal—for the government's national plan. The railway was absolutely essential for the achievement of an integrated, transcontinental Dominion. And yet was not the dead weight of its costs too great for a few million Canadians to bear? Ahead lay the dwindling markets, the falling prices, the inevitably reduced government revenues of the depression; ahead loomed also the dangerous prospect of that social unrest and political disaffection which depressions seemed to breed so quickly. In the next few months—or longer, if the slump continued—the very idea of a viable transcontinental Canadian state would be subjected to savage and continuous pressure. Belief in the future would be terribly tested; but, in the last analysis, it was only this faith in the possibility of a united and prosperous Canada to which the government could appeal. It plunged resolutely ahead. Despite the protracted resistance of the opposition in Parliament, the twenty-two and a half million dollar loan was voted. The Canadian Pacific Railway, with the goal of completion already in sight, resumed its rapid western advance.

And yet, as the year 1884 drew slowly towards its close, it was obvious that difficulties were rapidly, ominously mounting. The ordeal of the depression served to increase critical resistance to federal policies in the provincial governments of Ontario, Quebec, and Nova Scotia. This eastern political opposition was serious; but, in one important way, the prospect of trouble in the north-west was more serious still. If it began to seem really probable that the north-west would not become the homeland of a prosperous and contented people, then there was no point whatever in the Canadian Pacific Railway or its new loan, and no validity in the conception of a transcontinental Canadian nation. The north-west was the crucial test of the Canadian nationalist design; and in the north-west the first buoyant sense of purpose and conviction had suddenly and utterly vanished. All the three important elements in the population of the prairie country—the new white settlers, the *Métis* or French half-breeds, and the Indians—had now become restless with sullen resentments and grievances.

The white settlers, many of whom had been half-ruined by

crop failures and deflated land values, were clamouring against government policies. The Indians, who had lost their old spacious freedoms and the support of the buffalo hunt, had been forced to undergo the highly painful process of adjustment to life on the reserves. The *Métis* had fled westward to the Saskatchewan after the end of the Red River Rising and they now saw their old way of life threatened in its final retreat by a new onrush of white settlement. They were pressing extravagant claims for land upon the government; and they had recalled their old leader, Louis Riel, to direct their agitation for the redress of grievances. The return of this equivocal, though able and determined, half-breed to the north-west, darkly portended trouble for the future. But it was not the only ominous circumstance of 1884. Before the year was out the Canadian Pacific Railway was once more in alarming financial straits. The twenty-two and a half million dollar loan had gone. All other possible sources of funds had been hopelessly, fruitlessly explored. And almost in despair the Company turned back again to the nation which had given it birth.

The crisis of the north-west and the crisis of the railway arrived shatteringly together. It was certain now that further heavy sacrifices would be necessary to save the railway and the national plan; and yet already the whole country seemed to be breaking apart under the divisive strains which the national plan had imposed. The government, after having yielded to the importunities of the Canadian Pacific Railway less than a year before, was terrified of the dangers of appearing before Parliament for another loan. It was readier, though still reluctant. to grant the demands of the *Métis*; and early in 1885 it established a royal commission to distribute compensation to the half-breeds for their share in the Indian title to the land. Yet even this great concession could not save it from the crisis which Riel, for his own purposes, seemed determined to hurry on. On March 26th, in the snow near Duck Lake, between the two branches of the Saskatchewan, Riel's *Métis* met the North-West Mounted Police in the first armed encounter of the

9. Sir John A. Macdonald, First Prime Minister of Canada

10. Sir George Stephen—Lord Mount Stephen—First
President of the Canadian Pacific Railway

Rebellion; and, on the same day, in Ottawa, George Stephen faced the virtual certainty that there could be no further government relief for his railway. 'I need not repeat how sorry I am', he wrote to the Prime Minister, Macdonald, 'that this should be the result of all our efforts to give Canada a railway to the Pacific Ocean. But I am supported by the conviction that I have done all that could be done to obtain it.'

The outbreak of the North-West Rebellion and the imminent collapse of the Canadian Pacific Railway together rocked Canada with a stunning blow. Yet the very extremity of the peril roused the nation as nothing else could, and put into the hands of the government the effective means of averting national defeat. The disaster which threatened to overwhelm the Dominion in the spring of 1885 was not single but dual. It was composed of two separable problems which could be treated separately and in sequence. The nearly completed railway could be used to bring about the quick defeat of the rebellion; and the triumphant pacification of the north-west would provide the best of all possible justifications for the railway. It worked—almost as if it had been a successful stratagem. Some of the militia units which marched down to eastern railway stations on the rainy Monday of March 30th reached Winnipeg on the night of April 4th; and only a week later, before the Rebellion had had any real chance to spread or gather strength, the first of the Canadian army's three striking columns began its laborious march north from the mainline of the Canadian Pacific Railway towards the Saskatchewan River. The white settlers, who had been so ready to agitate only a few months earlier, would have nothing to do with armed revolt. Riel was left with his own *Métis* and the support of a few small, wandering bands of Indians; and when, on May 12th, the half-breed stronghold at Batoche was taken by storm, the back of the Rebellion was really broken.

Without any question, the rapid suppression of the Rebellion saved the railway. For weeks during that troubled spring and early summer of 1885 it had been almost hourly in peril of

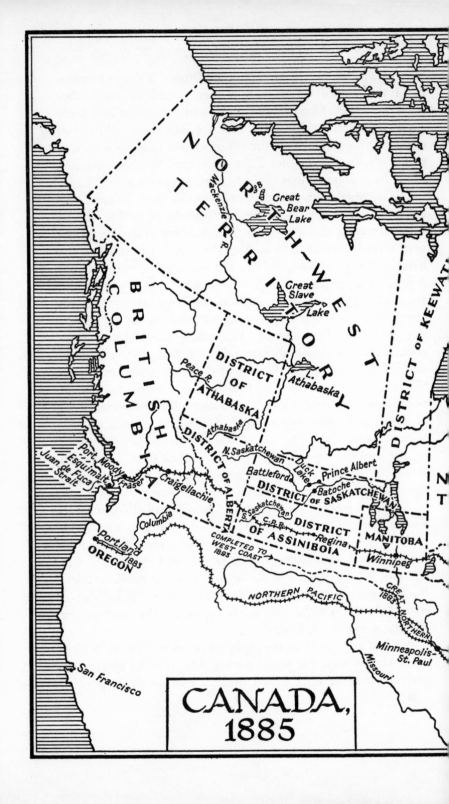

CANADA,
1885

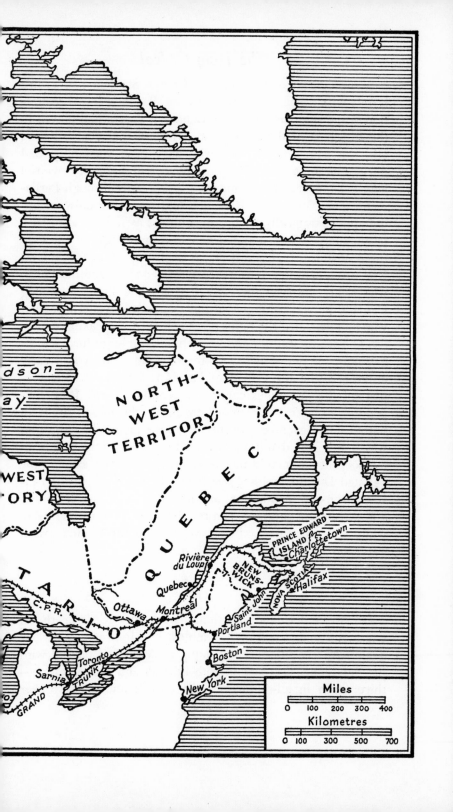

NORTH-
WEST
TERRITORY

Hudson
Bay

WEST
TORY

QUEBEC

ONTARIO

C.P.R.

Ottawa

Montreal

Quebec

Rivière
du Loup

NEW
BRUNS-
WICK

PRINCE EDWARD
ISLAND
Charlottetown

NOVA SCOTIA
Halifax

Saint John

Portland

Toronto
Sarnia
GRAND TRUNK

Boston

New York

Miles

0   100   200   300   400

Kilometres

0   100   300   500   700

bankruptcy and total ruin; and George Stephen had grown frantic with despair and apprehension. But the general realization of the key part which the Canadian Pacific had played in the transport of the troops and defeat of the rebels silenced criticism which would otherwise have been vociferous; and during the summer of 1885, the second, still more controversial loan in support of the Company slipped easily through Parliament. The North-West Rebellion had saved the railway; but unhappily, tragically, it did other things as well. It aroused a passionately serious national debate over the fate of the captured *Métis* leader, Louis Riel. To English-speaking Canadians, Riel was a contumacious, twice-convicted rebel and murderer, who richly deserved the capital penalty; to French-speaking Canada, he was a misguided but courageous western patriot, who had defended the rights of a small French-speaking minority, and whose frailties and misfortunes amply justified a mitigation of his punishment. All through the summer and early autumn, while the Canadian Pacific raced towards its completion, the dangerous controversy continued and Riel's impending execution threatened to cleave the nation apart in hatred. On November 7th, far out in the mountains, at a spot which Stephen determined must be called Craigellachie in memory of his clan's meeting-place and battle slogan, the bearded Donald Smith drove home the last spike in the railway's transcontinental line; and nine days later, on November 16th, while the autumnal sun rose late over plains which were white with hoar frost, the sprung trap in the Regina prison gave and Riel dropped to his extinction.

II

On November 22nd, less than a week after Riel's death, an enormous mass meeting assembled in Montreal to protest against his execution. The Champ de Mars was packed with people; a long succession of both Liberals and Conservatives—thirty-seven in all—addressed the crowd; and each speaker seemed almost to be attempting to outdo the others in the violence of his denunciations of the 'hangman's government' at Ottawa. It looked as if the whole of French Canada, irrespective of political affiliation, had united in a solid and furious bloc of opposition to the Dominion's government and the rest of its people. It looked, for a time, as if the nation was about to suffer what everybody had always dreaded and tried so hard to avert—a permanent political division along 'racial' lines. *Le Parti National* was formed, with Honoré Mercier as its leader, and both Liberals and Conservatives in its ranks. It was true that the composite character of the new association gradually weakened. It began to take on the appearance of an extreme wing of the Liberal Party. But, at the same time, it was undeniably growing in strength. Early in 1887, Honoré Mercier and his Liberal-Nationalists formed a provincial government; and the long rule of the Conservatives in the Province of Quebec appeared to have come to an end.

Mercier was one of the new young men, the angry and reckless young men, who were now rising to popularity and prominence out of the very failures, disappointments, and frustrations of Canadian national life. They heightened the tensions of the Dominion's politics; they increased its exasperation. Up to that point, what Macdonald and his government had chiefly feared were the economic and financial consequences of the depression and the results of provincial opposition to federal policies and powers. Mercier added the bitter acid of racial passion to economic discontent and Dominion-provincial controversy. He did more than this. He brought with him the possibility—almost the probability—of a renewal of those old disputes between French- and English-speaking Canadians over language, schools, and religious institutions which had paralysed the affairs of the old Province of Canada and which everybody had hoped to end by the division of powers at Confederation. The danger of a break-up of the union under the hammer blows of a variety of disruptive forces was now greater than ever. Macdonald was confronted by hostile men as well as by adverse circumstances. His back was to the wall.

Mercier's first act of defiance was to organize the resistance of the provinces to the federal government. He had no difficulty in drumming up his league of provincial discontent. The premiers of five provinces—including his own—were ready and willing to volunteer. Nova Scotia had suffered so much from the slump that it had actually elected a government pledged to effect the secession of the province from the union. New Brunswick was troubled by many of the same long-range and short-term economic distresses which had driven its sister province to such extreme action. Ontario had been for several years engaged in a furious quarrel with the Dominion over the extent of provincial legislative powers and over the exercise of federal controls on provincial legislation. Manitoba had become wildly indignant at the repeated disallowance, by the Dominion, of provincial railway charters designed to break the western traffic monopoly enjoyed by the Canadian Pacific Railway. Late in the autumn of 1887, at Mercier's invitation, the five premiers and their delegations met in a highly disgruntled conclave at Quebec City.

Their purpose was simple and revolutionary. They intended to remodel the British North America Act with their own hands, for their own purposes, and to their own complete satisfaction. Up to that point, in the absence of any precise provision in the constitution, the British North America Act had been amended by the imperial Parliament on the receipt of a joint resolution from the Senate and the House of Commons of the Parliament of Canada. The authority which the Dominion had thus acquired in the initiation of constitutional amendments was now emphatically denied by an indignant chorus of provinces. Confederation, they claimed in effect, was the result of a compact between the provincial governments of British North America; and now, after twenty years of bitter experience, it was open to the provincial governments to meet again and revise the terms of the contract exactly as they chose.

The Long Ordeal

In the days that followed, the delegates attacked the business of revision with a vengeance, freely altering political institutions and happily lopping off Dominion powers. Then, having made a virtually new constitution, they hopefully sought to have it converted into law by the imperial Parliament.

Here they soon found themselves in an impasse of defeat. The second 'Quebec Conference' was not a conference of all the governments of Canada, nor even of all the provincial governments of Canada, for both British Columbia and Prince Edward Island, as well as the Dominion itself, had taken no part in its deliberations. It was constitutionally impossible for the imperial Parliament to pay the slightest attention to the twenty-two resolutions which had been so solemnly drawn up at Quebec. The compact theory of Confederation had been tacitly but conclusively repudiated. The vainglorious presumption of the provincial premiers had met defeat. And yet these humiliating negative results were not the only results of the notorious interprovincial conference of 1887. It had gone far to prove a gloomy truth about the new transcontinental Canada. It had demonstrated only too clearly that the gristle of Confederation had not yet hardened into bone and that, in times of trouble, the solid political union for which the Canadians had hoped was only too apt to break apart in a congeries of wrangling governments.

The organization of the provincial protest movement had been Mercier's first work. His second was the renewal of the old, hateful cultural conflict which had been briefly and dramatically revived by the execution of Riel. The Jesuits' Estates Bill which passed through the Quebec legislature in the summer of 1888 ostensibly did no more than compensate the Society of Jesus for its properties which had been escheated to the Crown after the British Conquest. The Bill had other and more disturbing implications, however. It raised the old question of the public endowment of religious bodies, a question which many people believed had been settled for all time a generation before by the secularization of the Clergy Reserves.

It awakened Protestant apprehensions about the position of the Roman Catholic Church in Canada. And finally—and this was perhaps one of the most important consequences of the whole controversy—it brought forward a second vehement and reckless young man, the independent Conservative D'Alton McCarthy.

McCarthy became the provocative champion of the demands and assumptions of Protestant English-speaking Canada in much the same way as Mercier had already done for those of Catholic, French-speaking Quebec. He was firmly convinced that French Canada had become a distinctive, exclusive, and aggressive bloc which threatened to destroy all hope of a real Canadian unity. He and his associates failed to induce the wary federal government to disallow the Jesuits' Estates Bill; but this failure simply whetted his appetite for further combat. He attacked the special guarantees enjoyed by the French language in both Manitoba and the North-West Territories. He helped to raise the contentious question of Manitoba's dual system of public schools. The whole of Canada was suddenly thunderous with controversies which seemed to have both the intolerance of a religious war and the savagery of a tribal conflict. And the moderate men, who had made the country and were trying desperately to hold it together, appeared likely, at any moment, to be thrust contemptuously aside.

III

In the meantime the long ordeal of the depression continued. The slump had already nearly prevented the completion of the Canadian Pacific Railway. It had broken the settlement boom on the prairies, encouraged the North-West Rebellion, reduced immigration and helped to leave the western plains an empty and profitless wilderness. Already the hopes of the Canadians were almost at the point of breaking; but the depression had not yet finished its labour of frustration. Under its grinding pressure the development of a diversified eastern industry slowed down and the protective tariff began to appear to many as a ponderous and crushing burden. All the country's major economic and developmental policies had in succession become vulnerable; and the fundamental question, which the depression had always threatened to pose to Canadians, had now been asked and demanded an answer. Was the very idea of a separate, viable Canada a gigantic mistake? Should Canadians blindly and vainly seek the impossible any longer? Or, before their half-formed country broke apart under the pressure of its own centrifugal forces, should they not seek a new position and new external relations in the English-speaking world?

Macdonald refused to accept the idea of defeat. He was determined to continue his charted course. And yet the failures of his foreign policy, his inability to obtain any commercial concessions from the United States, undeniably increased popular discontent and left the national policy of protection still more vulnerable to criticism. The Washington Treaty of 1871, which the republic had proceeded to abrogate at the earliest possible moment, came to an end in 1885; and the Canadian Government, following the diplomacy which had succeeded so well in the Reciprocity Treaty of 1854 and which Macdonald had resumed with only limited success in 1871, attempted to exchange the liberty of its inshore North Atlantic fisheries for tariff concessions in the American market. An Anglo-American Joint High Commission, on which Sir Charles Tupper, the second Canadian High Commissioner in London, was the Canadian representative, sat at Washington during the winter of 1887–8, and debated the problem of the fisheries. But the Americans absolutely refused to consider a trade treaty; and the only result of the Conference was an unimportant set of regulations governing the commercial privileges of American fishing vessels in Canadian waters. The utter intransigence of the American protectionists had defeated the plans of the Canadian moderates. And their failure gave encouragement and hope to the extremists who now demanded a revolutionary change in Canadian national policy.

The Long Ordeal

After some (but not a great deal of) consideration the Liberal Party decided to put itself at the head of this growing body of dissidents. The Liberals had already lost three elections in succession; and they and their new leader, the bookish, eloquent French-speaking Canadian, Wilfrid Laurier, were anxiously on the look-out for a new and popular policy. Freer trade relations with the United States seemed to be exactly what was required. During 1887 a non-political agitation for commercial union with the republic had gained a surprising amount of support among urban groups and farmers' associations; and in a formal amendment to the budget resolutions of 1888 the Liberal Party committed itself to the policy of Unrestricted Reciprocity with the United States. Unrestricted Reciprocity was supposed to be a modified form of Commercial Union which would leave Canada in control of its tariff against the rest of the world. Yet, whether or not this theoretical distinction represented a real difference, Unrestricted Reciprocity obviously meant a violent and unqualified break with the basic principles of the national policy.

It would certainly force Canada to discriminate against a wide range of British manufacturers, sharply reduce the revenue from customs which was the main resource of Canadian public finance, put Canada's control of her own commercial policy in jeopardy, and, in general, weaken the economic and possibly the political defences of her autonomy. The implications of the Liberals' new programme for the whole future of the Dominion in North America were so sinister that a great many people drew back in alarm and consternation; and the radicalism of Unrestricted Reciprocity inspired an equally radical counter-movement in the direction of Empire trade. The Imperial Federation League, which up to that time had not been very popular in Canada, acquired a sudden new vitality. To many Canadians, British imperialism seemed the logical opposite of the hated American continentalism; and in the House of Commons D'Alton McCarthy extolled the merits of imperial preferential trade.

The Long Ordeal

Macdonald wanted neither of these extremes. Tariff preferences in the United Kingdom or a good trade treaty with the United States would have delighted him equally; but he had no intention of submerging Canada's economic identity in a free-trade system within either the British Empire or the North American continent. He was determined to negotiate on nationally self-respecting terms. And yet, in the face of the Dominion's existing distresses and uncertain future, how long could he possibly hope to do this? It seemed to be becoming increasingly obvious all the time that the United States would do business with Canada only on some extreme economic basis such as that of Unrestricted Reciprocity. Was the American Government really eager to defeat the Canadian national policies? Was it attempting to drive home to Canadians the hopelessness of any other course but that of unconditional economic surrender to the United States? Macdonald suspected that this was the republic's true purpose; and the curious, equivocal negotiations which went on between the two governments in the autumn and winter of 1890–1 give colour to the suspicion. The Canadian Government was inveigled into a series of secret, confidential trade talks; and then, after hopes had been successfully roused, the American Department of State repudiated the negotiation in a humiliating disavowal which was given the widest possible publicity.

It was this contemptuously cynical manœuvre which sharpened the issues of Macdonald's last election—the general election of 1891—into a single vital point of dispute. The United States, Macdonald contended, was secretly determined to use all economic pressure and all economic inducements to force Canada into annexation. Were not the Liberals, in advocating that the Dominion submerge itself in a continental commercial union dominated by the republic, really assisting the foreigner in his plans, and hurrying the country towards the foreigner's objectives? The fact that an important Liberal journalist in Toronto had actually written a private pamphlet suggesting a variety of ways in which the American Government could injure Canadian economic interests enabled Macdonald to infer the existence of a positive conspiracy; and the obviously revolutionary implications of the Liberals' plan of Unrestricted Reciprocity gave him the chance of denouncing it as the precursor of annexation and the tacit abandonment of the whole idea of a distinct and separate Canadian nation. His fundamental purpose, he told the electors in a last manifesto, was that 'of building up on this continent, under the flag of England, a great and powerful nation'. He had given his life to this work. And his final effort to preserve it, in the winter election of 1891, really killed him. He broke down at Napanee, in the midst of a crowded speaking-tour, a little over a week before the poll. From this collapse there was no real recovery; and on June 6th he died. The Conservatives won the election; but the Canadians lost the founder of their country.

IV

The general election of 1891 was the most important general election in Canadian history. The policy of Unrestricted Reciprocity was a fundamental attack upon the conception of an economically independent Canada; and it was launched at the very moment when all the other distresses and tribulations from which the young Dominion was suffering had reached a climax of intensity. The campaign for Unrestricted Reciprocity, for the surrender of the whole idea of a strong, diversified Canadian economy, could hardly have been better timed. Canada had been almost overwhelmed by a long series of reversals and misfortunes. And yet the instinct for survival, the desire for self-determination were strong. And in a last, almost despairing effort, they had triumphed.

They had triumphed, but the troubled and angry Canadians hardly realized it. The fact that they had passed the dangerous culmination of their difficulties was not yet apparent to them. Outwardly their situation seemed as gloomy and agitated as ever. The depression still continued; the great prairie country was still empty; and, worst of all, the rancorous quarrels between Dominion and provinces, Protestants and Roman Catholics, and French- and English-speaking Canadians, had once more been renewed and aggravated by the ominous commencement of the Manitoba schools question.

During the session of 1890 the Manitoba legislature had abolished the legal guarantees for the French language in the Province and had established a new uniform system of non-sectarian schools, to the support of which all citizens, irrespective of their religious beliefs, would be obliged to contribute. The Roman Catholic minority strongly objected, of course, so the new schools act; but it failed to upset the measure in the courts and it failed equally to persuade the federal government to resort to disallowance. There was, however, a means of redress still left. By the terms of both the British North America Act and the Manitoba Act, a religious minority might appeal to the Dominion against a provincial statute which adversely affected its educational rights and the Dominion might intervene with its own remedial legislation. The Roman Catholic leaders and supporters now urged the Dominion to use its constitutional powers on their behalf; and the federal Conservative government, grown seriously weaker under the rule of the four prime ministers who followed Macdonald in rapid succession, and itself fatally divided on the question of Manitoba's schools, was finally manœuvred into a position in which remedial legislation seemed the only possible policy. The 'coercion' of Manitoba was the principal issue of a new election —the general election of 1896; and in it the Conservative government went down to defeat.

The long span of Conservative rule, which had lasted, with one brief intermission, from Confederation, was over. And, as it chanced, the long ordeal of adversity, through which the Canadian nation had been passing, was also drawing towards its close. It had been a trial which would be long remembered. It had left the scars of lingering resentments and hatreds on the Canadian spirit; it had had more outward, obvious effects on the law and custom of the Canadian constitution. The relative positions of the Dominion and the provinces were never again to be exactly what the Fathers of Confederation had designed and Sir John Macdonald had attempted to realize. A new constitutional balance of power in the Dominion had been established, partly as a result of the political resurgence of the provinces during the 1880's, and partly as the direct consequence of a series of crucial decisions in the Judicial Committee of the Privy Council. This British Committee, which remained the supreme court of appeal for the Empire, continued as the final authority for constitutional cases under the British North America Act; and by means of several highly questionable judgments it effectively frustrated the plain intentions of the Fathers of Confederation and fundamentally altered the letter and the spirit of the British North America Act.

And yet the Dominion still stood. And the Canadian people still clung with determination to their design of transcontinental nationhood. The frontal provincial attack on the constitution had failed. The frontal attack on the national development policies had been defeated with equal conclusiveness; and although the Canadians had been divided by rancorous religious and 'racial' quarrels, they had also gained in their sense of identity and consciousness of maturity. The nation which a generation or two before had been still engaged in the primary business of establishing its school systems and its universities, was now producing scholarly and artistic societies, creative literary talents, literary critics and historians. In French-Canada the historian, François-Xavier Garneau, had already inspired a patriotic literary movement in which Octave Crémazie and Louis Fréchette were the most conspicuous figures; and in the early 1880's a group of serious and accomplished English-speaking poets—Charles G. D. Roberts, Archibald Lampman, Duncan Campbell Scott, and Bliss Carman—made their first appearance in print. For the first time the scholars and artists began to draw together in groups; and, with Lord Lorne's support, the Royal Society of Canada and the Royal Canadian Academy were founded in 1882.

12

THE TURNING OF THE TIDE

I

West of the Ontario—Manitoba boundary, the Pre-cambrian Shield, which had pressed to the edges of Lakes Huron and Superior, veered gradually northward. The undulating plateau of scarred and broken rocks, with their mingled shades of grey, dull blue, and deep red-brown, seemed slowly to subside into the black, rich earth. The thick forests of birch and poplar, spruce and pine, thinned out mysteriously, dwindled, and finally disappeared. The land flattened out in dead levels that extended unvaryingly westward towards a remote skyline. The endless repetitions of the enormous, monotonous landscape seemed to flaunt its unqualified uniformity and yet, at the same time, concealed subtle but important varieties and differences. As it stretched onwards towards the mountains, the prairie plateau rose gently through three distinct levels of altitude, from the Red River valley of Manitoba to the high plains of the future Province of Alberta. The land varied from the rich, black, wooded soils of the northern park belt, through the dark brown earth of the second, more southerly soil zone to the semi-arid, short grass country which lay in a great triangle in south-western Saskatchewan and south-eastern Alberta.

The land was empty. In southern Manitoba, where the Canadian Pacific Railway's network was densest, there was a thin, continuous scattering of colonists; and further west a narrow band of settlement followed the tracks of the main line or the branches which extended northward in the future Saskatchewan and Alberta. But these were simply small patches of human activity in the midst of an unconquered natural dominion. The land lay unoccupied and inert; and its untouched passivity seemed the conclusive, irrefutable proof of the failure of the design of a transcontinental Canada. For a quarter of a century world circumstances had been persistently hostile to the Canadian national experiment. The whole undertaking was stopped dead in frustration. The Canadian people were sunk deep in discouragement and apathy.

And then, when it seemed as if people had given up all hope or expectation of betterment, an almost incredible but rapidly spreading change began. World circumstances had been adverse for so long that Canadians hardly believed they could be anything else. But now, almost at a stroke, they became benignantly favourable. And, amid all the advantages which seemed to descend in a veritable shower, one tremendous piece of good fortune arrested everyone's attention. The great marching column of frontiersmen and settlers which had been travelling for generations over North America had at last turned sharply north-west into Canada. In the United States the frontier had crossed the continent and reached the Pacific. But in Canada the frontier was still the 'hither edge' of vast expanses of unoccupied free land. It was Canada's hour. Canada had captured the imagination of the Western World. It had become the land of hope and opportunity. And the Canadian north-west, which had seemed for decades the final proof of the Dominion's failure, became at once the happiest index of its new good fortune and its new success.

The settlers swarmed into the region. They made little effort to distinguish between lands which were fitted for agriculture and those that were best adapted to ranching. More and more they concentrated upon the great export specialty of wheat; and in this first prosperous decade of the century everything

11. Victoria with British Columbia Legislative Building, Empress Hotel and business district in the foreground

12. Red Island, Newfoundland, showing the hospital ship *Lady Anderson* in the centre of the harbour

seemed to encourage and speed their enterprise. They could draw readily upon the experience which many of their number had already gained under very similar circumstances in the United States. The main problems of homesteading and 'dry farming' in a rolling grassland region with a severe, semi-arid climate had already been largely solved; the machinery and equipment necessary for the production of wheat and flour on a large scale—reapers, steel-roller mills, elevators, and box-cars—had all been produced and tested by the time the new prairie country needed them.

Even the special and peculiar necessity of the Canadian north-west—the need of a spring wheat which would mature safely within the short northern growing period—had been successfully filled. Red Fife, the hardy prolific wheat which had been brought to Canada from Scotland by Duncan Fife early in the nineteenth century, was the first wheat used on the prairies; but in 1908 Charles E. Saunders, the Dominion Cerealist, succeeded in producing a new variety called Marquis which had all the fine milling qualities of Red Fife and which also matured about a week earlier and with a higher yield. In an incredibly short space of time, and without any dismal apprenticeship of trial and error, the new north-west was ready to go into full-scale production. The markets of Great Britain and western Europe, enlarged by the great and increasing masses of urban, industrial workers, opened capaciously to receive the golden torrent of grain that was pouring out of the prairies. The price of wheat went steadily up. The costs of ocean freight and insurance sank with equal steadiness.

Wheat was making the West. And the West was rapidly making a nation. The influx of immigrants into the prairie country, the satisfaction of their wants, and the sale of their products abroad were at once the principal causes and the main manifestations of the new prosperity; but it was a national, rather than a regional prosperity, and wheat was the golden hinge upon which the door now opened easily for the inrush of transcontinental success. The headlong occupation and exploitation of the agricultural north-west was accompanied by a revolution of equal magnitude in eastern and central industry. In the first decade of the twentieth century the net value of manufacturing production increased more than two and one-half times; and the mature, diversified national economy, based on an east-west axis and united by east-west, all-Canadian transport, was visibly becoming a triumphant reality. Only a little more than a decade before the Canadian Pacific Railway had been attacked as a huge and unnecessary incubus upon the resources of the Canadian people; but in 1902 its main line from Winnipeg to the head of the lakes was choked with an avalanche of wheat seeking a way eastward to tidewater. As late as the general election of 1891 protection had been denounced as an artificial and costly barrier against the natural, north-south trade routes of North America; but now the bursting cargoes of grain and the packed trains of manufactured goods that shuttled briskly back and forward across the continent on the east-west transport system were obviously making an integrated and prosperous Canada.

In 1905 an event occurred which seemed to prove that an integrated Canada had been already made. In that year the creation of the two new prairie provinces of Saskatchewan and Alberta was almost a public, formal announcement that the task of nation-building was complete. Apart from the lonely, sentinel island of Newfoundland, all the provinces of the old British North America had now joined the Canadian union. A linked chain of provincial governments and an organized network of economic activities now extended from ocean to ocean; and, although in many regions the density of population was extremely low, the northern half of the continent had at last been occupied by the Canadian people. In the decade from 1901 to 1911 the population of the Dominion rose from 5,371,315 to 7,206,643. It was a gain of nearly two million people; and, as might have been expected, well over a million of the new Canadians were distributed through the three prairie provinces and British Columbia. The peopling of the western plains was the most spectacular feature of the period; but this romantic population movement had an almost equally important counterpart in the east, where the persistent exodus from the farms to the industrialized cities and towns was making a new, much more urbanized Canada.

Over this rapidly changing scene of almost magical achievement there presided the tall, slender, elegant figure of the nation's first French-speaking Prime Minister, Sir Wilfrid Laurier. With his gracious urbanity, his inspiring eloquence, his air of easy distinction and effortless accomplishment, he might almost have seemed a magician who had brought all this success into glittering existence with a few swift passes of his enchanter's wand. And yet it was not, as might have seemed probable only a decade earlier, by any novel arts of magic that the Liberals were ushering in the new era of Canadian prosperity. A decade or more before they would have been ready to leave the Canadian Pacific Railway to its fate and eager to abandon the national policy of protection. But by the time Sir Wilfrid formed his first government these doctrinaire free-trade views had been quietly and unostentatiously dropped; and it soon became clear that, although the arrival of the new régime had coincided with a change in economic circumstances, it certainly did not portend any important changes in policy.

The Liberals laid no irreverent hands upon the tariff. They soon became earnest advocates of the vital importance of all-Canadian transport. In fact, the adjustments and innovations for which Sir Wilfrid was responsible tended rather to strengthen the idea of national development on an east-west axis and to accentuate the all-Canadian, anti-continental, and pro-British elements of the national design. The party which, a generation before, had denounced the Canadian Pacific Railway as a wanton and stupendous piece of folly, now sponsored the building of two new all-Canadian transcontinentals—the Canadian Northern and the National Transcontinental–Grand Trunk Pacific; and there could hardly have been a more complete repudiation of the Liberals' old idea of commercial union with the United States than the British preference, one-quarter lower than the general tariff, which W. S. Fielding introduced in the budget of 1898.

II

On the 5th of June 1897 Wilfrid Laurier (he was to become Sir Wilfrid only a very short time later) sailed from Canada for England. Both the transatlantic voyage itself and the occasion which prompted it were alike symbolic of a decided change which was already beginning in the development of the Dominion. Laurier, who had spent his entire adult life in Canadian public affairs, was crossing the Atlantic Ocean for the first time; and the Diamond Jubilee, to which he was bound as the head of the Canadian delegation, was the first completely imperial occasion in the long, sixty-year span of Queen Victoria's reign. It was true that ten years before the royal celebrations had been accompanied by a conference of representatives of the Crown and self-governing colonies at Westminster; but, in the main, the Golden Jubilee of 1887 was a domestic British occasion, almost a 'Little England' affair. The pageant of 1897 was a much more richly diversified, all-embracing spectacle of the range, strength, and variety of the Empire; and the soldiers of the Canadian contingent—Grenadiers, Highlanders, Governor-General's Body Guards, and troopers of the Royal Canadian Mounted Police—marched through the streets of London in an enormous procession which included most of the creeds and races of the world.

In all this huge and glittering assembly Sir Wilfrid—his knighthood was one of the Jubilee honours—was a not inconspicuous figure. In person he was easy, gracious, and distinguished; and, unlike his fellow prime ministers who each represented only a single, separate Australasian or South African colony, he stood for a union of seven British provinces in a single transcontinental state. The accolade of his knighthood, the attentions which he received on every side, were marks of the public recognition of his country's coming of age; and his own first venture into strange lands and his prominent presence among the statesmen of the Empire were also signs, in their own way, of Canada's acceptance of the burdens and responsibilities of maturity. For decades, for generations, British North America had been preoccupied, almost obsessed, with the exacting problems of its own internal development; but now, with a strange, victorious sense of accomplishment and self-realization, the Canadians could afford to lift their eyes from the immediate task and look abroad. Sir Wilfrid Laurier was, quite literally, looking abroad for the first time; and the curious mixture of national and imperial themes which informed his public addresses during the Jubilee was a fairly accurate anticipation of the mingled interest and perplexity with which the Dominion was to face the dangerous external world of the twentieth century.

At home, in the domestic sphere, the sunshine of success seemed to be everywhere. Abroad, in the larger arena of world affairs, the long shadows of evil things to come lay heavily everywhere. The sustained improvement in the nation's well-being was matched by the progressive deterioration of the state of the world; and the Britannic peace, from which both British North America and Canada had profited so much, almost without being aware of it, was now obviously threatened by rival imperialistic ambitions and impending imperialistic wars. The troubled world into which the Canadians were peering eagerly yet anxiously, for what was really the first time, was obviously a difficult and dangerous place. And two events— the South African War and the Alaska Boundary Dispute— which occurred fairly early in the period, proved only too clearly how much the new imperialism might cost the Dominion in inward quarrels and outward sacrifices.

The Laurier government decided, in the end, to send a Canadian contingent to South Africa. It was a decision really enforced by an aroused electorate which was now passionately concerned in the affairs of the outside world and determined to have at least a small share in their settlement. Canadian participation in the Boer War proved that Canada was no longer a dependent, irresponsible protectorate; it proved that the Anglo-Canadian alliance could now be extended the other way across the Atlantic to Great Britain's immediate advantage. These demonstrations abroad of the Dominion's new-found and confident sense of maturity were important; but so also were the heavy costs which they entailed at home. A furious controversy broke out between the great majority of Canadians, who wanted troops to be sent to South Africa, and a small, vociferous French-speaking minority which did not. The break in national unity was serious enough; and the gradual realization that it had been incurred without any compensating national benefit was almost equally disturbing. It became clear, in short order, that Canadian assistance in imperial wars was not to be repaid by British support for Canadian claims in the Americas. In 1901 the equal rights which Great Britain had by treaty with the United States in the ownership and control of the future Panama Canal were surrendered, without compensation and against Canada's protests, to the republic; and in 1903 the British representative in the judicial tribunal which had been appointed to settle the disputed boundary between Canada and Alaska voted against his Canadian colleagues and in favour of the American case.

The world of the twentieth century, with its power politics and diplomatic pressures, was evidently a harsh and dangerous place. Yet Canada was now deeply, inextricably involved in its affairs. She was conscious, in her new maturity, of a variety of external associations and interests which it was her business to promote and defend. How, as a member of the British Empire-Commonwealth, could she best undertake these responsibilities and exert this influence? It was not a question to which a single, obvious answer was immediately forthcoming, for the evolution of the Empire-Commonwealth rested somewhat ambiguously in mid-passage. The 'responsible government' which had been won over half a century before now embraced the whole range of domestic concerns; it even included some important aspects of foreign relations, as Laurier clearly indicated when in 1909 he established the new Department of External Affairs. Special provisions had long before been made in the imperial Foreign Office for the protection of Canadian interests, particularly in the realm of trade; and ever since the appointment of the first High Commissioner in London, Canadian diplomats, in Europe as well as in North America, had been taking a larger and larger share in the negotiation of treaties relating immediately to Canada.

All this was true; but it was also true that ultimate authority and responsibility for imperial foreign policy and defence still rested in the hands of the British Government. In the past Canada had been in no hurry to acquire these sovereign powers, for in the nineteenth century her first and hardest task was survival in a continent dominated by the United States; and for this purpose British diplomatic and military support was absolutely essential. But now, in the twentieth century, circumstances were obviously changing. It was true, of course, that Canadians had been deeply angered by the aggressive, 'big-stick' methods by which the new imperialistic United States had forced its will in Panama and Alaska. But the thought of annexation to the republic no longer attracted or frightened them as it had before. They had complete confidence in the success of their own national experiment; and they believed that Canada should now accept her proper responsibilities and exert her proper influence in the world at large. The terms of the Anglo-Canadian alliance would obviously have to be revised. For Canada there would have to be a new imperial relationship and a new international status.

Yet what was the new status to be and what form should the imperial relationship take? Obviously there were two principal ways in which the development of the Empire-Commonwealth could be consciously shaped in the light of the swift rise of the new Dominion. Either the existing trend towards decentralization could be equitably and logically continued, or the Empire could be more effectively centralized on a more truly co-operative basis. The most extreme form which this centralization could take—a supra-national imperial organization operating through federal institutions—was almost equally distasteful to both Liberals and Conservatives in Canada. Their view of the institutional structure of the Empire was invincibly plural rather than unitary; they both believed that whatever measure of imperial unity was desirable could best be achieved through the co-operation of separate governments, separately organized. Yet behind this general agreement on the political organization of the Empire-Commonwealth there lurked scarcely less significant differences. Laurier and the Liberals, who wished to enlarge their country's sphere of independent action, disliked military commitments and preferred detachment from imperial councils. Robert Borden, the new Conservative leader, who believed in a unitary system of defence and foreign policy provided it were organized on truly co-operative lines, was prepared to accept new military responsibilities in return for an effective voice in the framing of a really collective imperial foreign policy.

In 1909 the alarming realization of Germany's rapid progress in naval construction, which produced a 'naval scare' throughout the Empire, brought the Canadian controversy about defence and foreign policy to a head. To many people it seemed obvious that the Dominion, confronted with the increasingly dangerous aspect of world affairs, could maintain its state of colonial unpreparedness no longer. Whether the nation pursued its own separate course, or whether it co-operated in a common imperial system of foreign policy and defence, it must, in any case, accept the burdens of its own vaunted political maturity and provide for its own protection. It was true, of course, that an extreme group of French-Canadian 'nationalists', led by Henri Bourassa, objected violently to defence measures of any kind on the ground that, in effect, they would be simply contributions to the imperialistic wars of the great powers; but this kind of parochial nationalism, with its large admixture of the spirit of isolationism and dependence, won only a minority of supporters throughout the country.

The great bulk of Canadians agreed that defence was necessary, but differed as to the ways in which it could best be provided. In his Naval Service Bill of 1910, Sir Wilfrid proposed the creation of a small Canadian navy of cruisers and destroyers which would be under the independent control of the Canadian Government but which could be put at the disposal of the imperial Admiralty in time of war. Robert Borden countered with the idea of an immediate emergency contribution of capital ships to the imperial navy, and the subsequent arrangement of a common system of defence and foreign policy in which Canada would have an appropriate voice. The resulting controversy, which was spread over the next few years, proved again how hard the Canadian people found it to solve the complicated problems of the new imperial relationship and to decide upon the position from which they would face the perils of the twentieth-century world.

III

Over ten years before, on a still, snowy night in early February, 1899, the poet, Archibald Lampman, lay dying in his house in Ottawa. His death broke up the small, intimate group —Duncan Campbell Scott, William Wilfred Campbell, and Lampman himself—which formed the creative core of the literary circle of the capital. It tragically weakened, though of course it did not end, the literary movement led by Charles G. D. Roberts, Bliss Carman, Scott, and Lampman, which was the strongest Canadian movement of the late nineteenth and early twentieth centuries. Roberts and Carman had long literary careers ahead of them. Scott, who, after Lampman, was the ablest of the leaders, had much of his best work yet to do. But Lampman was their chief; and his poetry epitomizes the group's greatest collective achievement, which was the sensitive and reflective rendering of the contours, colours, and moods of the Canadian landscape.

In a single generation the horizons of this landscape had been enormously expanded. In a single generation the very achievement of national success had created a greater awareness of the young country's depth of experience in time. In the northwest, far away from the tidal reaches of the Bay of Fundy and the pleasant river valleys of the Ottawa countryside, which Roberts and Lampman celebrated, lay another Canadian nature, huge, primitive, ungainly, and sometimes cruel, with harsh rhythms and emphatic accents. Beyond the opportunities and rewards and relatively easy conditions of the first decade of the twentieth century, lay a past, three hundred years in length, of effort, struggle, and endurance, most of which had already passed from recollection into history. The endless variety of the regions of the Canadian scene, the suddenly appreciated interest of the record of history, were rich sources which more and more Canadian writers, scholars, and artists were trying to exploit.

Two new historical enterprises on a large scale—the biographical series, the *Makers of Canada*, and a national and regional history in many volumes, *Canada and Its Provinces*—were both begun during this period. Gilbert Parker was using picturesque French-Canadian *habitant* life and the costumed romance of the Anglo-French struggle in America as the themes of his tales and novels. Ralph Connor (Charles W. Gordon) found the setting for his stories in the harsh western mining frontier which he had come to know as a young clergyman; and Robert W. Service fashioned his smoothly turned ballads out of the obvious excitement and romance of the last and most northerly of the Pacific coast gold rushes, the 'trail of '98' to the Yukon. The new Canadian north-west did not succeed in evoking a different literary *genre*, such as the 'bush-ballad' poetry of Australia; it did not become the setting or the inspiration of work which challenged the quality achieved by Lampman and his friends. To a very large extent the stream of

The Turning of the Tide

books about Canada and the Canadians which swelled in volume during the first decade of the century was a rather obvious, optimistic, popular response to the growing demand of a people who had suddenly become aware of all that their country contained and all that it had been through.

This awakening sense of nationhood, complacent and truculent in character, yet tentative and diffident as well, was the transcendent feature of the period. The attainment of the national objectives, set so long ago, had largely created it; and the most important victory in this national accomplishment was unquestionably the settlement of the west. The west had been the mainspring of success; and the new nation which it was bringing into being was different from the old, different from what its authors had probably expected it would be, more complicated, contradictory, and perplexing in unexpected ways. The settlement of the prairies had set up a variety of strange new tensions in the body politic—tensions between west and east, between farmers and town and city dwellers, between direct simple democratic practices and the solidly established, venerable political systems of the old-time Liberal and Conservative parties. In the summer of 1910, when Sir Wilfrid travelled for the first time through the new prairie country, he was met everywhere by crowds of determined and argumentative farmers, the members of a dozen vigorous new grain growers' associations, who had western interests to represent, western grievances to air, and western demands to make. Nearly a thousand farmers from all parts of the country assembled in Ottawa's largest theatre on a December day in the same year to force the agrarian programme of the new Canadian Council of Agriculture upon the attention of the government. The march of the grain growers had begun; and the invasion of the capital was to have strange and permanent effects upon the familiar Victorian landscape of nineteenth-century Canadian politics.

The west had created new contradictions, new and exciting tensions. But it had done far more than that. It had also promoted a new and dominant sense of national unity. And in the general election of 1911, which supplied a political punctuation mark for the first decade of Canada's century and brought about the downfall of Sir Wilfrid Laurier's fifteen-year-old Liberal government, this robust feeling of Canadian nationhood found startlingly vehement political expression. The very violence of the outburst may have surprised the Canadians themselves; it certainly left Sir Wilfrid and his colleagues discomfited and nonplussed. They had fondly believed themselves to be the discoverers of a popular policy which would unquestionably win them success at the polls for the fifth time in succession. Impressed by the rumblings of discontent which marked the decline of the boom, and distinctly worried by the peremptory demands of farmers in general and westerners in particular for a lowering of the tariff, the Liberal government succeeded, at the beginning of 1911, in negotiating a new reciprocal trade agreement with the United States. Unlike the proposals of commercial union which had been made twenty years before, the new trade agreement was not financially or politically dangerous. But it permitted reciprocal free trade in a wide range of manufactured goods as well as in the natural products for which Canada had always hoped to get free entry into the American market. And in this vitally important respect it was a sharp departure from the national policies of the past.

It was precisely this apparent departure which the Canadian people was moved, by the strongest inner compulsion, to reject. In the last fifteen years the design of a transcontinental Dominion had magnificently succeeded; and in the eyes of most Canadians the national policies of development had unquestionably been the main factors in that success. They had clung to these policies through blackest failure and deepest doubt; and now, when their devotion had been completely vindicated, why should they alter or modify the instruments of their triumph? Why should they compromise their national achievement by a dangerously dubious agreement with a foreign power which had always proclaimed 'Manifest Destiny' and made no secret of its continental ambitions, and which was now dominating the affairs of the Americas with the 'big-stick' politics of imperialism? These big-stick methods had already been openly turned against Canada in the Panama negotiations and the Alaska boundary dispute. Was the reciprocity agreement a more insidious example of the same imperialist diplomacy? 'Canada', said President Taft with indiscreet ambiguity, 'stands at the parting of the ways.' The Canadians did not believe that they had arrived at a crossroads. They were convinced that they were already half-way down the broad highway to success. And in the election of 1911 they shook off the leadership of those who seemed to be trying to divert them from their course.

The election of 1911 made history. It also became literature. A Professor of Economics and Political Science at McGill University, named Stephen Leacock, who was just beginning to acquire a reputation as a humorist, immortalized the contest in two sketches, 'The Great Election in Missinaba County' and 'The Candidacy of Mr. Smith'; and these became the concluding chapters in what was perhaps his greatest work, *Sunshine Sketches of a Little Town*.

13

WAR ABROAD AND CRISIS AT HOME

I

The new Prime Minister, Sir Robert Borden, was a man very different from his two famous predecessors, Sir John Macdonald and Sir Wilfrid Laurier. Borden's square, rather solemn countenance, with its heavy eyebrows and melancholy moustaches, contrasted oddly with the fine sensitive lines of Sir Wilfrid's face or the lively ruggedness of Sir John's features. Sir Robert's deep, almost lugubrious voice could give delicious ironic point to the good stories which he liked to tell; but he could hardly emulate Laurier's suave, gracious urbanity or Macdonald's jaunty, offhand friendliness. There was an habitual deliberation in Borden's manner, an instinctive gravity in his approach. He would reach conclusions and form policies slowly, cautiously. But, once a decision had been taken, he would, in all likelihood, carry it out with vigour and conviction. Once a position had been occupied he would probably defend it with stubborn tenacity.

In the early summer of 1912 he sailed, with a few of his Cabinet colleagues, for England. His mission was a highly significant one. He was seeking a solution of the problem of the Dominion's external relationships—the problem which was to dominate Canadian politics for the next quarter-century; and, in one supremely important way, he was better fitted than either of his more famous predecessors for the task. He was much closer to Macdonald's informed awareness of the main currents of British and world politics than he was to Laurier's rather parochial and suspicious Canadianism; but he held the conviction, which neither Laurier nor Macdonald had really reached, that henceforth Canada would be inevitably and inextricably involved in the troubled world of international affairs. His reading and his travels had convinced him that the peace of western Europe was seriously menaced by Germany; and he was determined that Canada should take part in the defence of an order in which her interests were vitally engaged. In the past the foreign policy and defensive system of the Empire had been unified under the control of Great Britain; but now, when the Mother Country was becoming simply *primus inter pares* of a galaxy of nations, the same unity must be achieved by different methods. Henceforth imperial defence and foreign policy must be a collective system in which each co-operating partner would exert his proper influence and accept his proper share of responsibility.

It was this plan which Borden proceeded to lay before the Liberal government of Great Britain in the summer of 1912. He talked with the Prime Minister, H. H. Asquith, and his colleagues; he had several long discussions with the First Lord of the Admiralty, Winston Spencer Churchill, a stout, youngish man, not yet forty years old, who had already had an extremely varied and strenuous career in the army, journalism, letters, and politics. Churchill had, of course, forsworn his original Conservative allegiance because of his opposition to Chamberlain's plans for tariff reform within the Empire-Commonwealth; and neither he nor the other Liberal ministers seemed as eager as Chamberlain had been to exchange a part of Great Britain's control of foreign policy in return for a Dominion contribution to imperial defence. Yet the need for increased and unified defence seemed obvious and urgent. It was difficult now to shrug away Canada's demands as unreasonable; and Borden returned home in the belief that something effective could be done. Late that autumn, in the Canadian House of Commons, he introduced his Naval Aid Bill, which called for the immediate, emergency contribution of three capital ships to the imperial navy.

For over three years now the Canadian people had been debating, arguing, and quarrelling over the question of naval defence. The troubled passage of the Naval Aid Bill provided one more proof of how deep and persistent were the divisions of opinion which the subject had created. In the spring of 1913 the Bill passed the House of Commons, but after an extremely prolonged and obstructive debate which was only ended by the adoption, for the first time, of closure rules. The Bill then went to the Senate, and there it stuck. After fifteen years of Sir Wilfrid's nominations, the Liberals commanded a large majority in the Senate; and this triumphant opposition proceeded firmly to reject Borden's Bill. Sir Robert had, of course, suspended the implementation of the Laurier measure in the confident expectation of the passage of his own; but next year he did not reintroduce his Bill, for he had the best of reasons for fearing another rejection by the Senate. It was 1914. Laurier's small Canadian fleet of cruisers and destroyers had not been built; Borden's three capital ships for the imperial navy had not been laid down; and the Canadian naval service consisted solely of a couple of training vessels. The crisis was upon western Europe and time was running out.

II

The War of 1914–18, the first of the World Wars of the twentieth century, seemed to reconcile all these frustrating dissensions in a determined and purposeful national concord. On the 4th August 1914 every Canadian took for granted that his country was at war with the German Empire. It might have been, as it had been in the past, a largely detached acceptance of a legal fact; but this time it carried with it a sense of the direct responsibility of participation. Every Canadian assumed that his country was at war; every Canadian—or almost every Canadian—assumed that his country must make a direct and positive contribution to the achievement of victory. And in that double recognition the nation's coming of age was manifested more dramatically than ever before. The isolation and irresponsibility of colonial dependence were over. For better or for worse, Canada had accepted the burdens of maturity and entered the great society of nations.

The sailing of the first Canadian contingent to England on the 1st October 1914 was an event of curious symbolic significance. For generations and centuries armed men had been crossing the Atlantic in warships and transports. It was almost exactly two hundred and fifty years since the soldiers of the Carignan-Salières regiment had first paraded through the streets of Quebec; and from then on, at irregular but frequent intervals, the white- and blue-clad veterans of France and the redcoats of England had been borne up and down the River of Canada. Long ago, the whitecoats had vanished. A century elapsed; and then, one autumn day in 1871, the redcoats marched down to the quays of Quebec singing 'Auld Lang Syne'. For two hundred years the long procession of men and armaments had come westward across the ocean from Europe. Then it had slackened and stopped; and now, after nearly half a century, the tide had reversed and was beginning to flow the other way.

Rapidly it gained in volume and speed. The Canadian contingent which sailed on the 1st October 1914 was the largest armed force which up to that time had ever crossed the Atlantic Ocean; and of the six hundred and twenty-eight thousand Canadians who enlisted in the services during the four years of the war, four hundred and twenty-five thousand went overseas. Some joined the little fleet of coastal patrol vessels and anti-submarine craft which, at long last, formed the nucleus of the Canadian Navy; a good many more saw service in the Royal Flying Corps; but by far the greatest number of the Canadians who made the eastward journey across the ocean were khaki-clad soldiers who fought the war in the first large army that the new Canada had ever put into the field. In the autumn of 1915, when the Second Division arrived in France, the force was transformed into a separate Canadian Corps. Under its two commanders, Sir Julian Byng, and his successor, the Canadian, Sir Arthur Currie, it reached a total of four divisions; and for over three and a half years, from the rainy day in February 1915 when the first battalions went ashore at St. Nazaire to those final moments of victorious pursuit in November of 1918, it endured the relentless and sanguinary attrition of the trench warfare of western Europe. At Ypres, St. Eloi, Mount Sorrel, and Courcelette, the Canadians established a reputation as the storm troops of assault; and at Vimy, on a dreary morning of sleet and snow in April 1917, they fought their way up towards the crest of the ridge from which Walter Allward's Canadian War Memorial now looks serenely out over the landscape.

The War of 1914–18 was the first of the total wars. It involved the entire community, and its resources, both material and human; and Canada's participation in it was at once an expression of national growth and a cause of further and rapid national development. The boom, which had brought the sustained hum of success to the nation in the first decade of the century, had slowed down ominously and come to a jarring stop in the years immediately before the war. Painful adjustments might have been necessary; but after 1914 the mere thought of painful adjustments was forgotten in the face of the enormous and increasing demand of the allied powers for war materials and supplies. Almost as if there had been no pause at all, the economy resumed its steady onward march towards expansion on a transcontinental scale and integration on a strong east-west axis. Production of base metals, of wood pulp and newsprint, expanded enormously under the stimulus of war-time orders. High prices for wheat brought prosperity to the prairie provinces and hastened the settlement of their still unoccupied lands. Factories in central Canada were working night and day to fulfil contracts for munitions and aeroplanes and to satisfy the voracious demands of a domestic market deprived of most of its usual imports from overseas.

The advance from the simple, staple-producing commercialism of the nineteenth century to the complex, diversified industrialism of the twentieth proceeded at a speed which became almost headlong. The demands of war were transitory but stupendous. Their long-term consequences were bound to be highly important; their short-term effects were upsetting in the highest degree. The federal government, called upon to preside over the multifarious and jostling activities of a total war effort, found itself strangely, frighteningly alone and on its own, in a chaotic world whose traditional supports seemed to have vanished unaccountably, and whose familiar methods and routines had become pitifully inadequate in the face of the new and unnatural problems which crowded on every hand. It was a shock to realize that the supposedly never-ending stream of British capital imports, which had financed Canadian development all during the nineteenth century, had finally run dry. It was painful to have to acknowledge that the primitive Canadian system of taxation, with its old-fashioned reliance on excise taxes and customs duties, was totally incapable of supporting the vast expenditures of war time. It was perhaps most disturbing of all to be forced, by an aroused and clamorous public opinion, to cope with the hideously novel problems of food scarcities, rationing, profiteering, inflation, and high prices. The government, appealing for the first time for direct financial support from the Canadian people, introduced the popular Victory Bonds; a newly established income tax successfully removed a share of the rising incomes of war time; but the various regulations and controls which were set up to keep the expansive economy in check failed to satisfy public opinion, and the growth of class feeling and social unrest portended serious trouble.

In the meantime there could be no doubt about the magnitude of the Dominion's war effort. On the economic as well as on the military side, Canada's contribution had been on a scale befitting a principal rather than a subordinate; and the country which had made it had no longer any reason for accepting a subordinate's position. Only a few years before, Sir Robert Borden had agreed to accept a part of the burden of imperial defence in return for a share in the determination of imperial foreign policy. The plan for imperial reorganization which he had tentatively broached to Asquith and Winston Churchill in the summer of 1912 had failed because of Borden's complete inability to perform his own share of the bargain by getting the Naval Aid Bill through the Canadian Parliament. He had negotiated from weakness then; but in the meantime the Empire had endured two terrible years of war; and the abortive gift of the three capital ships had been given a hundred times over by Canada's contribution to the conflict. Surely the price had now been paid. Surely the Dominion deserved its place in the councils of Empire. By 1916 Borden, who was not uncritical of imperial military organization and strategy, was vigorously and peremptorily demanding a share in the direction of the war. The fall of Asquith and the arrival of Lloyd George to power in Great Britain opened the way for this change, as well as for so many others, in the imperial war effort. In the mid-winter of 1917 Sir Robert left Canada for continuous weeks of conference with the War Ministers in London; and the subsequent establishment of the Imperial War Cabinet and the Imperial War Conference brought about the effective realization of the Borden conception of the Empire-Commonwealth.

III

Sir Robert sailed from England in May. It was an agitated and excited Canada to which he returned; but perhaps the most disturbing element in the whole situation was the fearful determination which he had reached in the privacy of his own mind. Nearly a year and a half before, at the beginning of 1916, he had announced that Canada's objective was a total of five hundred thousand men in the armed services. Eighteen months had elapsed since then—eighteen months of appalling slaughter on the western front in Europe and declining voluntary enlistments in Canada; and Borden had left England with the conviction that conscription was the only equitable and effective solution of the problem of reinforcements. It was, in the light of all Canadian history, a highly dangerous resolve. Ever since, in 1855, at the time of the Crimean War, the first efficient militia force had been established, Canada had relied upon voluntary enlistment; and, at the beginning of the War of 1914–18 everybody, including Borden and Borden's government, had assumed that service in the Canadian armed forces would continue to be voluntary.

Yet, for the last few months, criticism of both the equity and the efficiency of the voluntary system had been growing in intensity and volume. Voluntary enlistment, these critics declared vehemently, condoned inequality of sacrifice and encouraged division at home, yet failed to maintain the Canadian Corps effectively in France. From the beginning of the War Canadians had differed, not so much about the justice of the conflict or the necessity of Canada's participation in it, as about the nature and the extent of the contribution which Canada should make. These differences of opinion became obvious in the varying regional responses to the call to arms. Towns gave relatively more than countryside, and West more than East to the armed services; but these variations, though they were not inconsiderable, were dwarfed in importance by the crucial difference between the contributions of English-speaking and French-speaking Canadians. English Canada, consciously proud of the Dominion's newly achieved maturity and its novel place of importance in world affairs, identified itself closely and sympathetically with the allied cause. French Canada, concerned above all with the defence of its own vulnerable minority culture in North America, looked always with a certain measure of detachment on the affairs of western Europe. French-Canadian enlistments were proportionately lower than those of any other major Canadian group. And it was this contentious disparity, which sprang from the old cultural division and seemed likely to exacerbate it, that added emotional bitterness to the debate over conscription.

For nearly two decades the question of Canada's position and responsibilities in the external world had been seriously dividing Canadians. Under the pressure of repeated disputes concerning foreign policy and defence, the sense of solidarity growing out of the successful achievement of the old national objectives had been repeatedly strained and weakened. Now it broke; and, in the main, it broke along the scarred lines of the cultural fractures of the past. Organized labour and organized agriculture both opposed or criticized the Military Service Act which now introduced conscription; but from the first, French Canada stood out as the most formidable single source of opposition; and, as the troubled months of 1917 sped swiftly by, Quebec's spiritual isolation in the midst of an increasingly aroused and unified Dominion, became more and more tragically obvious. Sir Wilfrid declined to join the Union Government which Borden hoped to establish as a political expression of the unified national determination to implement conscription and complete the war effort. Laurier no doubt believed that the old-fashioned, nineteenth-century party loyalties would prove strong enough to protect the distinctive position which French Canada had taken. The event proved how completely wrong he was. Led by the westerners and some Ontario Liberals, Sir Wilfrid's followers deserted him to carry out the national purpose in Borden's national administration. In the midst of the apparently dissolving wreck of the great party which he had led for thirty years, Laurier stood virtually alone; and the general election, which came in December 1917, served merely to emphasize his loneliness and estrangement. The Union Government swept the country. So far as Parliamentary seats were concerned, Canadian Liberalism had almost become identified with Quebec; and Laurier had been forced back into the fortress of his own province with the lifeguard of his own people.

War Abroad and Crisis at Home

At home, the new nation was encountering strains and stresses which were ominous for the future. Abroad it was winning prestige and recognition which seemed to realize all the ambitions of the past. The last three months of the war—the period from August to November which became known as 'Canada's Hundred Days'—gave the Canadian Corps repeated opportunities to show its fighting qualities in the massive operations of Foch's counter-offensive; and the Peace Conference at Paris—the first great international conference at which Canada had ever been represented—presented Borden with a uniquely favourable chance of introducing his young country to international society. With both naïve enthusiasm and tough persistence, the Canadian delegates sought to exploit the double advantage of their position. As a recognized secondary power, their country was granted representation in the formal deliberations of the Conference; and—what was infinitely more important—it participated in the inner councils of the great powers through its membership in the British Empire delegation, which was virtually a continuation of the Imperial War Cabinet. The Canadians made the most of all the Paris Peace Conference had to offer; and they similarly regarded the first great security system, the League of Nations, as a heaven-sent opportunity for acquiring status and achieving international recognition. Canada was admitted to the League as an original member with separate representation in the Assembly and in the International Labour Organization, and the right of election to one of the non-permanent seats in the Council. Canada signed and ratified the Peace Treaty in her own right.

In 1872, for the first time, a British North American legislature had given formal approval to a treaty negotiated by the government of the United Kingdom. That Treaty was the Washington Treaty of 1871, the legislature was the Parliament of Canada; and the Canadian Parliament's ratification extended only to the clauses in the Treaty which immediately concerned Canada. That was nearly half a century ago now;

and the Dominion, in its onward career towards international recognition, had gone a long way in those fifty years.

IV

On the 21st June 1919, one week before the plenipotentiaries of the world's powers assembled in the Hall of Mirrors at Versailles to sign the Peace Treaty, a large and angry crowd was gathering in the broad avenues of central Winnipeg, the capital of the far-away Province of Manitoba. For over a month, ever since May 15th, Winnipeg had been paralysed by a general strike proclaimed by the Trades and Labour Council of the city in support of the demands of the metal and building trades. Behind this particular dispute lay the general determination of radical western labour, already expressed in the formation of the One Big Union, to abandon the old craft organizations in favour of modern industrial unionism; and behind the O.B.U. was the obviously spectacular advance of Canadian industrialism, the evident growth of working-class unrest in Canada during the last years of the war, and the vague hopes and ambitions which the Russian Revolution had awakened in the labour force of the entire Western World. It was a bitter, resentful, and reckless crowd which gathered that June day in Winnipeg. Parades had been forbidden by the city authorities; but a parade of strikers had been announced, and the crowds assembled defiantly to watch it. There were arguments, street fights, mob demonstrations. The Mayor read the Riot Act; a force of Royal Canadian Mounted Police, special constables, and militia was hastily got together; and the scarlet-coated horsemen, with drawn pistols, galloped down Main Street through a fighting, screaming crowd.

The Winnipeg strike was broken and defeated; but the very fact that it had happened at all was, to many people, a sanguinary proof that the old nineteenth-century Canada had been irrevocably buried in the vast upheaval of the War. An unfamiliar and intimidating landscape now confronted the nation.

War Abroad and Crisis at Home

Abroad, the Britannic peace, under which British North America had proudly and placidly sheltered itself for so long, had yielded place to an untried and rather frightening system of collective security. At home, the well-known Canadian community of Liberals and Conservatives, English and French, had suddenly become an angry and turbulent society agitated by violent class feelings and radical politics. The crisis over conscription, which had for a while reawakened and intensified the nation's ancient cultural division, had been, apparently, merely a deceptively familiar prelude to the outbreak of other and more savage dissensions; and the break-up of the Liberal Party, which had occurred during the negotiations for the Union Government, began to look alarmingly as if it were simply the first phase of the disintegration of the entire nineteenth-century Canadian party system. Radical labour had suffered a savage check at Winnipeg; but agrarian radicalism was flowing freely and aggressively in the new United Farmers' organizations in Ontario and the West, and in the national Progressive Party which, with Thomas A. Crerar as its leader, was formed in January 1920. A new national party, the first since Confederation! A progressive programme, styled challengingly a 'New National Policy', which seemed mockingly to dismiss Macdonald's national policies as the broken-down meaningless instruments of a vanished past!

For a while it looked as if the old political parties would be swept from the field like companies of rustics fighting with pitchforks and matchlocks against machine-guns. In the first years of the 1920's every circumstance, political and economic, seemed to reveal the onrush of a new and strangely different order of things. The peace was followed by a sudden depression which revived the economic discontents and grievances of wartime and roused a fresh clamour for government intervention and control. In the midst of this unexpected renewal of social unrest, the Union Government, which only a few short years before had been the proud recipient of an overwhelming expression of national confidence, was drifting rapidly, hopelessly, into unpopularity and discredit. Its temporary Liberal friends deserted it, its war-time leader, Sir Robert Borden, was obliged to retire; and his successor, Arthur Meighen, was confronted, not merely by the militantly confident Progesssives under Crerar, but also by an unaccountably rejuvenated company of Liberals, captained by a new leader, a short, bulky, youngish man with an earnest voice and an air of serious purpose, called William Lyon Mackenzie King. King, who had had a good deal of experience of labour problems and who had gone so far as to write a book, *Industry and Humanity*, upon the subject, expressed the new gospel of public ownership and social reform with more apparent authority and conviction than Crerar. Under this fashionable verbal onslaught, Meighen, who kept talking the superannuated language of tariffs, was quickly put upon the defensive; and in the general election of 1921 his following in the House was calamitously reduced to fifty. The Liberals, miraculously restored to health and vigour, captured one hundred and seventeen seats. After the apparent break-up of Liberalism only four years before, it was astonishing; and what was perhaps even more astonishing was the success of the Progressives. In the new House they mustered sixty-five, fifteen more than the Conservatives.

V

Yet, surprisingly enough, the peaceful revolution never really arrived. The fact that it did not may be ascribed in part at least to the pacifying presence of the new Prime Minister, W. L. Mackenzie King. King had a settled preference for delay, an ingrained attitude of caution, a sure instinct for patient calculation. His ability to deflate the significance of any situation, to reduce the drama and tension of every episode, to flatten out the ups and downs of politics into a prosaic, unexciting level of monotony was a talent which approached positive genius. He could always find some unexceptionable reason—the burden of war-time debt, the prohibitions of the

constitution, the precarious position of his party in the House—
to justify the postponement of a programme of governmental
regulation and social security. He discovered moreover, as time
went on and he grew more agile in avoiding action, that the
pressure for change, which had seemed so compelling in the
last years of the war and the first of the peace, was rapidly
lessening. The return of prosperity had taken a good deal of
the enthusiasm out of the campaign for the paternal welfare
state; and the Farmer-Progressives, the not too appropriate
leaders of the radical cause, were soon divided by cross-purposes
and bedevilled by conflicts of personalities. In Ontario, the
United Farmers were driven from power after only one term
of office; and in the general federal election of 1925 the Progressives' following fell from sixty-five to twenty-eight seats.
There could be no doubt of it. In domestic politics, Canada was
going back comfortably, uneventfully, to the habits of the past.

Exactly the same thing was happening in foreign affairs.
King, who was in many ways a faithful follower of his old
French-Canadian leader, showed a Laurier-like instinct for
withdrawal from the entanglements of international relations.
It was true, of course, that Sir Robert Borden and his colleagues
had been equally apprehensive of the vast and vague obligations of the Covenant of the League of Nations; and the
attempts of the Liberals to whittle down Canada's commitments under Article X were simply continuations of the previous, very similar efforts of the Conservatives. Borden had dis-
trusted the new collective security system of the League; but
he had instinctively relied upon the old Anglo-Canadian
entente and he had sought to work out a common foreign policy
for the Empire-Commonwealth. King disliked these familiar
imperial associations as much as he disapproved of the international relationships of the League: and the Chanak incident
of 1922 markedly increased his distrust. At Chanak, on the
Dardanelles, advancing Turkish forces came face to face with
British troops guarding the international zone along the straits:
and Great Britain, obliged to take a stand without the advan-

tage of previous consultation with the Dominions, abruptly invited them to give her military support in defending the peace settlement in the Middle East. King replied that the dispatch of a contingent was a matter of such importance that it could be decided only by the Canadian Parliament. The crisis blew over, Parliament was not called; and at the subsequent Conference of Lausanne, where a new settlement with Turkey was negotiated, Canada was not represented and did not consider herself involved. The Chanak incident and its sequel thus gave King an opportunity of announcing, very ostentatiously, Canada's complete withdrawal from British politics in Europe; and in the negotiation of the Halibut Treaty of 1923 for the protection of the halibut fisheries off the Pacific coast, he served blunt notice that Canada had no need for British assistance in its relations with the United States and that henceforth the Dominion would do its own negotiating in North America.

This cautious retreat from the problems of the international order and the welfare state had a suitable tactical diversion in the so-called 'constitutional crisis' of 1926. The general election of 1925 had sharply reduced the strength of the Progressives, slightly cut down the number of Liberals; and it had left the Conservatives the largest single group in the House. King, supported generally by the Progressives, continued to govern, though with difficulty; and in June 1926, when a Conservative motion censuring the scandalous abuses recently revealed in the Department of Customs and Excise was being debated, the Liberal minority government was obviously in great distress. The Prime Minister took the highly unusual step of requesting a dissolution before the termination of the debate; and Lord Byng, the Governor-General, refused. King angrily resigned; Meighen, the Conservative leader, agreed to form a government; but three days later he was defeated by a single vote. The general election which followed was enlivened by several constitutionally righteous sham-battles. King, in his efforts to obtain a dissolution, had tried repeatedly to appeal over the Governor-General's head by urging Lord Byng to communicate with the Secretary of State for the Dominions in Great Britain before reaching a final decision. The Governor-General, who showed a more scrupulous regard for Canadian autonomy than his Prime Minister, declined the advice; but this did not prevent the Liberals from basing a part of their electoral campaign on the charge that Lord Byng's refusal was an insupportable interference by Downing Street in Canadian public affairs.

Yet behind the grandiose humbug of the 'constitutional crisis' and the self-satisfied optimism of the boom, there were other, deeper forces at work. For a quarter-century the Dominion had been going through the painful business of adjusting itself to its new national stature and its new international role. Half-eagerly, half-reluctantly, with impetuous advances and occasional timorous retreats, it had been drawn into the sorry mess of twentieth-century international affairs. It had experienced to the full all the thrilling and agonizing growing-pains of its rapid progress, through the settlement of the west and the development of eastern industry, towards industrial diversification and social and political maturity. Despite the apparent lull in world affairs and the apparent return to old-fashioned normality in domestic politics, the forces which were making the new Canada had by no means ceased to operate. The 'Locarno Spirit' would not diffuse itself beneficently over Europe much longer. The Wheat Pool, that greatest manifestation of the co-operative feeling of the new Canadian West, was to come to grief in the catastrophe of the depression only a few years later. Circumstances were about to change, and change drastically, in the world at large. Circumstances were already changing, more quietly and inconspicuously in Canada. The first quarter of the twentieth century had begun in Canada with the settlement of the west. It was ending in the discovery of the north; and the north was to carry forward the advance towards national maturity one long stage further. It was to be the great new factor in Canadian development. And already it was rousing the interest and firing the imaginations of the Canadians.

War Abroad and Crisis at Home

Perhaps better than anyone else, the painters of the Group of Seven expressed this new northward orientation of the Canadian people. J. E. H. MacDonald, A. Y. Jackson, Arthur Lismer, Lawren Harris, F. H. Varley, Franklin Carmichael and Franz Johnson formed an informal association of artists who did not 'pin a label' on their movement until one of its best-loved and most talented members, Tom Thomson, had died. At the beginning these painters were united simply by a common desire to escape from a 'foreign-begotten technique' and a European way of looking at things; but it was strange how swiftly their purpose of 'making a Canadian statement in art in Canadian terms' carried them out of the cities, and past the gentle landscape of the St. Lawrence valley, and up into the north. They came to realize that inhabited Canada was simply 'a long, thin strip of civilization on the southern fringe of a vast expanse of immensely varied, virgin land'. They found bold contours, sweeping rhythms, massive formations, breathless atmospheric clarity and richness of colour. Alone and in companionable groups, they explored it all—Algonquin Park, Georgian Bay, the Laurentians, Algoma and the Lake Superior country, the Gulf of the St. Lawrence, the Nova Scotian coast, the Rocky Mountains, and the Canadian Arctic. They worked for months in the north, camping out in tents, living in abandoned box-cars and log cabins, travelling about in canoes and railway hand cars, and painting in all weathers and temperatures. They painted boldly, with a technique of great freshness, simplicity, and force, trying to capture the immensity, the ruggedness, and the vividness of the country they had come to love so well.

Their association had been formed before the war. It was resumed with the coming of peace; and in the early 1920's, through annual exhibitions of their work at the Toronto Art Gallery, the Group of Seven became increasingly well known. No movement in Canadian art or literature had ever before aroused so much curiosity, wonder, discussion, and enthusiasm. The poets born in the 1860's—Lampman, Roberts, Scott, and

Carman—had been admired as individuals; the earlier painters—Nicholas Krieghoff, Paul Peel, James Morrice, Homer Watson, A Suzor-Coté, and Clarence Gagnon—had won their reputations in isolation. But here was a purposeful group, a consciously native movement which defiantly proclaimed its Canadianism. It demanded that art should embody the character and spirit of the Canadian scene. Above all, it dramatically called attention to the enormous country which formed most of the Dominion's territorial inheritance, the north. And already the north, with its base and precious metals, its sources of energy and power, its essential components of twentieth-century industrialism, was doing strange things to the Canadian nation.

14

AN END AND A BEGINNING

I

In October 1926, when he sailed to attend the Imperial
Conference in London, the Prime Minister, W. L. Mackenzie King, was in a mood of peculiarly exalted satisfaction. From Belle Isle, in a departing message, he informed the
Canadian people that he proposed to follow a course 'of good
will above all things' at the approaching Conference; and a
few days later, at a dinner given by the Canada Club at the
Savoy Hotel, he declared that there was no man in existence
for whom he felt a warmer personal regard or a deeper affection than for Lord Byng. Admittedly there were several good
and substantial reasons for the Prime Minister's magnanimity.
He had overcome the appalling danger of the customs scandal
with the masterly device of the constitutional crisis. He had
snatched victory from the gaping jaws of defeat. The Governor-
General, whose successor, Lord Willingdon, had already been
announced before the crisis in June, had returned to England
by the end of September. Meighen, who had led the Conservative Party into defeat in the September general election, had
resigned, not merely the office of Prime Minister, but also the
leadership of the Conservative Party; and the most formidable
antagonist of King's political career had in effect been
removed.

King had left one triumph in Canada. He was on his way

to another triumph in the United Kingdom. It was not, of course, in any exclusive sense, his own personal achievement which was about to be completed; he simply happened, by the crowning mercy of that wonderful year of good fortune, 1926, to be once again at the head of affairs when the long labours of his predecessors and himself reached their appointed conclusion. The political theory of the Empire-Commonwealth was about to catch up with its empirical political practice. The Dominions, those new nation states of which Canada was the most conspicuous, were now to have their political maturity openly acknowledged and their autonomy formally announced. Henceforth, as the eloquent sentences of the *Report* of the Imperial Conference of 1926 made abundantly clear, there was to be a new British Commonwealth, a Commonwealth characterized by the three guiding principles of equality of status, freedom of association, and common allegiance to the Crown. The last territorial restrictions, the last unimportant legal limitations, on Canadian sovereignty, annulled in principle by the generalizations of the Report of 1926, were to be abolished in fact by the Statute of Westminster of 1931. The Governors-General of Canada were not in the future to be responsible to the government of the United Kingdom or to any department of that government. They were to be simply and solely representatives of the Crown.

So far at least as Canadian domestic affairs were concerned, the Imperial Conference of 1926 did not do a great deal more than cover practice with theory and convert custom into law. It was in the matter of foreign policy, in the arrangements for diplomatic representation and treaty-making, that the real innovations were made. It was here too that King's own contribution was greatest and his personal views were most clearly apparent. The Imperial Conference of 1923, using the Halibut Treaty as an acceptable precedent, had already provided for the negotiation of bilateral treaties by individual members of the Commonwealth. The Conference of 1926 made similar provision for multilateral treaties, and for Commonwealth representation, by means of one or several separate delegations, at international conferences; and it suggested, using the need of a Canadian mission at Washington as an illustration, that some of the Dominions might soon establish diplomatic representatives abroad. It was a comprehensive and flexible set of arrangements which permitted a wide measure of latitude and a real freedom of choice. Sir Robert Borden would have welcomed the declared principles of the new British Commonwealth just as enthusiastically as King. He would have used its novel machinery in one way. King employed it in an emphatically different fashion.

Borden, to the end of his career, had welcomed close imperial association and worked for a common imperial policy. King was suspicious of both. He disliked the implications of 'centralization'; he feared the commitments of a common front. For him and for two other prominent Liberals, O. D. Skelton, the Deputy Minister of External Affairs, and J. W. Dafoe, the editor of the *Winnipeg Free Press*, both of whom were not uninfluential in the formation of Liberal foreign policy, separation from the foreign policy of the United Kingdom was desirable, in the first place, as the logical completion of Canadian autonomy. It was only slightly less desirable in practice as the one sure means of escaping from the ramifying and dangerous entanglements of British diplomacy. King was determined to use the diplomatic machinery devised for the new Commonwealth to effect Canada's final liberation from these perilous toils. Laurier had followed the negative method of avoiding imperial commitments. King would pursue the positive course of a separate Canadian foreign policy. He had no intention, of course, of setting up a large-scale network of Canadian missions abroad; it would be foolish and dangerous to commence in such a grandiose fashion. But a sensible beginning could be made by sending representatives to a few of the countries with which Canada had important relations, and by gradually strengthening the Department of External Affairs at Ottawa. In the years 1927-9 the first Canadian missions abroad were

An End and a Beginning

established in Washington, Paris, and Tokyo; and in Ottawa the Department, which was only twenty years old in 1929, began to recruit the able staff which was to serve it so efficiently for the next quarter-century.

The year 1928 provided a most imposing public occasion for the ostentatious display of the nature of the new British Commonwealth, the international status of the new Canada, and the separateness of the new Canadian foreign policy. That summer the General Treaty for the Renunciation of War as an instrument of national policy—the 'Briand-Kellogg Pact'— was to be signed in Paris; and King hastened in person to take advantage of this favourable diplomatic opportunity. He crossed the ocean in the *Ile de France*, in the company of Frank B. Kellogg, the joint author of the treaty, a gratifying circumstance which inspired reflections on the peaceful accord of the North American continent. In Paris, in the Salle des Horloges, on the Quai d'Orsay, King savoured to the full the pleasant sensations, which only one Canadian Prime Minister, Sir Robert Borden, had previously experienced, of signing a great international agreement in brilliant surroundings and in the presence of delegates from nearly fifteen of Canada's new sovereign peers. From Paris King proceeded to Geneva, where he took part in the deliberations in the Council of the League of Nations, for Canada had been elected to one of the non-permanent seats in 1927. In the League Assembly, which opened immediately after, in September, he delivered an edifying talk on the undefended boundary between Canada and the United States as an illustration of the spirit of the Briand-Kellogg Pact. Only three years later the peace of the Versailles and Washington Treaties was to be broken. But King, like so many others, detected no sign of the approaching rupture. His satisfaction was unruffled. In his view there was not a cloud in the sky.

An End and a Beginning

The economic horizon presented the same appearance of prosperous serenity. The economy which was to totter with such sickening suddenness in October 1929 stood with what seemed unshakeable stability. King, R. B. Bennett, the new leader of the Opposition, Liberals, Conservatives, manufacturers, urban workers, grain growers—everybody—had the utmost confidence in the continuance of prosperity. Prosperity was the natural, normal condition of the Canadian economy; and the Canadian economy had reached its final perfected form in the exploitation of the grain-producing prairies and in the solid achievement of the east-west axis. It was true that the development of the north and the rise of twentieth-century industrialism were producing strange, lucrative, but also disturbing cross-currents in this great principal movement of Canadian growth; but these, however interesting, seemed as yet to be not much more than eddies in the main stream. The west had made a prosperous and united Canada. The west was continuing to ensure a prosperous and united Canada. There had, it was true, been a brief, unhappy moment of hesitation and uncertainty in the early 1910's and again in the early 1920's. But in each case the economy had quickly and splendidly recovered and the familiar onward march had been resumed along the familiar transcontinental east-west lines. The boom in which the golden torrent of wheat had been the main enriching force, had lasted now for nearly thirty years. Was there any reason to feel that it would not continue indefinitely? Prices for wheat were good. Population increased and settlement expanded on the prairies. Canada's share of the export market in wheat shot up to approximately 50 per cent; and the Wheat Pool, a large collective enterprise organized by the western farmers on a voluntary contract basis for the orderly and unspeculative marketing of the wheat crop, stood at the height of its confidence and power.

An End and a Beginning

Yet within this familiar and popular drama of Canadian development, which was still playing to crowded and enthusiastic houses, there were a number of increasingly distracting sub-plots. The original national economic unity, which had been planned after Confederation and achieved in the first decades of the twentieth century, was now threatened, not merely by the inherent precariousness of the world market for wheat, but also by the rapid advance of new developments in the Canadian economy itself. The old economic internationalism, based on regional specialization and an efficient division of the world's labour force, was obviously yielding before the upsurge of economic nationalism; and Canada itself, an excellent specific example of the new assertive tendency, was moving still more rapidly forward to greater diversification and greater industrial maturity. The enormous possibilities of hydro-electric power in the nation's youthful and turbulent river system, the aluminium, nickel, and other base metal resources which lay hidden in such huge quantities in the complex ore-bodies of the Precambrian Shield, were making the Dominion richer and much better adjusted to the industrialism of the twentieth century.

The economy grew stronger and more diversified; but, at the same time, its new trades and industries were steadily qualifying and complicating the old, simple economic unity. The opening of the Panama Canal, the growth of the port of Vancouver, the construction of a great network of paved highways, and the immense development of gasoline-motor traffic by road, river, and airway, all helped to reduce the importance of the old transcontinental railways. The wheat of the west had moved eastward to Montreal and across the ocean; but the staple products of the new north mainly found their way southward to the capricious and uncertain markets of the United States. The west had promoted national unity; but more and more the north seemed to encourage regional diversity, provincial inequality; and Alberta, Saskatchewan, and the Maritime Provinces had to look enviously on while Ontario, Quebec,

British Columbia, and to some extent Manitoba reaped the chief benefits of the developments of the 1920's. Some of the provinces, in their own right, had become powerful economies. They began to play an increasingly important part in the social and economic life of the post-war world.

The rise of the provinces was the obverse side of the apparent decline of the Dominion. In international relations and especially in the politics of the British Commonwealth, the Dominion certainly maintained its role of confident leadership; but in domestic affairs its air of preponderating authority had just as definitely vanished. In a series of crucial decisions in the early 1920's the Judicial Committee of the Privy Council had flatly and firmly declared that the vast expansion of federal powers which had taken place during the War of 1914–18 was constitutionally justified only by the emergency of war time and must cease with it. The formidable barriers of the constitution fenced the Dominion out of the dangerous but politically attractive fields of economic control and social welfare; and King, whose traditional Liberalism was qualified mainly by a benevolently theoretical feeling of social obligation, retreated behind these limitations with alacrity. The federal government sponsored a provincially administered system of old age pensions and contributed substantially to its support; but apart from this it ostentatiously declined to have anything to do with the new social services. An obvious constitutional vacuum was created into which the provinces—particularly the wealthier provinces —rushed with conviction and vigour. They were developing their resources, improving their services, assisting their people, assuming a bewildering variety of new functions and responsibilities; and during the 1920's their total governmental expenditures exactly doubled.

Then, with significant but unheeded warnings, came the stock market collapse of October 1929. The economy, caught off balance by the repeated shocks of that autumn, slid slowly and protestingly down the long decline of the depression. In the period 1929–33 the value of the world's export trade, in which Canada then gained over one-third of its national income, declined by nearly 50 per cent. The prices of the nation's staple raw materials, which still constituted about two-thirds of these vital exports, were particularly hard hit; and it was the primary producers and, above all, the grain growers in the western prairies, where the misfortunes of falling prices and contracting markets were accompanied by the calamities of drought, soil drifting, wheat rust, and repeated crop failures, who bore relatively the heaviest burden of the depression. The coming of the slump not only ended the thirty prosperous years of the 'wheat boom'; it also brought down a ragged, sombre curtain on wheat's long primacy in the Dominion's affairs. Wheat was the last—and the greatest—of the Canadian single export specialties, whose history had begun long ago when Champlain first sailed up the 'River of Canada' to barter furs with the Indians; and with the passing of wheat's old predominance, the nation passed definitely from one economic age to another. The depression was at once the last agony of the old industrialism and the first crisis of the new. It raised political as well as social and economic problems. What remedies would a free-enterprise society use to cure its trouble? And how were they to be applied in a federal state?

At first it seemed certain that only the most safely traditional methods would be considered and that they would be carried out with the most conservatively scrupulous regard for the niceties of the federal constitution. The fact that the care of 'hospitals, asylums, charities, and eleemosynary institutions' had been enumerated among the powers of the provinces at Confederation had always appeared to King as an argument of conclusive finality. During the slump of the early 1920's he had insisted that unemployment was the concern of the municipalities and provinces and not of the federal government. During the angry debate on unemployment in the session of 1930 he was still sheltering himself behind the increasingly artificial limits of the constitution; and, in a moment of blazing indiscretion, he enormously exaggerated the error of his evasion of responsibility by declaring furiously that even if his government might give financial assistance to some provinces for unemployment relief, it would not give 'a five-cent piece' to any Conservative provincial government in the country.

It was easy for Richard Bedford Bennett, the new Conservative leader, to argue that unemployment had ceased to be simply municipal or provincial in scope and had assumed truly national proportions. It was relatively easy for him to make the unemployment problem the major issue of the general election of 1930. It was not too difficult, in the circumstances, to win the election, though not by any huge majority, on the confident boast that he would 'blast his way' into the markets of the world. The explosive metaphor was well suited to a person of his vehement energy. He was a tall, portly, solemn, vigorous man, devoted to his country's interests, earnest and utterly sincere in all he did, with a purposeful will to achieve, and an enormous confidence in his own powers. He treated the government of Canada as if it were a single public department under his own exclusive guidance. He rated his colleagues and lectured his followers like a domineering pedagogue and harangued the House with a torrential and overpowering eloquence. Zeal, determination, wilful purpose—all the youthful qualities were there in large quantities; but, on the whole, the policies they served were venerably traditional. It was true that he was ready to spend public money with a Keynesian generosity which shocked that still old-fashioned financier King; but his sharp increases in the Canadian tariff, and the preferential agreements which he negotiated at the Imperial Economic Conference held in Ottawa in 1932, were measures of unimpeachable fiscal orthodoxy. Bennett had, in fact, fallen back upon the past—upon the old Conservative policy of protection and the still older policy of imperial preference.

The Canadians watched all this with rapidly increasing restlessness and misgiving. Their mood, like that of most other westerners in the early 1930's, was one of impatient discontent and readiness for radical experimentation; but this general leftward movement, common to the whole English-speaking world, was not the only, nor perhaps the deepest, current in the thought of Canadian public men, scholars, journalists, and writers at that time. Like so many others, the Canadian critics were holding up to sharp inspection, if not to ridicule, the economic system, the political order, the social structure, the philosophy, morality, art, and literature of their own day and the immediate past. They were doing all this in much the same ways as their fellows in other parts of the English-speaking world; but they were doing something else as well. They were revolting not only against a system, an age, a fashion, or a convention; they were also revolting against their entire agrarian and colonial past. In a period when, for really the first time, their consciousness of maturity had been strengthened by every obvious circumstance of their position and by the open or tacit acknowledgements of the rest of the world, they could look upon the past and present with the perceptions of knowledge and experience. The idealism, the hope, the naïve simplicity, the simple-minded uncritical acceptance with which the Canadians had viewed their long career of hard work and direct action and material success, had at length been succeeded by an attitude of critical realism.

It was perhaps in journalism and literature that this new mood of anger, sophistication, irony, satire, and critical objectivity found its clearest expression. The revolt against colonial Victorianism sometimes took the form of direct contemptuous attacks upon such poets as Lampman and his contemporaries; but it was even better exemplified in the new and much wider range of themes and styles which the younger writers were exploiting. E. J. Pratt, the most important of the new generation of poets, was finding his subjects in the familiar sources of nature, Canadian history, and contemporary heroism and drama; but the smooth serenity and the vague diffuse philosophizing of much of the work of the poets of the late nineteenth and early twentieth century were lost in his terser, more concentrated style, his sharper, more contemporary images, his complex, shifting variety of moods. In his sombre novels of the western prairies, Frederick Philip Grove was painting a picture of pioneer farming very different from that of the facile, hopeful romances of previous decades; and Hugh MacLennan and Morley Callaghan were finding themes, barely discoverable for Canadians of a previous generation, in the life of the ports and cities of eastern and central Canada. Satiric poets such as F. R. Scott and L. A. MacKay were enlivening the pages of the new magazines, the *Canadian Mercury* and the *Canadian Forum*, with amusingly acid comments on the contemporary scene.

It was in these highly favourable circumstances, when the nation was revelling in a new intellectual freedom and experimentally trying out its powers with a new-found confidence, that the protest movement of the 1930's gathered strength and speed. It was an attack both against free enterprise, which no longer seemed able to provide a good living out of the bounty of Canadian nature, and against nineteenth-century Canadian federalism which had left the Dominion with restricted functions and the provinces with crushing responsibilities, and appeared incapable of performing the tasks of government which the twentieth century required. In the provinces a series of electoral upsets brought new governments, and sometimes completely new parties, such as the *Union Nationale* in Quebec, and Social Credit in Alberta, to power; and in the federal field, a new third party, the Co-operative Commonwealth Federation, which combined the agrarian radicalism of the Progressives with the urban socialism of British Labour, came into existence in 1932–3. The language of the social service state grew more fashionable. Keynesian economics gained in authority. The reform of the Canadian constitution became a popular game in which politicians, lawyers, historians, and economists joined with enthusiasm.

An End and a Beginning

On the 2nd January 1935, as if to emphasize the fact that the New Year was to be one of long-awaited reform and happily restored well-being, the Prime Minister of Canada addressed his fellow citizens in the first of five radio broadcasts to the nation. This new and ingratiating technique of taking an entire people into a political leader's confidence had, of course, become fairly familiar by this time; Franklin D. Roosevelt, the new President of the United States, had employed it with striking success in his 'fireside chats'. But the Canadians had never before heard the method used on such a scale, and for such an obviously important purpose, by one of their own statesmen. Bennett, as he faced the microphone, seemed full of his old superb confidence. His voice was earnest, magisterial, admonitory, yet beneficently purposeful and warmly encouraging. The time had come, he declared in the first broadcast, for a radical change in the policy of the government. Unrestricted capitalism, a Liberal doctrine which people like King defended, must be cured of the faults which permitted the few to exploit it to the disadvantage of the many. How it could best be corrected and reformed was a problem for which he had evolved a satisfactory answer; and in the four broadcasts which followed he proceeded to describe in detail the labour statutes, economic controls, and social security measures of which his reforming programme was composed.

It was Bennett's most magnificent piece of political audacity. Time was running out. The existing Parliament had only a little over six more months to go; and nobody knew better than the Prime Minister how great was the likelihood of his defeat in the approaching general election. In the past four years everything, both nationally and internationally, had gone from bad to worse. The deepening distress of the depression in Canada had been matched by the steady deterioration of international affairs. The Japanese invasion of Manchuria had for the first time broken the peace and the post-war settlement; and the impunity with which the aggressors in the Far East had defied world opinion was an all too obvious encouragement to attacks against the collective security system in western Europe. In Germany the mendicant adventurer from Munich had confirmed his grasp on political power by the slaughter of the political purge of the summer of 1934; and in Italy Mussolini was obviously intent upon bringing on a crisis in his relations with Abyssinia. The primitive political conditions which were rapidly thrusting their way up through the elaborate organization of world government were beginning to frighten many. Abroad, it looked as if the danger of armed aggression might be real, as if the post-war settlement might fail after all.

At home, the outward aspect of affairs was even more ominous. Unless some desperate final effort could retrieve its fortunes, the failure of the Bennett government seemed foregone and its defeat inevitable. Yet it had already acted earnestly and energetically. Disdaining to use its limited constitutional obligations as a justification for parsimony or inaction, the Dominion had rushed to rescue the provincial governments overwhelmed with the burden of unemployment relief. The huge sums of money—unconditional subsidies, loans, grants-in-aid—which the federal government had made available had saved the weaker provinces from bankruptcy and the people of Canada from the worst physical distress. The Conservative palliatives had been applied on a most generous scale; but the Conservative cures had been strikingly old fashioned and singularly ineffective; and with the prestige of the National Recovery Administration rising in the United States and the Co-operative Commonwealth Federation (C.C.F.) extolling the cause of social planning in Canada, the popular demand for a modern and positive attack on the depression became almost irresistible.

Bennett was disposed to yield to it. From the days of Sir John Macdonald the Conservatives had often shown a readiness and an ability to use the power of the state daringly and imaginatively in the general interest. The *laissez-faire* Liberals of the nineteenth century had looked on aghast while Macdonald had resolutely carried out his national policies. What was to prevent Bennett from devising a new national programme for the industrial Canada of the twentieth century and thus picking up the gauntlet of challenge flung down by Woodsworth and the C.C.F. before the timid King could make up his mind to venture forward? Politically it was a tempting prospect. It might even be an act of wise and necessary statesmanship. Some of Bennett's closest advisers counselled him to take the adventurous course; and the fact that the Judicial Committee of the Privy Council, apparently reversing the previous trend of interpretation, had in two recent crucial cases given the Dominion authority over radio broadcasting and airways, seemed to suggest that the way of daring might be constitutionally feasible. An agreement for the revision of the British North America Act with provinces, most of which were politically opposed to the Dominion, was clearly impossible. But was it necessary? Characteristically, Bennett decided to push forward alone. In the name of the national emergency he would make a frontal attack upon the constitution.

For a while it looked as if he might succeed. The legislation of the Bennett 'New Deal'—three statutes based on the draft conventions of the International Labour Organization, an Employment and Social Insurance Act, a revised Natural Products Marketing Act, and amendments to the Criminal Code, the Companies Act, and the Farmers' Creditors Arrangement Act—were pushed through the House during the session of 1935 against only relatively feeble and embarrassed opposition. Despite the serious breakdown in his own health, Bennett seemed for the moment to have regained the initiative and recovered political strength. But this last-minute conversion of a man who, both personally and politically, had seemed for so long to embody the very antithesis of the doctrine he was now proclaiming, was too much for the Canadians. The 'New Deal' lost Bennett the allegiance of many veteran supporters without gaining the support of even a few declared enemies. The bulk of the electors remained suspicious of the sincerity of the Conservatives and doubtful of the wisdom of the Socialists. They wanted something benevolently forward-looking but eminently safe. They chose King; and in October 1935 King was swept back again into power by a comfortably satisfying majority.

At once there was a slackening of pace which became a pause for prudent reflection and reconsideration. The nation was slowly led back again into the safe, the middle way. Extravagant and ill-considered adventures in domestic politics had been tacitly condemned by the results of the general election; and—as the fate of the proposed oil sanctions against Italy clearly proved—dangerous heroics abroad could be repudiated even more completely and unequivocally by the new government. In the early days of October, when the Canadian election was roaring to its conclusion, the League of Nations had declared Italy guilty of aggression against Abyssinia; and G. Howard Ferguson, the Canadian High Commissioner in London and the leader of Canada's delegation to the Assembly, had urged the League to show the world that it meant business and would no longer be scoffed or laughed at. Ferguson, whose appointment to London was a political one, retired as soon as the results of the election were known; but his successor, W. A. Riddell, Canada's permanent representative at Geneva, who believed that the new King Cabinet had authorized a strong policy of resistance to Italian aggression, took the initiative in proposing the imposition of sanctions on the key commodities of oil, coal, iron, and steel. On December 1st Riddell was repudiated by the Canadian Government. The Canadian Government announced that the Riddell proposal represented merely Riddell's own personal opinion and not the views of the government of Canada. All efforts, creditable and discreditable, to stop Mussolini failed miserably. The League died of this final exhibition of its shameful powerlessness; and in September 1936, when King himself headed the Canadian delegation to the Assembly, he pronounced a typically Canadian panegyric over the corpse. Canada had never accepted the political commitments of the Covenant; she now repudiated the economic commitments. She was free.

In domestic politics it was not necessary to resort to the extreme measure of repudiation; it was only necessary to mark time. The twin problems of capitalism and federalism, of the welfare state and the Canadian constitution, had been given concrete form in the famous test cases of the Bennett 'New Deal'; and it was not until 1937 that the Judicial Committee of the Privy Council finally delivered its judgment on the validity of the legislation. Bennett, who held the natural assumption that the national Parliament of a great state ought to be able to deal with a great national emergency, had tried to justify his controversial statutes by appealing both to the Dominion's residuary authority to legislate for the peace, order, and good government of Canada, and to its enumerated powers to regulate trade and commerce and to implement the nation's treaty obligations. In the event, his hopes were completely falsified. The fond assumptions which he and others had built on the airways and radio broadcasting cases proved entirely illusory. The gradual and systematic transformation of the Canadian constitution, which had been begun by Lord Watson and Lord Haldane, was now majestically completed by their successors in the Judicial Committee of the Privy Council. Virtually the whole of the Bennett 'New Deal' was declared to be *ultra vires* of the Parliament of Canada. The frontal attack upon the constitution had failed. The more deliberate approach, beloved by King, was obviously required; a thorough and impartial investigation of the nature of the constitutional problem was an essential preliminary to all action; and in 1937 a Royal Commission on Dominion-Provincial Relations was appointed to examine the suitability of the division of powers at Confederation in the light of the economic and social changes of the past seventy-five years. King surveyed the future with confidence. The Commission could not possibly report for a year or two; and, in the meantime, the depression was slowly but unmistakably lifting.

An End and a Beginning

It was very different abroad. If the air was perceptibly lightening in Canada, it was darkening swiftly and angrily in Europe. And in this atmosphere of rising tension and danger, Canada stood apart in an attitude of deliberately non-committal detachment. Her obligations to both the Commonwealth and the League of Nations had been repudiated; and, although she had insisted on her autonomy and her diplomatic separateness, she made no attempt to control events herself or even to arm effectively for her own defence. The Canadian people, though they were at one in their concern and apprehension for the future, were far from unanimous about Canada's proper course; and King, who wished above all to reconcile their differences and preserve their unity, stubbornly refused to give anything but the most tentative and hesitating lead. It was not until the early spring of 1939, after the final extinction of Czechoslovakia, that he publicly recognized Canada's inability to stand aside if Great Britain were directly and violently attacked. He promised that there would be no conscription for overseas service; he went so far as to scout the idea of a Canadian expeditionary force being sent to Europe; and, as late as the last summer of the peace, he was still repeating that, when the moment of crisis came, the Canadian Parliament would make its decision in the light of all the existing circumstances, domestic and foreign. It was in this unreal atmosphere of inaction, evasion, and illusion, that the Canadian people approached September 1939. The real, the vital decisions had already been made in the privacy of their own hearts and minds.

13. The Parliament Buildings of Canada and the Ottawa River, with pulp-wood logs for the paper industry in the foreground

14. Oil derrick in the prairies

15

TRIAL BY BATTLE

I

'Que Dieu bénisse le Canada!' They were the words which Queen Elizabeth had spoken in a last farewell to the Canadian people as she and King George VI sailed from Halifax at the end of their Dominion-wide tour in the early summer of 1939. They were the words echoed by Ernest Lapointe, King's principal French-Canadian associate, in the eloquent conclusion of his speech in the brief session of the Canadian Parliament which, nearly three months later, authorized Canada's entrance into the Second World War.

It was not until September 7th, four days after the British declaration of war against Germany, that Parliament met. Even then, at the moment of decision, King's policy retained much of its old aspect of indefiniteness and ambiguity. Not until September 9th, the second day of the debate, did he announce that the passage of the Address in reply to the Speech from the Throne would be followed by an immediate declaration of war against the German Reich; and his frequent references to economic co-operation with Great Britain, and the brief phrases in which he appeared still to scout the idea of a Canadian expeditionary force, all suggested a limited and partial participation. Yet the cautious determination with which King sought to avoid any 'hasty or premature pronouncement' was balanced by the warm advocacy with which

Lapointe supported the government's policy once it had been unequivocally announced. Lapointe was a lawyer; and much of what he had to say was a lawyer's brief proving the impossibility of neutrality to his French-Canadian fellow citizens. But there was much more in his speech than this. He began by reminding the members of the House that their King was at war and that they were there to decide whether they would make his cause their own; he ended by recalling Queen Elizabeth's last farewell, in French, to the Canadians, 'Que Dieu bénisse le Canada. . . . Yes, God bless Canada. . . . God save Canada's honour, Canada's soul, Canada's dignity, Canada's conscience.'

Late that Saturday night the address was voted. Later still the cables carried the decision of Canada's Parliament to Canada's King in London. On Sunday, September 10th, King George formally gave his approval to the Proclamation declaring that 'a state of war with the German Reich exists and has existed in our Dominion of Canada as and from the tenth day of September, 1939'; and on Monday morning the Canadian people awoke to the knowledge that, once again, for the second time in a quarter-century, it was at war with Germany. A nation that could be warlike enough on occasion, and yet was on the whole profoundly unmilitary by tradition, Canada was extremely badly prepared for the ordeal which lay ahead. The armed services were just beginning to be rescued from the state of irresponsible neglect in which they had lain so long; and for the past few years the Canadian people had been persistently deluded by the evident assumption of the authorities at Ottawa that for Canada the next war would certainly be a 'limited-liability' war. There were serious material deficiencies and mental obstacles; there was the false, delusive calm of the 'phony' war; but, even so, the Canadians came to grips with the realities of their position with surprising quickness. In December the government signed an agreement with Great Britain, Australia, and New Zealand to set up an extensive Commonwealth Air Training Plan in Canada and to contribute four-fifths of its trainees; and in the same month the first of the three 'flights' of ships which were to carry the First Division of the Canadian Army to Great Britain sailed from Halifax.

With King's cautious support, rather than his resolute leadership, the Canadians had moved a surprisingly long distance in a few weeks. But the policy which the Dominion had adopted, active and direct, yet sensible and realistic in character, was essentially a typically Canadian 'middle-of-the-road' policy which could be readily attacked from the two traditional Canadian extremes. On the one hand, Maurice Duplessis, the Premier of Quebec, denounced Canada's participation in an imperialistic war which threatened the autonomy of his Province; and on the other, Mitchell Hepburn, the Premier of Ontario, deplored the feeble inadequacy of the federal government's effort in a conflict which the Canadian people wished to be waged with the utmost vigour. Duplessis obligingly went to the country in a provincial general election, was attacked in full force by the federal Liberals, and was resoundingly defeated. Hepburn was not so accommodating; but the electoral trial of strength which he showed no signs of seeking in the provincial field King determined to bring on in the nation as a whole. He obtained a dissolution from the Governor-General; and the eighteenth Parliament of Canada was abruptly ended on the very day on which its sixth and last session had commenced. The 'Addled Parliament' of James I, which passed no statutes, had its burlesque analogy in the 'addled parliamentary session' of Mackenzie King, which did not even resume its proceedings after the first day's dinner recess. Yet this unceremonious dismissal of Parliament did not disturb the satisfied equanimity of the Canadian electorate; and, in the general election which followed towards the end of March, the Liberal government was easily returned and with a slightly larger majority than before.

It was not a domestic farce, but an overseas tragedy, which finally shook the Canadian war effort out of its deliberate pro-

gress, and the Canadian people out of its complacent contentment. On April 9th, exactly a fortnight after the general
election, the invasion of Denmark and Norway began; and in
the next two months the German armies swept with appalling
swiftness and violent efficiency over the whole of north-western
Europe. Denmark, Norway, Belgium, and the Netherlands
were occupied and disarmed; and France, her army out-
generalled and out-fought, her people divided and demoralized,
abjectly surrendered. While the rest of the world looked on in
stunned silence and apprehensive inaction, the nations of the
British Commonwealth, Great Britain, Canada, Australia,
New Zealand, and South Africa, continued alone to bear the
enormous burden of the struggle against Hitler's Germany;
and Canada, which only a year before had been debating
whether she would ever again send an expeditionary force
across the Atlantic, suddenly discovered herself to be the
second power engaged in a major European War. A generation
before, with the best will in the world, she would not have been
able to play the part which had been so suddenly thrust upon
her; but in the meantime her swift advance to political and
industrial maturity had made it possible for her to undertake
tasks which beleaguered Great Britain was now unable, and
the neutral United States still unwilling, to perform. The
Dominion rapidly reorganized its war-time machinery of
government, immediately and vastly increased the size of its
armed services, and began the production, on a grand scale,
of almost all the materials and equipment of modern, mechan-
ized warfare. For a whole year, from June 1940 to June 1941,
Canada was Great Britain's senior ally.

It was a highly significant position—a position which neither
Canada nor any other Dominion had ever occupied before. It
might have led to a new kind of Commonwealth co-operation.
In the War of 1914–18 the old Anglo-Canadian alliance, extended for the first time to Europe, had taken institutional
form in the Imperial War Cabinet and the Imperial War Conference; and in the desperate crisis of 1940–1, Canada obviously

deserved a position of even greater authority and influence than that which she had occupied in these old war-time bodies. If King had wished to do so he might have insisted upon the creation of a Commonwealth Council, or frequent and regular conferences of Commonwealth Prime Ministers, which would have given Canada an appropriate voice in the political and military control of the war in Europe as well as valuable support in the negotiation of defence arrangements in North America. But King, whose mind harked back to the colonial projects and controversies of the days of Joseph Chamberlain, regarded all formal association with Great Britain as potential 'imperial centralization'. He was quite prepared, in order to avoid dangerous political contact with a nation in whose company Canada was in fact fighting a great war, to let Great Britain direct the war in Europe alone. He was quite convinced that he could negotiate successfully, alone, with the United States; and in August 1940, at Ogdensburg, on the American side of the St. Lawrence, he proceeded to do so with ready compliance. Repeatedly, in the past, he had declared that his government would make no commitments—above all, no permanent commitments—without the concurrence of Parliament; but now, on August 18th, after only a single night's reflection, he announced, with President Roosevelt, the establishment of a Permanent Joint Board on Defence for the North American continent.

If Canada could make unilateral defence arrangements with the United States, so could Great Britain, as the 'destroyers for bases' deal, announced on August 20th, two days after the Ogdensburg Agreement, clearly proved. This extremely hard bargain, by which Great Britain, in her desperate necessity, was obliged to cede the keys of the Atlantic in return for fifty quickly built, not very seaworthy, and largely obsolescent American destroyers, directly affected Canada, for bases in Newfoundland, as well as in Bermuda and the West Indies, were included in the deal. Ever since the delegates from Newfoundland had arrived for the Quebec Conference in the autumn of 1864, Canada had hoped and believed that the outpost island would some day become a province of the Dominion; and in his speech in the House in September 1939, on the eve of the declaration of war, King had declared that the integrity of Newfoundland and Labrador was essential to the security of Canada. But now, though the matter was of supreme importance for Canada's future territorial sovereignty, the Canadian government proved either unwilling or unable to prevent or to modify the grant of the ninety-nine-year Newfoundland lease-holds to the United States.

The Dominion was forced to stand by, a dissatisfied and disgruntled onlooker, while this transaction was completed. She was being gradually shouldered aside by the great nation which, while still neutral, was participating indirectly but forcefully through the device of Lend-Lease and the policy of 'all aid short of war'. Canada was not even invited—for nobody apparently considered the presence of Great Britain's senior English-speaking ally either desirable or necessary—to the dramatic meeting off Newfoundland in August 1941, which ended in the publication of the Atlantic Charter. It was only after this that Mackenzie King, as if to prove that the Prime Minister of Canada could also talk personally to the Prime Minister of the United Kingdom, hurried off, for literally the first time since the war had begun, to London. Even then he apparently made no attempt to insist upon a place and a voice for Canada in the making of policy; and by that time, in any case, it was probably too late. In June, Russia had already entered the war; the United States was to be precipitated into it in December. And Canada, who for a year had been the second power engaged in the conflict, became the submissive satellite of the Big Three.

II

In the spring of 1942 the Canadian people was asked whether it was prepared to free its government from the obligations of a famous promise, firmly but incautiously given. 'Are you in favour', the electorate was asked in an unparliamentary inquiry by plebiscite on April 27th, 'of releasing the government from any obligations arising out of any past commitments restricting the methods of raising men for military service?' The commitment, that there would be no conscription for overseas service, had been made before the war, confirmed at the first war-time session in September 1939, and confirmed again at the time of the provincial election in Quebec. The pledge had even, to make the matter doubly sure, been given solid statutory expression in Clause Three of the National Resources Mobilization Act. Yet now the government, confronted by the insatiable demands of total war, the ceaseless pressure of the opposition, and the anxious dissatisfaction of the citizens, was already beginning to chafe in embarrassment at the restrictions of its own promise.

It was the year 1942—the year in which the Grand Alliance recovered from surprise and defeat and regained the initiative. Already the search for manpower was growing steadily in intensity. Already, although it was obvious that the greatest efforts and the most costly ordeals lay in the future, the nation had accomplished much and undertaken more. With the assistance of the United States, great chains of bases for air transport from fortress North America to the eastern and western theatres of war had been constructed; and the Royal Canadian Navy, with its fleet of agile destroyers, corvettes, motor torpedo boats, and minesweepers, had taken over much of the perilous task of protecting the precious Atlantic convoys against the German submarine campaign. A hundred thousand young recruits had crowded into the Royal Canadian Air Force; and in January the Prime Minister had announced the creation oversea of a Canadian Army of two Army Corps— there had only been one in the War of 1914–18. The Canadians had made part of the vain sacrifice which ended in the surrender of Hong Kong on Christmas Day of 1941; and they were soon to bear most of the appalling losses of the frontal attack on Dieppe which was launched in the grey morning of the tragic 19th of August 1942.

It was in the light of these circumstances that the Canadian people considered the plebiscite of April 27th. The nation as a whole voted 64 to 36 per cent in support of the government's release from its commitments. In Quebec, to be sure, the vote was 72 to 28 per cent against the removal of the restrictions; but, in all the rest of Canada, it was 80 to 20 per cent in favour. The government obediently introduced legislation removing the limitations on conscription for overseas service from the National Resources Mobilization Act; but at the moment it made no use of its new negative freedom to make any positive changes in the conditions of mobilization. In the jingling formula of King, the policy of the government was 'not necessarily conscription, but conscription if necessary'. And yet, as the Grand Alliance recaptured the offensive everywhere and as the losses and ordeals which alone could achieve victory drew close, the time for these obvious evasions and delays was rapidly coming to an end. The Canadian Government, pressed by the acute national sense of inactivity and frustration to put a part at least of the Canadian Army into the allied attacks now opening up, was itself shortening the period in which postponement of policy would be possible. Before dawn on the 10th July 1943, while the long rollers of the Mediterranean crashed on the beaches and rocked the landing craft, the men of the First Division went ashore at the 'Amber Coast' near Pachino, Sicily. All during the hard autumn and winter that followed, the Canadians, now enlarged to the dimensions of a Corps, fought their difficult way up the Italian peninsula; and late in May 1944 their successful assault on the Adolf Hitler Line was the first stage in the great battle which ended only a few days later in the fall of Rome.

Two days after Rome fell, when the long and anxiously planned invasion of north-western Europe descended at last like an avalanche, other Canadians, the men of the Third Infantry Division, were racing across the beaches of the Bay of

Seine towards the strong points of the enemy's Atlantic Wall. Placed in the centre of the Second British Army's front, the Canadians formed part of that impregnable pivot which the massed German armoured divisions tried in vain to crack and upon which the American right wing of Montgomery's forces swung forward swiftly in a wide encircling sweep to the south and east. The First Canadian Army crashed its way into Falaise and struggled to close the gap through which the trapped German Armies were desperately seeking to escape from the cauldron of their encirclement. The shattering allied victory in the Battle of Normandy sent the Wehrmacht reeling back across north-western Europe and the British, American, and Canadian forces speeding after them in swift pursuit. General Crerar's Army entered Dieppe in triumph and swept up the Channel coast; and then, as the German front reformed and stiffened in resistance, the Canadians settled down to that grim, protracted advance, past fortified dikes, canals, and flooded fields, which ended in the occupation of the Scheldt estuary and in the freeing of the port of Antwerp.

The losses of the Normandy bridgehead, of Caen, Falaise, and the Scheldt estuary did not stand alone. To them were added those other losses which the First Canadian Corps, still with the Eighth Army in Italy, had suffered as it drove up the Adriatic Coast towards the plains of Lombardy. It was these casualties, the heavy price of invasion, advance, and victory, that precipitated the political crisis which everybody in Canada had expected or feared since the beginning of the war and which most people had hoped and tried to avoid. Reinforcements were necessary to recruit the depleted and exhausted Canadian forces in Europe; but where, in the face of declining voluntary enlistments, were those reinforcements to be got? Over sixty thousand troops had been called up and were available for service in Canada; and, after the plebiscite and the amendment of the National Resources Mobilization Act, it had been perfectly possible for the government to employ these men, not only for home defence, but also for overseas service. Was this the desperate moment when that solemnly granted permission must be acted upon? Colonel J. L. Ralston, the Minister of Defence, flew to Europe, visited the Canadian forces in Italy and the Netherlands, learnt the full disquieting story of their losses and necessities, and flew back again to Ottawa, bearing with him the grievous burden of a firm resolve. For him the famous phrase 'not necessarily conscription, but conscription if necessary' was not a comforting formula but a definite promise for which the condition had now been unquestionably met. On the 19th October 1944 he proposed to the War Committee of the Cabinet that conscription for overseas service should be enforced and that fifteen thousand men recruited under the National Resources Mobilization Act should be dispatched at once to reinforce the Canadian Army in Europe.

For over a month the government and the nation moved protestingly, tortuously, but apparently inevitably towards a major political crisis. King believed that conscription would destroy Canada's war-time concord and damage its future unity irremediably; he was determined to avoid the extreme measure of compulsion—and to demonstrate publicly that he had tried to avoid it—by every means in his power. Time might be consumed, effort wasted, consistency abandoned, reputations injured, and careers ruined; but at all costs—or nearly all costs—the simple, straightforward, and unforgettable decision must not be taken. For ten days the Cabinet fruitlessly debated the Defence Minister's proposal and argued over the manpower figures; and then, on November 1st, the argument was ended without warning when King suddenly decided to take advantage of the resignation which Ralston had submitted two years before. Ralston's withdrawal was the first sacrifice made to the unity of the government and the unifying policy of voluntaryism; and a new Minister of Defence, General A. G. L. McNaughton, the first Commander-in-Chief of the Canadian Army, took office pledged to make a final effort to discover volunteers.

For three weeks McNaughton tried, where Ralston had tried before him. In three weeks McNaughton failed, as Ralston might have predicted that he would. On November 22nd, when Parliament met, it seemed obvious that the voluntary policy had finally been proved bankrupt. It seemed almost certain that the conscriptionist ministers would resign, the government would be defeated, and the nation would be split asunder by a disastrous repetition of the catastrophe of 1917. Yet none of these things happened. For King, having tried all expedients, exhausted all possibilities, and thwarted all advocates of compulsion, was finally prepared to yield to military necessity. Not without qualification, of course; even yet the simple, unforgivable, unforgettable decision of 1917 would not be repeated. The promise, though the nation had permitted its retraction, would still, in form, be kept. Conscription, as a general principle with general applications, would not be adopted; but sixteen thousand conscripts under the National Resources Mobilization Act would be sent overseas immediately as an emergency reinforcement for the Canadian Army. The astonished Cabinet, including the French-Canadian members, accepted King's proposal; Parliament accepted it; the nation in bewilderment accepted it also. The Liberal government was miraculously through in safety, and the crisis was over.

Something else, something vastly more important, was over as well. The great battles in the Rhineland were ending; the German armies broke in pieces; and the Third Reich fell apart in collapse.

III

In the spring of 1945 Mackenzie King led a large delegation, in which every shade of Canadian political opinion was represented, to the Conference at San Francisco. Canada had fought the war under the generalship and political direction of the great powers. She had been obliged to look on, at a respectfully discreet distance, while the great powers laid the bases of a new general security system at Dumbarton Oaks; and now, at the invitation of the 'Big Four', who referred to themselves modestly as the 'sponsoring powers', her statesmen were travelling to San Francisco to say, in Canada's right, what they thought of the projected world political organization.

For some time there had been very little doubt about what Canada's position would be. A little over a year before, in January 1944, Lord Halifax, the British Ambassador to the United States, had declared in a speech in Toronto that the future peace of the world would largely depend upon the maintenance of a balance of power among the 'Big Four' of the War; and he appealed to Canada to assist in making the British Commonwealth a fourth power which would have equal authority, and could exercise equal influence, with the 'titans', Russia, the United States, and China. Such an appeal offended not only King's settled and inveterate dislike of 'imperial centralization', but also his new-found enthusiasm for collective security. The great powers with which Canada was most closely associated either through family relationships or common frontiers had planned and agreed upon a new international organization; and, in the eyes of the Canadian Government, it seemed obvious that the best conceivable guarantee of the preservation of peace lay in this organized continuance of the war-time Grand Alliance. King rebuked Lord Halifax in a tone of earnest, high-minded candour. 'We look forward therefore', the Prime Minister declared, 'to close collaboration in the interests of peace not only inside the British Commonwealth but with all friendly nations small as well as great.' The cordiality of Canada's welcome to the United Nations stood in odd contrast with the judiciously qualified expressions of esteem with which she had assisted at the interment of the old League.

King had no desire to acquire for Canada a position of possible influence inside a collective Commonwealth. He preferred to accept a more subordinate place in a general international organization. The domination which the great powers were determined to exercise in the post-war world and which they had so candidly avowed in the plans adopted at Dumbarton Oaks and Yalta was the price which smaller nations would have to pay for the 'Big Four's' support of collective security. It was a very large price for a more than slightly doubtful promissory note; but King was prepared to pay it on Canada's behalf. The pre-eminence of the few great powers would have to be granted and acknowledged; but, in the view of the Canadian Government, this admission did not necessarily mean that all nations which made it must accept a position of common political inferiority. There was, in the opinion of the Canadian Government, a small but clearly distinguishable group of powers, powers which stood midway between nations of acknowledged political pre-eminence and those of admitted political subordination, powers which had clearly demonstrated their readiness to accept responsibility and their capacity to perform essential functions in international affairs—'middle powers', in short, which deserved to be placed in a distinct and recognized category of their own. Canada was obviously one of the principal members of this group; and at San Francisco, King and his colleagues sought to ensure that Canada should be given a preferred place in the councils of the great powers and a larger share of the authority they exercised. In this endeavour the Canadians gained only a limited and qualified success. It was decided, in the end, that the Assembly, in electing the non-permanent members of the Security Council, should have due regard, 'in the first instance', to the capacity of the nominated states to perform the functions of the post. It was also determined, however, that 'equitable geographical distribution' was a consideration which should guide the Assembly in its choice; and, as the future history of the United Nations showed, this second requirement was to frustrate some of the hopes of what King called the 'secondary powers with world-wide interests'.

The sober, practical realism which the Prime Minister and

his colleagues had shown at the San Francisco Conference was a faithful reflection of the relieved but unexcited mood of the Canadians in the years immediately after the peace. There was to be no renewal of those visionary hopes for the future, that confident belief in the possibility of a better order, both national and international, which had inspired the new parties, the new programmes, the bitter social unrest and the intense political excitement which had been so characteristic of Canadian affairs in the period after the First World War. The disintegration of the Liberal Party in 1917 and the catastrophic defeat of the Conservatives in 1921 had seemed, in that first post-war age, to foreshadow the break-up of the whole nineteenth-century Canadian political system; but the new postwar election of 1945, which once again safely returned King and the Liberals to power, showed no hint of impatience with the past or revolutionary zeal for the future. The National Unemployment Insurance Act, which had been passed in 1941 after a necessary amendment to the British North America Act, and the subsequent provision of Family Allowances for all children under sixteen, took much of the urgency out of the pre-war demand for greater social security; and although some of the basic recommendations of the Royal Commission on Dominion-Provincial Relations were not implemented, the worst of the financial difficulties which plagued the modern Canadian federal state were settled by the tax agreements negotiated by the Dominion and the provinces during the war and renewed after the peace. The relatively slow post-war recovery of Europe, the necessity of maintaining Canada's overseas markets with loans, and the consequent difficulty of squaring accounts with the United States in cash, brought on an acute exchange crisis between Canada and the republic in 1947. Even this, however, was of relatively short duration; and it was speedily forgotten in the continuance of a domestic prosperity which had falsified so many gloomy prophets and nervous fears. Times were good at home; abroad, it was hoped, conditions would gradually become better. The rehabilitation of a war-worn world, the secure establishment of a new and effective collective security system, would certainly be a slow and difficult business; and Canada, like other nations, would have to be content with limited objectives and small gains. It was a sober, sensible state of mind; and it may have helped to reduce the violence of the disillusionment that followed.

Almost as soon as the war ended, the process of disillusionment began. On the 5th September 1945 Igor Gouzenko, an obscure cipher clerk in the Russian Embassy at Ottawa, left his employment unobtrusively and for ever. He carried with him a mass of documents which corroborated beyond all doubt the truth of an important message which he felt he must somehow communicate to the Canadian people. That evening he appeared at the editorial offices of an Ottawa newspaper. Next day he sought an interview with the Minister of Justice, Louis St. Laurent. It was not until the city police discovered agents of the Soviet Embassy attempting to enter the cipher clerk's Ottawa apartment that anybody took Gouzenko's story at all seriously; and it was not until the Royal Canadian Mounted Police had put together a formidable collection of his statements and documents that the Canadian Government decided to act. The evidence, assembled by a Royal Commission of inquiry, of an extensive Russian spy ring operating in Canada, and the subsequent trial and conviction of eight Canadians and others, shocked and bewildered as well as angered the nation. It was the first phase in the rapid decline of the great war-time prestige of the Soviet Union; and it was followed quickly by other episodes which showed Russian obstruction and implied Russian ill will. These negative signs of hostility were bad enough; but infinitely worse was the growing positive evidence, culminating in the terrifying *coup d'état* in Czechoslovakia, of an expansive and aggressive revolutionary purpose. Even the careful, guarded post-war reliance on the new collective security system was shaken; and the nations of western Europe and North America drew together for defence.

For Canada, situated geographically between the United

States and the Soviet Union, and now, with unhappy and un-
enviable literalness, 'a middle power', there was, of course, no
choice. During the winter of 1947 the war-time association of
the Dominion and the United States was renewed and the
Permanent Joint Board on Defence took up its combined defensive arrangements once again. A return to a continental system
for the defence of fortress North America was a natural first
response to the danger of Soviet aggression; but, to most
Canadians it was not a satisfactory response, for it did not
guard Canada's overseas interests, nor include her overseas
allies. On the strongest historic grounds the Dominion disliked
the thought of being separated from Great Britain and western
Europe just as much as she objected to the prospect of becoming
a solitary North American protectorate of the United States.
In her view, a transatlantic reply would be the only effective
reply to the Russian defiance; and the association of powers on
both sides of the ocean, which began to take shape after the
formation of the Brussels Pact in 1948, suited both her historic
interests and her existing position very satisfactorily. Canadian
statesmen took an active and interested part in promoting the
new union; and towards the end of April 1949 the North
Atlantic Treaty, which L. B. Pearson had signed for Canada a
few weeks before, was ratified by the Canadian Parliament.

Six months before, Mackenzie King had resigned the office
of Prime Minister and retired from the leadership of the
Liberal Party. His political career had lasted over thirty years.
He had seen his country gain national sovereignty, achieve
industrial maturity, and acquire international recognition. He
had reached high office at a time when the League of Nations
had yet to face its first trials; he left it when the first hopes for
the United Nations were already fading; and throughout the
almost uninterrupted violence in which Canada had become
of age, he had tried to maintain the nation's essential inner
harmony.

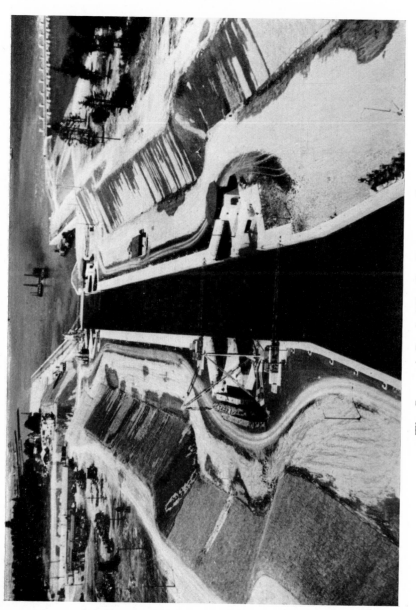

15. The Iroquois Lock, The St. Lawrence Seaway

16. The city of Toronto

16

THE FIRST ELIZABETHAN AGE

I

Around the front arch of the main entrance to the Peace Tower and the Parliament Buildings at Ottawa, ten stone coats of arms stood out in high relief. At the top, in the centre, the shields of the two central provinces—the maple leaves of Ontario and the fleurs-de-lis of Quebec—were joined to form a crown for the arch. On the right the arms of the western provinces—the buffalo of Manitoba, Saskatchewan's wheatsheaves, Alberta's mountains, and the effulgent sun of British Columbia—followed each other down the curve of the entrance. On the left the arms of the maritime provinces—New Brunswick's ship, the rampant lion of Nova Scotia, and the trees of Prince Edward Island—were ranged in a second descending row. The stone shields on each side of the arch were in perfect balance; but the emblems which they carried were unequal in number. For a long time the fourth shield on the left-hand side was blank. It had been left blank at the beginning. Its empty surface lay waiting for the day when the lions and unicorns of Newfoundland's coat of arms could be worked upon it. And its mere presence in the great arch of Canada's armorial bearings testified mutely but eloquently to the invincible hope that some day the entrance of the island province into Confederation would complete the original plan of a united British North America.

R

The First Elizabethan Age

Eighty-five years ago, in October 1864, two delegates from Newfoundland had arrived at Quebec to take part in the first discussions of a British North American federal union. Now after long delays, and repeated abortive negotiations, it looked at last as if the island were finally prepared to join. The times could hardly have been more propitious. The war had brought about Newfoundland's economic recovery; and the Commission Government, which had administered its public affairs since the financial collapse of 1933, began to look increasingly anomalous. The island people faced the problem of their constitutional future; and three obvious choices lay before them. The Commission Government could be continued for another five years at least; responsible government, as it had existed before 1933, could be restored with separate Dominion status; and, finally, Newfoundland could join the Canadian federation, as it had so often thought of doing in the past. In two referendums, held during the summer of 1948, the issue was squarely put before the people of the island. Commission government was eliminated in the first vote; in the second union with Canada was given a close majority over responsible government and a separate status. On the 31st March 1949, with six senators, seven members of the House of Commons and its own provincial legislature, Newfoundland entered Canadian Confederation.

The great design of 1864 was now complete. 'He shall have Dominion also from sea to sea, and from the river unto the ends of the earth.' It was true at last. The Dominion stretched from the outpost Atlantic island of Newfoundland to the shores of the Pacific; it extended all the way from the St. Lawrence, the River of Canada, to the northern cap of the world. And the achievement, in all its grandeur, had taken less than a century to finish. The union of the four original provinces had been largely the work of Macdonald. He had pushed expansion west and east by bringing in Manitoba, British Columbia, and Prince Edward Island; Laurier had filled in the gaps in the transcontinental structure with the addition of Alberta and

Saskatchewan; and now, after an interval of over forty years, the honour of introducing the tenth and last province into Confederation had fallen to William Lyon Mackenzie King. It was the last great work of his career. An ordinary yet curiously unusual man, courteous but friendless, unobtrusive but dominating, with odd dark complexities beneath his correctly commonplace exterior, he had made himself appear a political necessity without ever acquiring much respect or inspiring any great affection. He had been Prime Minister of Canada for a longer period than Sir John Macdonald; he had beaten Sir Robert Walpole's record for length of tenure as First Minister of the Crown. He had even lived long enough to see that lingering, hesitating tenth province finally complete the design of 1864 by entering Confederation.

On the 31st March 1949, when Newfoundland first took its place in the union, King had already retired; and his retirement marked the end of an era with a firmer punctuation mark than anything else could possibly have done. The last quarter-century—the boom, the depression, and the Second World War—had been the age of King. Under the superintendence of this tubby, mild-mannered, undistinguished little man, with his incredible talent for political longevity, the nation had come of age, acquired political and industrial maturity, grasped the last formal trappings of sovereignty, established its own independent relations with the rest of the world, fought the war with a strength second only to that of the greatest powers, and played a part of prominence in the troubled politics of the post-war world. Now this agitated but successful quarter-century was over. The career of its uninspiring presiding genius had ended; and a new generation was coming to grips with the problems of a new age.

Some of the principals had already appeared upon the national stage. George A. Drew, a vigorous and aggressive Conservative chieftain, replaced the last of the somewhat undistinguished and certainly unsuccessful war-time leaders of the opposition. A new Prime Minister, Louis St. Laurent, who, despite his years, was fairly fresh to Parliament and to office, now sat in the place which the veteran King had occupied for so long. For the second time in the century a French-speaking Canadian was presiding over the course of national affairs. The omens were favourable in the highest degree. It was nearly forty years since Sir Wilfrid Laurier had been defeated in the general election of 1911; and through the romantic haze of recollection and history, his long 'reign' of fifteen years seemed to stand out like a golden age of national success. He had prophesied, of course, that the triumphant accomplishment of that first decade would be continued throughout the nine that lay ahead. 'The twentieth century', he had declared—and it was perhaps the most famous of his sayings—'belongs to Canada.'

The vast material and moral developments of the past fifty years might have seemed to make Laurier's boast come true; but the national advance towards power, plenty, and creative self-expression had been neither so rapid nor so uninterrupted as his prophecy had implied. The progress of these first five decades had been held back by the stultifying frustrations of the great depression and hampered by the tragic losses of two great wars. Now these prolonged trials were ending as the first troubled fifty years drew towards their close. Would the commencement of the second half of the century see a repetition of the great burst of creative activity with which the first half had opened? Would St. Laurent direct the nation through a period of expansion as spectacular as that over which Laurier had presided? In June 1949, when the Liberal government faced the test of its first general election under the leadership of the new French-speaking Prime Minister, the electorate could hardly have expressed its hopeful trust more emphatically. The Liberal majority, greater than that which King had won at the height of his power, was like an overwhelming vote of confidence in the future.

The First Elizabethan Age

II

For a variety of reasons the confidence seemed justified. In more than one important way the opening of the second half of the century resembled the commencement of the first. The ten years from 1900 to 1910 had been marked both by the steady advance of Canadian domestic affairs and the progressive deterioration of world politics; and now the century's sixth decade saw the same curious and exciting mixture of national well-being and international troubles. N.A.T.O. was in itself an open admission that the great hope of the establishment of a new collective system, maintained and directed by the great powers, had failed. For years to come the world was to be locked in the uncomprehending dislikes, the sustained frustrations and menaces of the Cold War; and this state of continuous diplomatic low temperature was to be varied only by sharp and dangerous attacks of fever, such as the Korean War and the crisis in the Middle East. The two armed ententes into which the world was now divided were certain to give the highest priority to the stock-piling of strategic materials and the amassing of engines of destruction; but defence spending, formidable though it was, would not be the only strain on the world's productive capacities. The pent-up demands of populations frustrated by the prolonged austerities of war time would now unquestionably assert themselves; and under the driving power of these twin pressures the industrial machine of the Western World was to maintain for years a steady hum of prosperity.

Canada had responded eagerly and vigorously to the stimulus which the first decade of the twentieth century had brought. Could she make an equally effective reply to the invitations and demands of the 1950's? The north and west, the enormous domain which stretched 'from the river unto the ends of the earth', was a treasure-house whose riches had never been fully exploited, whose value even yet could be hardly guessed. Sir John Macdonald had staked his whole tremendous gamble for the future of Canada upon the promise of the north-west. The north-west had given British North America the three great staple products—furs, timber, and wheat—around which the history of its economic development could be largely written. The Precambrian Shield and the Great Plains had together made the fortunes of Canadians during the days of the old commercialism and the industrialism of coal and iron. But in the meantime a new industrial age had arrived and an economically more mature Canada had arisen. In what ways would the north-west help Canadians to realize their second great opportunity of making Laurier's boast come true?

Long before the war ended, before it had even begun, the evidence was already accumulating. Even in respect of coal and iron, those tested sinews of nineteenth-century industrial power, the nation was finding itself to be far better endowed than its citizens of previous generations had believed possible. Coal had always been available in abundance, though the country's principal mines were situated in Alberta, British Columbia, and Nova Scotia, economically far distant from the St. Lawrence valley; the known deposits of iron were not considerable; and both for fuel and ore the industrial machine of central Canada had been largely dependent upon imports from the United States. Now, with the exploitation of the resources at Steep Rock in northern Ontario and with the discovery of the enormous body of ore on the boundary between northern Quebec and Labrador, the whole position of affairs had suddenly and miraculously changed. The nation had found a place for itself in the old industrialism; it could face the competition of steam and steel. And yet, industrially, Canada was a creature of the twentieth, rather than of the nineteenth, century. It was more richly and variously endowed with the new metals, the new materials, the new sources of energy and power. The turbulent waters of the youthful drainage systems of the northern half of the continent were capable of producing vast supplies of hydro-electric power. The rocky uplands of the

The First Elizabethan Age

Precambrian Shield, which the artists of the Group of Seven had begun to depict a quarter-century before, had disgorged huge quantities of nickel, aluminium, and a long string of other base and precious metals. The Eldorado Mining and Refining Company's operations on Great Bear Lake, which made possible the federal government's atomic pile at Chalk River near Ottawa, was only the first of a series of uranium-mining enterprises; and in February 1947 the prolonged but indefatigable search for petroleum on the Canadian prairies led finally to the discovery of the Leduc oil-field, sixteen miles south-west of Edmonton.

The promise of the second half of the century lay partly in this heaped-up accumulation of material things. It lay equally obviously in the nation's growing human resources. And here also, as in so many other aspects of development, the sixth decade of the century saw a renewal of the amazing growth of the first. In the ten years 1901–11, the decade of the Laurier boom, the rate of increase of Canada's population was the highest in the world; only Australia had achieved a higher gain in 1911–21; and now after nearly thirty years of painfully deliberate growth, the nation was again approaching these buoyant records of the early years of the century. The census of 1951 revealed the fact that the rate of increase during the agitated 1940's had nearly equalled that of the comparable war-time decade of 1911–21. The marriage rate climbed sharply; the birth-rate was up; and immigration, which was not at first so significant a factor in the growth of population as it had been in the early years of the century, began again to assume huge proportions as the decade of the 1950's advanced. A total which kept getting close to half a million people was being added annually to the nation's human resources; and the population of the ten provinces, which the decennial census of 1951 had put at a little over fourteen million, reached seventeen million by the spring of 1958.

Early in February 1952, when the second half of the century was only a year old and when Canadians were just beginning

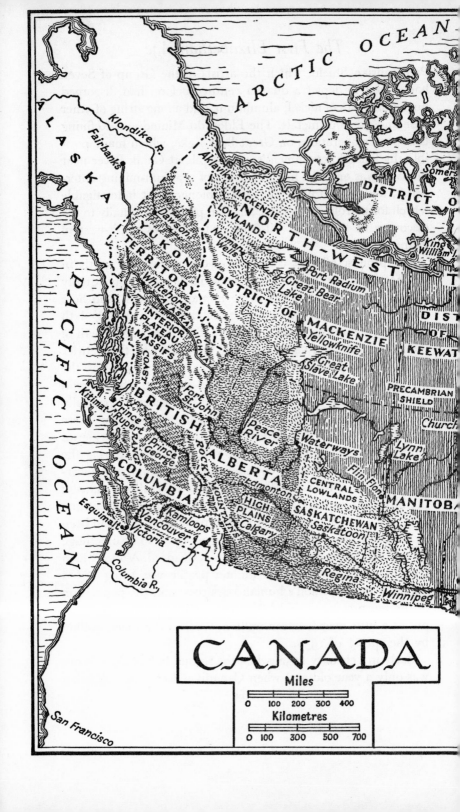

to realize that their country stood on the edge of a second spectacular expansion, their King, George VI, died. He was aged, not with years, but by the steadfast performance of a duty which he had never expected would be his; and his death, and the accession of his daughter, Queen Elizabeth II, seemed to mark the end of a period of endurance and bitter struggle and the beginning of a happy time of confidence and easy accomplishment. For England, a new Elizabethan Age had dawned; but Canada, the second of the Realms of the Commonwealth, had never known the reign of the first Elizabeth. In the dark early hours of the 24th March 1603, when the great Queen had died, the springtime which was to see Champlain venture up the River of Canada for the first time, had barely begun to blossom. The reign which commenced in February 1952 was the reign of Canada's first Queen Elizabeth. Would it, in fact, be a real Elizabethan Age? Would it bring to Canadians not only the territorial gains and material splendour of the reign of the first Elizabeth, but also something of its creative spirit?

For Canadians the question had become an important and exciting one. They had already begun a stock-taking examination of their existing achievement in the things of the mind and the spirit; they had already begun to inquire how they could make the way smoother for the accomplishments of the future. In the spring of 1949 a Royal Commission on National Development in the Arts, Letters, and Sciences had been appointed by the federal government. '. . . It is in the national interest', declared the Order-in-Council establishing the Commission, 'to give encouragement to institutions which express national feeling, promote common understanding, and add to the variety and richness of Canadian life.' During the next two years the Commissioners carried out a systematic review of Canadian achievement in letters, arts and scholarship, as well as a careful evaluation of the voluntary associations and federal agencies which tried to encourage and promote artistic and scholarly work. The Commission's *Report* affirmed the promising possibility of a genuine Canadian culture; but, at the same time, it effectively emphasized the fundamental difficulty with which Canadians had to contend in the maintenance of a conscious sense of identity and the expression of a distinctive point of view. Canada had escaped the continental empire of the United States and won autonomy inside the Empire Commonwealth of Great Britain; but the two imperialisms from which the Canadians had managed to liberate themselves were political, not cultural, in character. Political empires sometimes ended; cultural empires could be incredibly enduring. For generations and centuries Great Britain and the United States, the metropolitan centres of English-speaking civilization, had gone on imposing their virtues as universal standards, elevating their accomplishments into timeless masterpieces, and manufacturing cultural consumer goods, to their own exclusive specifications, and on a mass-production basis. A Canadian creative artist could gain admittance to these cultural empires only on their own terms and through the surrender of at least a part of his own tradition and special point of view. A Canadian theme or subject would be deemed worthy of acceptance only if it were either primitive and barbaric, and thus corresponded with the metropolitan dogma of what Canada must be like, or if it were laid in the outpost or frontier of the Dominion in which the metropolitan power happened currently to be interested for the purposes of economic or military exploitation.

The Royal Commission on National Development in the Arts, Letters, and Sciences—the 'Massey Commission', as it was called, after its chairman Vincent Massey, who in 1952 became the first Canadian-born Governor-General of Canada —believed that a great and positive effort should be made to end this state of affairs. The nation must intervene to encourage the growth of Canadian spiritual independence; and the solid support for state action was already in existence. Rapidly, obviously, Canada was ceasing to be the acquiescent cultural colony that it had been in the past. Visiting English lecturers and touring American theatrical companies were no longer admiringly regarded as the only possible sources of sophisticated entertainment. From the stock fictional characters of southern English villages and Midland towns, from the familiar figures of the American Big City and the American Deep South, the Canadians were turning away with the feeling that they could hardly do much worse in Canada and might conceivably do even better. The author who had felt that he must wash the local colour out of his play or novel, the scholar who had been informed in England that it would be fatal to reviews and sales if he admitted identification with a Canadian university on the title page of his book, were certain now of far more encouragement at home, and a good deal more attention abroad, than they had ever had in the past. Even so—and the Massey Commission emphasized the fact—a more deliberate co-operative attempt must be made to create vehicles for the expression of Canadian themes and opportunities for the development of Canadian talent. The Canadian Broadcasting Corporation, the National Film Board, and the other federal, provincial and municipal institutions, such as galleries, museums, libraries, and archives, were clearly not enough for the purpose. The Commissioners recommended that the federal government should establish a new national institution called the Canada Council, to which substantial sums would be appropriated for the support and encouragement of letters, arts, humane studies and social sciences in Canada.

There was a hopeful prospect of solid government aid. There was the inspiring reality of the far greater popular interest which Canadians were showing in the work of their own writers, artists, musicians, and scholars. A time of incentives and opportunities, an electric air of stimulus seemed suddenly to have come into being; and a new literary and artistic generation was responding to it with as much talent as ever before and with a far greater range and variety of expression and accomplishment. The poets, painters, and prose writers, creative and scholarly, built on solid foundations and appealed to already established audiences; but it was not so much in these traditional modes of expression as in music, drama, ballet, and opera, where almost no native tradition existed, that the most spectacular advances were achieved. The larger, richer cities now sustained choirs, symphony orchestras and a wide variety of musical organization; the little theatres, the repertory companies, the Dominion Drama Festival, and the Canadian Broadcasting Corporation—which was perhaps the most important single agency in the development of native talent—had brought into being a large company of able actors and musicians. In both Montreal and Toronto, groups of young musical composers appeared; the National Ballet Company and the Royal Winnipeg Ballet quickly attained a high level of accomplishment; and in the summer of 1953 the Stratford Shakespearian Festival, with its company of largely Canadian actors, opened for its first season in the pleasant riverside town of Stratford in southern Ontario.

III

Potentialities which had barely been discovered two generations before were rapidly being realized. At home the nation was freeing itself and finding itself in a wide variety of ways; abroad it was expressing its new-found sense of identity and voicing its distinctive point of view with a novel confidence and persistence. In the 1920's Canada had regarded the right to a separate foreign policy largely as the final essential attribute of sovereign independence. A separate foreign policy in order to make full Dominion status manifest, rather than Dominion status in order to carry out a separate foreign policy, was the formula in which perhaps her cloudy aspirations could have best been stated; and, so far as she had followed her own course in the fateful period between the wars, her policies had been hesitating, imitative, and negative to the last degree. All this was in the past. The experiences of the war and post-war diplomacy had finally broken down this sense of timidity and fearful detachment. Really, as well as theoretically, Canada's position was now her own.

And yet, of course, the world of the 1950's was a place coldly unsympathetic to the expression of independent views by the newly arrived 'middle powers' of the twentieth century. Under the divisive compulsions of the Cold War, the nations were separating themselves into two camps which were rapidly becoming armed camps; and over these two fearful, bewildered, and acquiescent divisions of humanity, the two super-powers, the United States and the Soviet Union, were assuming a large measure of direction and control. In 1949 the creation of N.A.T.O. had been an impressive demonstration of the political solidarity of West-European-American civilization; but, in the same year, this western diplomatic success had been matched in the Far East by the defeat of the Kuomintang and the victory of the Chinese People's Republic. At the mid-point of the century the fortunes of the two great rivals in the grand strategy of world politics were not unequally balanced; and the 1950's were to be a decade characterized by a determined search for allies, an eager pursuit of strategic advantages, and a desperate effort to outdo each other in the construction of bombs, missiles and other engines of mass destruction. In such circumstances, even the permanent members of the Security Council, apart from the super-powers, could hardly call their souls their own; and small and 'middle' powers, which did not look at all times as if they were ready to volunteer instantly in the just cause, were apt to be accused of the crimes of incipient 'neutralism' or 'anti-Americanism'.

There was tension all along the vast, vaguely defined borderland which separated Communist Eurasia from the Western World. In the late 1950's the Middle East was to become a principal potential source of danger; but at the beginning of the decade the Far East was the scene of even more explosive rivalries; and it was here, in June 1950, that the first armed breach of the uneasy post-war truce occurred. War was undertaken by the United Nations to stop armed aggression and to protect the southern Republic of Korea; but this defence of the new collective security system was complicated by the private American decision to insulate the island of Formosa by force, and by the apparent inclination of some leading Americans to broaden the scope of the conflict by an attack against Communist China. In the long confusion of cross-purposes and divided authorities which marked the conduct of the Korean War, Canada strove not unsuccessfully to follow a consistent line of policy. On the one hand, the Canadian Government was prepared to support the principle of collective resistance to aggression by contributing a brigade of its troops to the Commonwealth Division in Korea; but, on the other, it was equally anxious to keep the war concentrated on its original common purpose, and to prevent any drastic enlargement of its scope or change in its fundamental character. Like Great Britain, Canada was disposed to sympathize with India's championship of Asian nationalism; and both as a principal and as a supporter of others' efforts the Canadian representatives played a fairly active part in the diplomatic efforts to limit and terminate the war.

In the Middle Eastern crisis, which reached its climax on the 29th October 1956, when Great Britain and France sent their ultimatum to Egypt, Canada played both a more prominent and a more constructive role. The Suez affair, which bore a faint family relationship to the Chanak affair thirty-five years before, was precisely the kind of imbroglio from which King, in the period between the wars, would have retreated with the utmost alacrity in a cloud of postponements and disclaimers. This time Canada's lack of interest in Middle Eastern oil and Canada's infrequent use of the Suez Canal for shipping were not urged to justify an attitude of irresponsible passivity. Canadians were seriously concerned over the Suez crisis and deeply divided by it; and while there was shocked surprise at the violent suddenness of the Anglo-French intervention in Egypt, sharp criticism was also directed at the meddling and muddling of American foreign policy in the Middle East. This position of informed, independent, and critical concern was something new; but even more novel was the swiftness with which the distinctive Canadian attitude was translated into an effective line of policy. In the United Nations Assembly Canada abstained from voting on the American resolution requiring Great Britain and France to refrain from the threat or use of force on the ground that it offered no constructive alternative; and, at the next meeting of the Assembly, L. B. Pearson submitted the Canadian proposal for a constructive alternative in the shape of 'an emergency International United Nations force' which would bring about a cease-fire. Canada had dared to take the initiative on the highest level of policy; and it was this act which led slowly and protestingly to a relaxation of tension and which helped to win L. B. Pearson his Nobel Prize for Peace.

IV

During the Commons debate on the crisis, Prime Minister St. Laurent had been provoked into confessing how 'scandalized' he had been at the violent action of 'the supermen of Europe'. This indiscreetly angry ejaculation, which echoed so oddly the moral indignation in which professional Canadian nationalists used to indulge a generation before, hardly accorded with the mood of the Canadian people or the realities of the contemporary situation. The relative decline of Great Britain and the revolution which had taken place in the Commonwealth had emptied the old 'colonial' fears of all validity; and it was not the sinister imperialistic designs of the nations of western Europe but the vast preponderance of power enjoyed by the continental nations, the Soviet Union and the United States, against which Canada would have to try to guard itself in the future. One of the basic national objectives —autonomy inside the British Commonwealth—had been won so completely that young Canada had come to regard it with the disinterest born of complete familiarity. But autonomy

inside the Commonwealth had been only one of the two goals
of Canadian nationhood; the other object, still more fundamental and difficult of achievement, was survival as a separate
and independent nation on the North American continent.
And during the 1950's the difficulties of maintaining a national
Canadian identity in a continent dominated by the United
States were driven home to Canadians as they had not been
for nearly a century. The terrors of a mythical British 'imperialism' had now been completely replaced by the apprehensions of a very real American continentalism.

American continentalism, economic, political, military, was a
force as huge and varied as North America itself. Under the
complementary pressures and inducements of the Cold War
and the investment boom, Canadians felt themselves being
fitted smoothly into a continental defence system and a continental capitalist organization. They were worried, as they
had never been before, about the ownership and control of
their minerals, their sources of fuel and power, and about the
management and commercial policies of American industries
established in Canada. They were apprehensive of the outcome
of the negotiations over power developments on the Columbia
River and they had a resentful feeling that they had sacrificed
only too cheaply their hitherto exclusive and unbroken control
of the waterway of the St. Lawrence, 'The River of Canada'.
By the middle of the decade the interests of Canadian grain
growers were being seriously injured by the subsidized export
of American wheat abroad; and, when the recession began in
the autumn of 1957, the existing rigid quotas imposed on the
import of Canadian grains into the United States were supple-
mented by new 'voluntary' restrictions on the import of
Canadian oil and by threats of similar restrictions on Canadian
base metals. Quotas, 'voluntary' restrictions, tariffs and the
barbed-wire entanglements of the American customs administration seriously embarrassed Canada's economic development;
while, on the other hand, the extent of Canadian-American
co-operation in the necessary business of continental defence

sometimes roused concern among Canadians for their political sovereignty. In the north, Americans had been permitted to build and man radar installations; in the east they occupied the military bases in Newfoundland which Great Britain had granted by the destroyers-bases deal and which the island had carried with her, a serious limitation on Canadian sovereignty, into Confederation. In 1957 a plan for a unified system of continental air defences was put into operation by the American and Canadian governments.

This accumulation of concessions, injuries, and worries had been giving a critical edge to the Canadian nationalism of the 1950's; and to many Canadians it seemed that the vigorous new national spirit, in many of its manifestations, was only feebly and unimaginatively represented by the Liberal government. It was now a very old government which had lasted for the incredible space of over twenty years and which, when the notorious pipe-line debate began in the spring of 1956, had already forfeited some of the respect, and inspired much of the tedium and exasperation of abnormal longevity. The furious debate over the Bill for the construction of a pipe-line designed to bring huge quantities of natural gas down from the wells in Alberta to the urban markets of central Canada was an important episode in the government's slow decline. Rapidly the debate developed into a spirited defence of the rights of Parliament against the brutal use of the power of the majority by which the government sought to force its bill through the House at record speed. This was the major significance of the debate, but it had begun as a protest against the transference into American hands of the control of a new and important national economic undertaking. Half-acknowledged yet irrepressible, this defiant feeling was a vital element in the robust Canadianism to which the new Progressive-Conservative leader, John Diefenbaker, was appealing with such successful fervour. Everybody—Liberals, Conservatives, and newspaper wiseacres of all political opinions—expected the Liberals to win the general election of 10th June 1957. But the Canadian people had decided otherwise. And when the votes were counted, the Progressive-Conservatives, with 111 out of 265 seats, emerged as the strongest group in the new House.

That autumn Elizabeth II paid her first visit as Queen to her Kingdom of Canada and for the first time in history Canada's monarch assisted in person at the opening of the Parliament of the second Realm of the Commonwealth. 'I greet you as your Queen,' she said as she began the speech from the throne in the Senate Chamber on the afternoon of Monday, 14th October 1957. 'Together we constitute the Parliament of Canada. For the first time the representatives of the people of Canada and their sovereign are here assembled on the occasion of the opening of Parliament. This is for all of us a moment to remember. . . . I am proud to contemplate the great heritage of this nation—the minerals, the forests, the lands, the waters, the sources of power and energy which fire your ever-growing industries. But I am more proud to contemplate the spirit and ideas which brought this country to nationhood, and now, drawing reinforcement and enrichment from many lands and peoples, have given Canada a national character peculiarly her own. . . . I will call to your minds the words of the earlier Elizabeth when, more than three centuries ago, she spoke from her heart to the Speaker and members of her last Parliament and said "Though God hath raised me high, yet this I count the glory of my Crown, that I have reigned with your loves." Now here in the New World I say to you that it is my wish that in the years before me I may so reign in Canada and be so remembered.'

The Canadians had no doubt that in the new world of Canada the wish would be fulfilled. Their Queen had captured their imagination and caught their own mood by her reference to the earlier Elizabeth. In the few sweeping sentences of her speech she had triumphantly evoked the spirit of the first Canadian Elizabethan Age. Despite the return of unemployment and the evil effects of the recession in the United States, her Canadian subjects still looked eagerly forward to the

s*

promise of the future; and on the last day of March, when the early spring of 1958 began to break, they affirmed their confidence in the way open to liberal democracies by a great collective political act. The results of the general election of June 1957 had not been decisive; but by now the Canadians were impatient with indecisions, bored by the monotonous prolongation of Liberal rule, and obscurely eager for a more earnest and fervid type of national leadership. They transformed the general election of March 31st into a political revolution such as had occurred only twice before in Canada's history. The Progressive-Conservatives swept every province except Newfoundland; with 208 seats, they won the largest majority that any party had ever had in the Canadian House of Commons; they could boast that they had politically reunited the Canadian nation.

SOME SUGGESTIONS FOR
FURTHER READING

The following is not meant to be a systematic or comprehensive list of the principal works on Canadian history. It is rather a brief selective list of the more readable books, chosen chiefly from the publications of the last twenty-five years, and intended simply for those readers who may wish to pursue the study of Canadian history somewhat beyond the limits of the present small volume. The first section of the list includes books on Canadian history as a whole, or on one of its general themes; the three following sections, which correspond with the three main divisions of Canadian history, include studies of a somewhat more specialized character. Within each section the books are listed alphabetically, according to author.

I

GENERAL WORKS

Brebner, J. B., *North Atlantic Triangle, the Interplay of Canada, the United States, and Great Britain*. New Haven, 1945.
Buchanan, D. W., *The Growth of Canadian Painting*. London, 1950.
Careless, J. M. S., *Canada, a Story of Challenge*. Cambridge, 1953.
Creighton, Donald, *Dominion of the North, a History of Canada*. New edition. Toronto, 1957.

Some Suggestions for Further Reading

Dawson, R. M., *The Government of Canada.* Toronto, 1952.

Easterbrook, W. T., and Aitken, H. G. J., *Canadian Economic History.* Toronto, 1956.

Glazebrook, G. P. de T., *A History of Canadian External Relations.* Toronto, 1950.

Massey, Vincent, *On Being Canadian.* London, 1948.

Pacey, Desmond, *Creative Writing in Canada, a Short History of English-Canadian Literature.* Toronto, 1952.

Putnam, D. F., *Canadian Regions, a Geography of Canada.* Toronto, 1952.

Stanley, G. F. G., *Canada's Soldiers, the Military History of an Unmilitary People.* Toronto, 1954.

Wade, Mason, *The French Canadians, 1760–1945.* Toronto, 1955.

II

NEW FRANCE

Bishop, M. G., *Champlain, the Life of Fortitude.* New York, 1948.

Brebner, J. B., *The Explorers of North America, 1492–1806.* London, 1933.

Chapais, T., *The Great Intendant, a Chronicle of Jean Talon in Canada, 1665–1672.* Toronto, 1921.

Colby, C. W., *The Fighting Governor, a Chronicle of Frontenac.* Toronto, 1915.

Crouse, N. M., *Lemoyne d'Iberville, Soldier of New France.* Ithaca, 1954.

Graham, G. S., *Empire of the North Atlantic, the Maritime Struggle for North America.* Toronto, 1950.

Innis, H. A., *The Fur Trade in Canada, an Introduction to Canadian Economic History.* Revised edition. Toronto, 1954.

MacKay, D., *The Honourable Company, a History of the Hudson's Bay Company.* Revised edition. Toronto, 1949.

Wrong, G. M., *The Rise and Fall of New France.* Two vols. Toronto, 1928.

Some Suggestions for Further Reading

III

BRITISH NORTH AMERICA

Brebner, J. B., *The Neutral Yankees of Nova Scotia, a Marginal Colony during the Revolutionary Years*. New York, 1937.

Burt, A. L., *The Old Province of Quebec*. Toronto, 1933.

Campbell, M. W., *The North West Company*. Toronto, 1957.

Creighton, Donald, *John A. Macdonald, the Young Politician*. Toronto, 1952.

Creighton, Donald, *The Empire of the St. Lawrence*. Toronto, 1956.

Grant, W. L., *The Tribune of Nova Scotia, a Chronicle of Joseph Howe*. Toronto, 1920.

Kilbourn, William, *The Firebrand, William Lyon Mackenzie and the Rebellion in Upper Canada*. Toronto, 1956.

New, C. W., *Lord Durham, a Biography of John George Lambton, first Earl of Durham*. Oxford, 1929.

Trotter, R. G., *Canadian Confederation, its Origins and Achievement, a Study in Nation Building*. Toronto, 1924.

IV

CANADA SINCE CONFEDERATION

Borden, H. (ed.), *Robert Laird Borden: His Memoirs*. Two vols. Toronto, 1938.

Creighton, Donald, *John A. Macdonald, the Old Chieftain*. Toronto, 1955.

Gibbon, J. M., *Steel of Empire*. Toronto, 1935.

Hutchison, Bruce, *The Incredible Canadians, a Candid Portrait of Mackenzie King: his Works, his Times, and his Nation*. Toronto, 1952.

Schull, Joseph, *The Far Distant Ships, an Official Account of Canadian Naval Operations in the Second World War*. Ottawa, 1950.

Some Suggestions for Further Reading

Skelton, O. D., *The Life and Letters of Sir Wilfrid Laurier*. Two vols. Toronto, 1921.

Soward, F. H., *et al.*, *Canada in World Affairs, the Pre-War Years*. Toronto, 1941.

Stacey, C. P., *The Canadian Army, 1939–1945, An Official Historical Summary*. Ottawa, 1948.

Stanley, G. F. G., *The Birth of Western Canada, a History of the Riel Rebellions*. London, 1936.

INDEX

Index

Brown, George, 140, 168; John, 85, 86
Brussels Pact, 256
Buffalo, 114
Burgoyne, General John, 91
Butler's Rangers Regiment, 94
Byng, Sir Julian, Viscount Byng, 210, 220, 221, 224

Cabot, John, 12
Caen, 249
Callaghan, Morley, 234
Campbell, W. W., 201
Canada and its Provinces, 202
Canada Corn Act, 1843, 136
Canada Council, 268
Canada, Province of, established, 131; struggle for responsible government in, 133, 134, 135-7; reforms in, 140; tariff of, 145; political dualism in, 150; accepts Quebec plan, 156; joins Confederation, 157
Canada East, 150; West, 135, 150
Canadian Army, 247, 248, 249
Canadian Broadcasting Corporation, 268, 269
Canadian Corps, in World War I, 209-10, 215
Canadian Council of Agriculture, 203
Canadian Northern Railway, 195
Canadian Pacific Railway, receives charter, 170; construction of, 171; western lands, 172; financial difficulties of, 173-6; in North-West Rebellion, 177-80; settlement along, 191; success of, 194; and Liberal party, 195
Canals, 135-6
Canso, 54, 62, 63
Cape Breton, 15, 65, 69, 81; France retains by Treaty of Utrecht, 52; builds Louisbourg on, 52-3; Loyalists settle, 94; Scots immigration to, 117
Cape Diamond, 74
Cap Rouge, 74
Carignan-Salières Regiment, 27, 28, 41, 46
Carleton, Sir Guy, Baron Dorchester, 84, 85, 86
Carman, Bliss, 190, 201, 223
Carmichael, Franklin, 222
Cartier, Sir George E., 149, 157
Jacques, 11, 12, 13, 14, 16
Cartwright, Richard, 94
Casco Bay, 43, 49
Castine, 109
Cataraqui, 96
Cayuga Indians, 47

Chamberlain, Joseph, 245
Chambly, 31
Champlain, Samuel de, 18, 56; at Quebec, 16-17; War with Iroquois, 19; western explorations of, 20; defeated by Onondagas, 22; returns to New France, 24
Champlain's Company, 20
Champlain, Lake, 19, 27, 42, 43, 56, 73, 88, 91, 94, 108
Chanak incident, 219, 220
Charles I, King of England, 24; II, 34
Charlottetown, 152
Chaudière River, 43, 89
Chebucto, 64
Chignecto, Isthmus of, 64, 65, 66, 90, 98
Chinese People's Republic, 270
Churchill River, 56
Churchill, Sir Winston S., 207, 212
Church of England, 119, 120
Scotland, 119, 120
Civil War, American, 147, 154, 159, 163
Clergy Reserves, 119, 120, 122, 131, 140
Cobden, Richard, 133
Colbert, Jean Baptiste, 29, 37, 42
Columbia River, 103, 273
Commonwealth Air Training Plan, 242-3
Commonwealth of Nations, problems of defence and foreign policy in, 198-200; Borden conception of, 207; King's attitude to, 219-20; Imperial Conference of 1926, 225-7; in Second World War, 244-5; and United Nations, 252; Canadian autonomy in, 272
Company of New France, 22, 23, 24
Confederation, problem of British North American union, 149; Canada proposes, 151; Conferences discuss, 152-3; Quebec scheme of, 153-4; hastened by Great Britain and United States, 155-6; achieved in British North America Act, 157; Manitoba and British Columbia enter, 162; Provinces attack, 182-3; Alberta and Saskatchewan created, 194; Newfoundland joins, 258-9
Congregational Church, 82
Connecticut River, 92
Connor, Ralph, 202
Conscription, 213-14, 240, 248, 250-1
Conservative Party, in Province of Canada, 135; Macdonald leads, 140; proposes Confederation, 151; Pacific scandal, 166-7; adopts pro-

Index

Index

Index

Index

Index

Montcalm, Louis Joseph, Marquis de, 72, 73, 75, 76, 77, 78

Montgomery, General Bernard L., Viscount Montgomery of Alamein, 249

General Richard, 88, 89

Montgomery's Tavern, 125

Montmorency River, 74, 75, 77

Montreal, 30, 43, 49, 59, 61; first settlement in, 25; fur traders at, 56; rejects American revolutionary propaganda, 85–7; captured by American army, 89; begins northwest fur trade, 101; in War of 1812, 108; yields fur trade to Hudson's Bay Company, 112; in Rebellion of 1837, 124; and burning of Parliament buildings, 137; and railways, 143–4

Monts' Company, 17, 19

Moody, Parson, 63

Moose River, 41

Morrice, James, 223

Mount Sorrel, 210

Mouy, Charles de, Seigneur de la Meilleraye, 11

Murray, James, 84

Mussolini, Benito, 236, 238

Napanee, 188

National Ballet of Canada, 269

Film Board, 268

Nationalism, growth of economic, in British North America, 143; American and British influences on, 145–8; Confederation an experiment in, 157; difficulties of during the 'Great Depression', 167, 173, 175, 184–5; national objectives realized, 196–9, 203; in World War I, 215; economic changes in inter-war period, 229; in art and literature, 222, 233–4; and the United States, 273–4

National Resources Mobilization Act, 247, 248, 249, 250, 251

Transcontinental Railway, 195

Unemployment Insurance Act, 254

Natural Products Marketing Act, 237

Naval Aid Bill, 208, 212

Navigation Acts, 116

Neilson, John, 122

Nelson River, 56

New Brunswick, Province of, 66, 145, 159; established, 98; in War of 1812, 109; timber trade and shipbuilding in, 113–14; early society in, 117–18; granted control of

Crown revenues, 133; and Maritime Union, 149, 152; and Confederation, 156–7; at interprovincial conference, 182

New England, 25, 45, 49, 50, 63, 81, 82

Newfoundland, 37, 46, 113, 159; beginnings of fishery at, 12; English occupy Avalon peninsula, 15; Iberville attacks, 45; in Peace of Ryswick, 47; in Treaty of Utrecht, 51; in Treaty of Paris, 1783, 93; representative government in, 133; and Confederation, 156; American Bases in, 245–6; joins Confederation, 258

New France, its early character, 20–1; settlement and the fur trade, 24–5; becomes royal province, 28; reorganization of, 30–1; and westward expansion, 36–7; and forest warfare, 41; in Peace of Ryswick, 46–7; after Treaty of Utrecht, 50–52; and aggression in the interior, 55–6; weaknesses of, 57–8; government of, 61; desperate condition of, 73; ceded by Peace of Paris, 79

New Hampshire, 43, 81

Netherland, 33

New York City, 42, 94, 95

State, 18, 55, 67, 84, 94

Niagara, 100, 108, 114

Nicholson, Colonel Francis, 50

Nonintercourse Act, 105

Normandy, Battle of, 249

North, The, 221–8, 229, 262–3

North Atlantic Treaty Organization, 256, 261, 270

Northern Pacific Railroad, 166, 174

North-West Company, 101, 102, 103, 111, 112

Mounted Police, 176

Rebellion, 176–80

Territories, 147, 159, 160, 162, 184

Nova Scotia, Province of, 15, 131, 149, 175, 262; James I grants to Sir William Alexander, 23; surrendered to England by Treaty of Utrecht, 51; British neglect, 54; British reorganize and promote settlement in, 66; effect of New England immigration on, 80–2; in American Revolution, 86–8; after Peace of Paris, 1783, 90–3; Loyalist migration to, 94–6; partitioned, 98; failure to gain West Indies trade, 105; economic activities of, 113; immigration to, 117; responsible government in, 133–4, 136;

Index

Index

Index

Index

Da

E

A   D